INVESTMENT INFORMATION
A DETAILED GUIDE TO SELECTED SOURCES

MO

MANAGEMENT
INFORMATION
GUIDE : : 19

INVESTMENT INFORMATION
A DETAILED GUIDE TO SELECTED SOURCES

James B. Woy

[
Head
Mercantile Library
The Free Library of Philadelphia
]

GALE RESEARCH COMPANY · BOOK TOWER · DETROIT, MICHIGAN

(1970)

OTHER BOOKS IN THE
MANAGEMENT INFORMATION GUIDE SERIES
Write for Complete List

TRANSPORTATION—A Guide to Publications, Agencies, and Other Data Sources. Edited by Kenneth Metcalf, Henry Ford Museum.

BUSINESS TRENDS AND FORECASTING—A Guide to Theoretical and Technical Publications. Edited by James Woy, Mercantile Library, Free Library of Philadelphia.

PACKAGING—A Guide to Literature, Associations, and Educational Institutions Concerned with Containers and Packaging. Edited by Gwendolyn Jones, Librarian, St. Regis Paper Co.

GOVERNMENT REGULATION OF BUSINESS INCLUDING ANTITRUST—A Bibliography of Works Pertaining to Antitrust Division, Department of Justice, and to Major Regulatory Agencies of the Federal Government. Edited by Beatrice S. McDermott and Freada A. Coleman, Librarians, Dewey, Ballantine, Bushby, Palmer & Wood, and Winthrop, Stimson, Putnam & Roberts.

SYSTEMS & PROCEDURES INCLUDING OFFICE MANAGEMENT—A Guide to Literature and Bodies Concerned with Systems and Procedures Aspects of Organization and Management, including Office Management. Edited by Chester Morrill, Jr., Program Officer, Chief, Program and Management Branch, Army Comptroller Division, National Guard Bureau, Departments of the Army and Air Force.

ELECTRONIC INDUSTRIES—A Guide to Literature and Other Data Sources. Edited by Gretchen R. Randle, Librarian, The Thomas Newcomen Memorial Library, The Newcomen Society in North America.

INTERNATIONAL BUSINESS AND FOREIGN TRADE—A Guide to Literature and Bodies Concerned with the Procedures and Policies of Conducting Business with Other Countries. Edited by Lora Jeanne Wheeler, Librarian, The American Institute for Foreign Trade.

COMPUTERS AND DATA PROCESSING—An Annotated Guide to the Literature, Associations and Institutions Concerned with Present Day Input, Throughput and Output of Data. Edited by Chester Morrill, Jr., Program Officer, Chief Program and Management Branch, Army Comptroller Division, National Guard Bureau, Departments of the Army and Air Force.

FOOD AND BEVERAGE INDUSTRIES—A Bibliography and Guidebook. Edited by Albert Vara, Senior Professional Assistant, Business Section, Paley Library, Temple University.

COMMERCIAL LAW INFORMATION SOURCES—Edited by Julius J. Marke, Professor of Law and Law Librarian, and Edward J. Bander, Assistant Professor of Law and Associate Law Librarian, New York University School of Law.

ACCOUNTING INFORMATION SOURCES—An Annotated Guide to the Literature, Associations and Federal Agencies Concerned with Accounting. Edited by Rosemary R. Demarest, Chief Librarian, Price Waterhouse & Co., New York.

INVESTMENT INFORMATION—A Detailed Guide to Selected Sources. Edited by James B. Woy, Mercantile Library, Free Library of Philadelphia.

Library of Congress Catalog Card Number 79-118791

$11.50

Copyright © 1970 By
GALE RESEARCH COMPANY

CONTENTS

FOREWORD

Management processes continue to grow more complex and the range of factors relevant to contemporary decision-making mounts apace. Inevitably, the volume of published information and the number of institutions and agencies which aid in the identification of factual material increase correspondingly. The variety of materials, publications, and institutions useful in providing the factual basis for informed management judgments varies considerably from one field to another. Often, the businessman, government official, student, and librarian will lack a comprehensive and organized inventory of the resources available for fact finding in a particular field. One inevitable consequence is that the opportunity to apply appropriate factual information to the problem-solving process may be lost.

The MANAGEMENT INFORMATION GUIDE SERIES is being developed expressly in order to overcome this deficiency in basic business research tools. Each volume is edited by one or more individuals known to be expert in the subject matter of the field as well as in the information resources applicable to the problems of that field. Each is devoted to a topic of broad interest to business and professional personnel. Each work in the series is designed to direct the user to key sources by arranging, describing, and indexing published sources as well as the programs and services of organizations, agencies, and facilities, which in combination make up the total information scene of each of the fields covered.

PAUL WASSERMAN
Series Editor

INTRODUCTION

Investment periodicals and newspapers contain a great deal of financial data, but it is often difficult to remember exactly which publication contains which bit of statistical information. This volume is meant, therefore, to serve as an index to regularly recurring financial statistics. With one exception, the publications analyzed appear on a daily, weekly, or monthly basis, and they were selected because of their usefulness and wide distribution. While some of the material indexed may seem obvious, such as prices on the New York Stock Exchange, much of the data referred to is of a more specialized nature—-yields on the various stock and bond averages, for example.

The arrangement of entries is alphabetical throughout, with many cross references. In cases where identical information appears in more than one publication, the further arrangement is alphabetical according to name of publication.

Financial terms are explained briefly where necessary to avoid ambiguity, or where unusual data is involved. Also, if a heading used by a financial publication is unusual or unclear in some way, the wording of the heading is quoted in the appropriate entry.

It is hoped that this handbook will prove helpful to those who are unfamiliar with sources of investment information, as well as serving as a memory jogger for those who are experienced in the field.

November, 1969   James B. Woy

LIST OF PUBLICATIONS INCLUDED

BANK AND QUOTATION RECORD. William B. Dana Co., 25 Park Place, New York, New York 10007. Monthly. $75. a year.

BARRON'S. Dow Jones & Co., Inc., 30 Broad Street, New York, New York 10004. Weekly. $18. a year.

BOND OUTLOOK. Standard & Poor's Corporation, 345 Hudson Street, New York, New York 10014. Weekly. $120. a year.

COMMERCIAL AND FINANCIAL CHRONICLE. William B. Dana Co., 25 Park Place, New York, New York 10007. Twice weekly on Monday and Thursday. $90. a year (Thursday edition only is $26.).

MOODY'S BOND SURVEY. Moody's Investors Service, Inc., 99 Church Street, New York, New York 10007. Weekly. $250. a year.

MOODY'S HANDBOOK OF COMMON STOCKS. Moody's Investors Service, Inc., 99 Church Street, New York, New York 10007. Quarterly. $40. a year.

MOODY'S STOCK SURVEY. Moody's Investors Service, Inc., 99 Church Street, New York, New York 10007. Weekly. $144. a year.

NATIONAL MONTHLY STOCK SUMMARY. National Quotation Bureau, Inc., 116 Nassau Street, New York, New York 10038. Monthly. $84. a year. (Includes bound, semiannual, cumulative volumes.)

NEW YORK TIMES. 229 West 43rd Street, New York, New York 10036. Weekday edition, $37. a year. Sunday edition, $39. a year. Both editions, $75. a year. (Mail subscriptions.)

THE OUTLOOK. Standard & Poor's Corporation, 345 Hudson Street, New York, New York 10014. Weekly. $72. a year.

STANDARD & POOR'S EARNINGS AND RATINGS BOND GUIDE. Standard & Poor's Corporation, 345 Hudson Street, New York, New York 10014. Monthly. $34. a year.

STANDARD & POOR'S SECURITY OWNER'S STOCK GUIDE. Standard & Poor's Corporation, 345 Hudson Street, New York, New York 10014. Monthly. $24. a year.

TRENDLINE DAILY BASIS STOCK CHARTS. Trendline, 345 Hudson Street, New York, New York 10014. Weekly. $228. a year.

List of Publications (continued)

TRENDLINE'S CURRENT MARKET PERSPECTIVES. Trendline, 345 Hudson Street, New York, New York 10014. Monthly. $72. a year.

VALUE LINE INVESTMENT SURVEY. Arnold Berhard & Co., Inc., 5 East 44th Street, New York, New York 10017. Weekly. $167. a year. (Part one: "Weekly Summary of Advices and Index." Part two: "Selection and Opinion." Part three: "Ratings and Reports." Part four: "Special Reports".)

WALL STREET JOURNAL. Dow Jones & Co., Inc., 30 Broad Street, New York, New York 10004. Daily (business days). $30. a year.

INVESTMENT INFORMATION

INVESTMENT INFORMATION

ADR's (American Depository Receipts).

    SEE: Foreign stocks. . .

Acceptances, bankers'.

    SEE: Bankers' acceptances rates. . .

Acquisitions.

    SEE: Mergers and acquisitions. . .

Active stocks.

    SEE: High volume stocks. . .
           Most active stocks. . .

Activity.

    SEE: Volume of trading. . .

ADDRESS OF PRINCIPAL OFFICE (main corporate address for each of over 1,000 companies with actively traded common stock). MOODY'S HANDBOOK OF COMMON STOCKS. Published quarterly.

ADDRESS OF PRINCIPAL OFFICE (main corporate address for each of roughly 26,000 unlisted and listed corporations). NATIONAL MONTHLY STOCK SUMMARY. This information appears in semiannual cumulative volumes, dated April 1 and October 1.

ADDRESS OF PRINCIPAL OFFICE (main corporate address for each of about 1,400 leading companies). VALUE LINE INVESTMENT SURVEY. Part three: published weekly, a few industries each week.

Adjusted earnings per share.

    SEE: Diluted earnings per share. . .

Advance-decline line.

    SEE ALSO: Advances and declines. . .

ADVANCE-DECLINE LINE, AMERICAN STOCK EXCHANGE, DAILY, CHART (covers about two years. Measures cumulative difference between number of stocks advancing and number declining). TRENDLINE DAILY BASIS STOCK CHARTS. Published weekly.

ADVANCE-DECLINE LINE, NEW YORK STOCK EXCHANGE, DAILY, CHART (covers about four years. Measures cumulative difference between number of stocks advancing and number declining). TRENDLINE DAILY BASIS STOCK CHARTS. Published weekly.

ADVANCE-DECLINE LINE, NEW YORK STOCK EXCHANGE, WEEKLY, CHART (covers about five years. Measures cumulative difference between number of stocks advancing and number declining). TRENDLINE'S CURRENT MARKET PER-SPECTIVE. Published monthly.

ADVANCES AND DECLINES, BOND PRICES ON AMERICAN STOCK EX-CHANGE, DAILY (number of issues advancing, declining, and remaining un-changed on each of last four trading days). WALL STREET JOURNAL. Published on business days.

ADVANCES AND DECLINES, BOND PRICES·ON NEW YORK STOCK EX-CHANGE, DAILY (number of issues advancing and number declining on each of last three trading days). NEW YORK TIMES. Published weekdays.

ADVANCES AND DECLINES, BOND PRICES ON NEW YORK STOCK EX-CHANGE, DAILY (number of issues advancing, declining, and remaining un-changed on each of last two trading days, in each of following categories: foreign, domestic, all issues). WALL STREET JOURNAL. Published on business days.

ADVANCES AND DECLINES, STOCK PRICES ON AMERICAN STOCK EX-CHANGE, DAILY (number of issues advancing, declining, and remaining un-changed on each day of week just past). BARRON'S. Published weekly.

ADVANCES AND DECLINES, STOCK PRICES ON AMERICAN STOCK EX-CHANGE, DAILY (number of issues advancing, declining, and remaining un-changed on each of last two trading days. Labeled "The Summary"). NEW YORK TIMES. Published weekdays.

ADVANCES AND DECLINES, STOCK PRICES ON AMERICAN STOCK EX-CHANGE, DAILY (number of issues advancing, declining, and remaining un-changed on each of last six trading days). WALL STREET JOURNAL. Pub-lished on business days.

ADVANCES AND DECLINES, STOCK PRICES ON AMERICAN STOCK EX-CHANGE, WEEKLY (number of issues advancing and number declining, on a weekly basis, for each of last two weeks. Labeled "Market Breadth"). NEW YORK TIMES. Sunday edition.

ADVANCES AND DECLINES, STOCK PRICES ON NEW YORK STOCK EX-CHANGE, DAILY (number of issues advancing, declining, and remaining un-changed on each day of week just past). BARRON'S. Published weekly.

ADVANCES AND DECLINES, STOCK PRICES ON NEW YORK STOCK EX-
CHANGE, DAILY (number of issues advancing, declining, and remaining un-
changed on each of last two trading days. Labeled "Market Summary").
NEW YORK TIMES. Published weekdays.

ADVANCES AND DECLINES, STOCK PRICES ON NEW YORK STOCK EX-
CHANGE, DAILY (number of issues advancing, declining, and remaining un-
changed on each of last six trading days. Labeled "Market Diary"). WALL
STREET JOURNAL. Published on business days.

ADVANCES AND DECLINES, STOCK PRICES ON NEW YORK STOCK EX-
CHANGE, WEEKLY (number of issues advancing, declining, and remaining un-
changed during week just past). BARRON'S. Published weekly.

ADVANCES AND DECLINES, STOCK PRICES ON NEW YORK STOCK EX-
CHANGE, WEEKLY (number of issues advancing and number declining, on a
weekly basis, for each of last two weeks. Labeled "Market Breadth"). NEW
YORK TIMES. Sunday edition.

ADVANCES AND DECLINES, VOLUME ON AMERICAN STOCK EXCHANGE,
DAILY (trading volume in advancing stocks and in declining stocks, in number
of shares for previous day). WALL STREET JOURNAL. Published on business
days.

ADVANCES AND DECLINES, VOLUME ON NEW YORK STOCK EXCHANGE,
DAILY (trading volume in advancing stocks and in declining stocks, in number
of shares for previous day). WALL STREET JOURNAL. Published on business
days.

Agent, transfer.

    SEE: Transfer agents. . .

AIRLINES, COMMON STOCK EQUITY (PERCENT), YEARLY (for each of past
18 or so years, for each of about 17 leading airlines. Refers to common stock
as percentage of total capitalization. Labeled "Common Equity Ratio").
VALUE LINE INVESTMENT SURVEY. Part three: published weekly, a few
industries each week.

AIRLINES, PASSENGER LOAD FACTOR (PERCENT), YEARLY (for each of past
eleven years, for each of large airlines with actively traded common stock.
Refers to percentage of available seat miles actually used). MOODY'S HAND-
BOOK OF COMMON STOCKS. Published quarterly.

AIRLINES, PASSENGER LOAD FACTOR (PERCENT), YEARLY (for each of past
18 or so years, for each of about 17 leading airlines. Refers to percentage of
available seat miles actually used). VALUE LINE INVESTMENT SURVEY.
Part three: published weekly, a few industries each week.

American Depository Receipts.

    SEE: Foreign stocks. . .

American Stock Exchange advances and declines.

> SEE: Advances and declines, bond prices on American
> Stock Exchange. . .
> Advances and declines, stock prices on American
> Stock Exchange. . .

American Stock Exchange average.

> SEE: American Stock Exchange price level index. . .

American Stock Exchange bond prices.

> SEE: Bond prices on American Stock Exchange. . .

American Stock Exchange commission rates.

> SEE: Commission rates, major stock exchanges. . .

American Stock Exchange dividends.

> SEE: Dividends, amount, current, American Stock
> Exchange. . .
> Dividends, amount, indicated annual rate,
> American Stock Exchange. . .

American Stock Exchange earnings.

> SEE: Earnings per share, interim, American Stock
> Exchange. . .

American Stock Exchange index.

> SEE: American Stock Exchange price level index. . .

American Stock Exchange issues traded.

> SEE: Issues traded, bonds on American Stock Exchange. . .
> Issues traded, stocks on American Stock Exchange. . .

American Stock Exchange most active stocks.

> SEE: Most active stocks, American Stock Exchange. . .

American Stock Exchange new highs and lows.

> SEE: New highs and new lows, bond prices on American
> Stock Exchange. . .
> New highs and new lows, stock prices on American
> Stock Exchange. . .

American Stock Exchange new listings.

> SEE: New listings, bonds. . .
> New listings, stocks. . .

AMERICAN STOCK EXCHANGE PRICE LEVEL INDEX, DAILY, CLOSE (for
each day of week just past). BARRON'S. Published weekly.

AMERICAN STOCK EXCHANGE PRICE LEVEL INDEX, DAILY, HIGH-LOW-CLOSE (for each day of week just past). COMMERCIAL AND FINANCIAL CHRONICLE. Monday edition.

AMERICAN STOCK EXCHANGE PRICE LEVEL INDEX, DAILY, HIGH-LOW-CLOSE (for previous day). NEW YORK TIMES. Published weekdays.

AMERICAN STOCK EXCHANGE PRICE LEVEL INDEX, DAILY, HIGH-LOW-CLOSE, CHART (daily prices charted for about two years). TRENDLINE DAILY BASIS STOCK CHARTS. Published weekly.

AMERICAN STOCK EXCHANGE PRICE LEVEL INDEX, DAILY-YEARLY, CLOSE (closing price for previous day and same day one year ago). WALL STREET JOURNAL. Published on business days.

AMERICAN STOCK EXCHANGE PRICE LEVEL INDEX, MONTHLY, HIGH-LOW, CHART (monthly ranges charted for about five years). MOODY'S HANDBOOK OF COMMON STOCKS. Published quarterly.

AMERICAN STOCK EXCHANGE PRICE LEVEL INDEX, MOVING AVERAGE, CHART (200-day moving average is shown on daily chart covering about two years). TRENDLINE DAILY BASIS STOCK CHARTS. Published weekly.

AMERICAN STOCK EXCHANGE PRICE LEVEL INDEX, MOVING AVERAGE, CHART (200-day moving average charted weekly for about four years). TRENDLINE'S CURRENT MARKET PERSPECTIVES. Published monthly.

American Stock Exchange price level index, percentage change.

    SEE: American Stock Exchange price level index, weekly, percentage change. . .
        American Stock Exchange price level index, year to date, percentage change. . .

American Stock Exchange price level index, rallies and declines.

    SEE: Trading swings, American Stock Exchange price level index. . .

AMERICAN STOCK EXCHANGE PRICE LEVEL INDEX, WEEKLY, HIGH-LOW, CHART (weekly ranges charted for about two years). MOODY'S HANDBOOK OF COMMON STOCKS. Published quarterly.

AMERICAN STOCK EXCHANGE PRICE LEVEL INDEX, WEEKLY, HIGH-LOW-CLOSE, CHART (weekly prices charted for about four years). TRENDLINE'S CURRENT MARKET PERSPECTIVES. Published monthly.

AMERICAN STOCK EXCHANGE PRICE LEVEL INDEX, WEEKLY, PERCENTAGE CHANGE (for end of week just past. Included with data under "Mutual Fund Investment Performance Index"). BARRON'S. Published weekly.

AMERICAN STOCK EXCHANGE PRICE LEVEL INDEX, YEAR TO DATE, PER-CENTAGE CHANGE (up to end of week just past. Included with data under "Mutual Fund Investment Performance Index"). BARRON'S. Published weekly.

AMERICAN STOCK EXCHANGE PRICE LEVEL INDEX, YEARLY, HIGH-LOW, CHART (annual price ranges charted for about seven years). TRENDLINE DAILY BASIS STOCK CHARTS. Published weekly.

American Stock Exchange seat prices.

SEE: Exchange seats, prices. . .

American Stock Exchange short interest.

SEE: Short interest, individual stocks on American Stock
        Exchange. . .
      Short interest, total for American Stock Exchange. . .

American Stock Exchange stock prices.

SEE: Stock prices on American Stock Exchange. . .

American Stock Exchange stock splits.

SEE: Stock splits, American Stock Exchange. . .

American Stock Exchange ticker symbols.

SEE: Ticker symbols. . .

American Stock Exchange volume.

SEE: Volume of trading in bonds, individual bonds on
        American Stock Exchange. . .
      Volume of trading in bonds, total for American
        Stock Exchange. . .
      Volume of trading in stocks, individual stocks on
        American Stock Exchange. . .
      Volume of trading in stocks, total for American
        Stock Exchange. . .

American Stock Exchange volume trends.
      See: Upside-downside volume, American Stock Exchange. . .

Amsterdam Stock Exchange prices.

SEE: Stock prices on Amsterdam Stock Exchange. . .
      Foreign stock price indexes. . .

ANNUAL MEETING DATES (date of annual meeting for each of over 1,000 companies with actively traded common stock). MOODY'S HANDBOOK OF COMMON STOCKS. Published quarterly.

Applications for listing.

SEE: New listings, stocks, pending. . .

Arbitrary price-earnings ratio.

> SEE: Price-earnings ratio, individual stocks, arbitrary. . .

Argentine stocks.

> SEE: Stock prices on Buenos Aires Stock Exchange. . .

Asset totals.

> SEE: Banks, asset totals. . .
> Closed-end investment companies, asset totals. . .
> Insurance companies, asset totals. . .
> Mutual funds, asset totals. . .
> Savings and loan companies, asset totals. . .

Asset value per share, closed-end investment companies.

> SEE: Closed-end investment companies, asset value per share. . .

Asset value per share, mutual funds.

> SEE: Mutual funds, asset value per share. . .

Assets, cash.

> SEE: Cash as current asset. . .

Assets, current.

> SEE: Current assets. . .

Australian stocks.

> SEE: Stock prices on Sydney Stock Exchange. . .
> Foreign stock price indexes. . .

Authority bonds.

> SEE: Public authority bonds. . .

AUTOMOBILE COMPANIES, MARKET SHARE (PERCENT), YEARLY (for each of past 18 or so years, for each of four largest U.S. automobile producers, shows output of cars relative to total U.S. production). VALUE LINE INVESTMENT SURVEY. Part three: published weekly, a few industries each week.

Average, American Stock Exchange.

> SEE: American Stock Exchange price level index. . .

Average, most active stocks.

> SEE: Most active stocks, New York Stock Exchange, average closing
> price. . .

Averages, Barron's.

    See entries beginning "Barron's. . ."

Averages, Dow-Jones.

    See entries beginning "Dow-Jones. . ."

Averages, foreign stocks.

    SEE: Foreign stock price indexes. . .

Averages, Moody's.

    See entries beginning "Moody's. . ."

Averages, mutual fund.

    SEE: Mutual fund averages. . .

Averages, National Quotation Bureau.

    See entries beginning "National Quotation Bureau. . ."

Averages, New York Stock Exchange (indexes).

    See entries beginning "New York Stock Exchange. . ."

Averages, New York Times.

    See entries beginning "New York Times. . ."

Averages, Standard & Poor's (indexes).

    See entries beginning "Standard & Poor's. . ."

Averages, Value Line (indexes).

    See entries beginning "Value Line. . ."

Balance sheets, dates of latest available.

    SEE ALSO: Fiscal year ending month. . .

BALANCE SHEETS, DATES OF LATEST AVAILABLE (for individual corporations with bond issues). STANDARD & POOR'S EARNINGS AND RATINGS BOND GUIDE. Published monthly.

BALANCE SHEETS, DATES OF LATEST AVAILABLE (for about 4,300 individual corporations with stock issues). STANDARD & POOR'S SECURITY OWNER'S STOCK GUIDE. Published monthly.

Bank for Cooperatives bonds.

    SEE: Banks for Cooperatives bonds. . .

Bank stock average, Moody's.

    SEE: Moody's New York bank stock average. . .

Bank stock averages, Standards & Poor's.

SEE: Standard & Poor's stock group indexes. . .

BANK STOCKS, DIVIDENDS, AMOUNT, INDICATED ANNUAL RATE (for each of about 150 over-the-counter bank stocks). BARRON'S. Published weekly.

BANK STOCKS, DIVIDENDS, AMOUNT, INDICATED ANNUAL RATE (for each of about 150 over-the-counter bank stocks). NEW YORK TIMES. Published weekdays.

BANK STOCKS, DIVIDENDS, AMOUNT, INDICATED ANNUAL RATE (for each of about 150 over-the-counter bank stocks). NEW YORK TIMES. Sunday edition.

BANK STOCKS, DIVIDENDS, AMOUNT, INDICATED ANNUAL RATE (for each of about 150 over-the-counter bank stocks). WALL STREET JOURNAL. Published business days.

BANK STOCKS, EARNINGS PER SHARE, INTERIM (latest interim earnings for each of about 150 over-the-counter bank stocks). BARRON'S. Published weekly.

BANK STOCKS, PRICES, DAILY (bid and asked prices for previous day for each of about 150 over-the-counter bank stocks, with former bid). NEW YORK TIMES. Published weekdays.

BANK STOCKS, PRICES, DAILY (bid and asked prices for previous day for each of about 150 over-the-counter bank stocks, with net change in bid). WALL STREET JOURNAL. Published on business days.

BANK STOCKS, PRICES, MONTHLY, CLOSE (bid and asked prices for end of month prior to month of publication for each of about 750 over-the-counter bank stocks. Banks are arranged geographically by state). BANK AND QUOTATION RECORD. Published monthly.

BANK STOCKS, PRICES, MONTHLY, CLOSE (bid and asked prices for thousands of unlisted bank stocks are interfiled with other stock prices, in alphabetical order). NATIONAL MONTHLY STOCK SUMMARY. Published monthly.

BANK STOCKS, PRICES, WEEKLY, CLOSE (bid and asked prices for each of week just past, and bid price for end of previous week, for each of about 150 over-the-counter bank stocks). BARRON'S. Published weekly.

BANK STOCKS, PRICES, WEEKLY, CLOSE (bid and asked prices for end of week just past for each of about 150 over-the-counter bank stocks). COMMERCIAL AND FINANCIAL CHRONICLE. Monday edition.

BANK STOCKS, PRICES, WEEKLY, HIGH-LOW-CLOSE (range of bid prices for week just past, for each of about 150 over-the-counter bank stocks). NEW YORK TIMES. Sunday edition.

BANK STOCKS, PRICES, YEAR TO DATE, HIGH-LOW (range of bid prices for current year for each of about 150 over-the-counter bank stocks). BARRON'S. Published weekly.

BANKERS' ACCEPTANCES RATES (PERCENT), DAILY (bid-ask rates on prime bankers' acceptances for 30 days, 60 days, 90 days, 120 days, 150 days, and 180 days. All rates quoted separately for each day of the month prior to month of publication). BANK AND QUOTATION RECORD. Published monthly.

BANKERS' ACCEPTANCES RATES (PERCENT), DAILY (bid-ask rate for one to 180 days. Under "Money" heading). NEW YORK TIMES. Published weekdays.

BANKERS' ACCEPTANCES RATES (PERCENT), DAILY (bid-ask rate for one to 180 days "quoted by one dealer." Under "Money Rates" heading). WALL STREET JOURNAL. Published business days.

BANKERS' ACCEPTANCES RATES (PERCENT), WEEKLY-YEARLY (bid-ask rates for end of week just past, for previous week, and for same week one year ago. Under "Economic and Financial Indicators" heading). BARRON'S. Published weekly.

Banknote rates, foreign.

   SEE: Foreign banknote rates. . .

BANKS, ASSET TOTALS, YEARLY (for each of past 18 or so years, for each of about 40 leading banks). VALUE LINE INVESTMENT SURVEY. Part three: published weekly, a few industries each week.

BANKS, BOOK VALUE PER SHARE, CURRENT (for many individual banks, interfiled with other stocks). STANDARD & POOR'S SECURITY OWNER'S STOCK GUIDE. Published monthly.

BANKS, BOOK VALUE PER SHARE, YEARLY (for each of past eleven years, for each of large banks with active common stock). MOODY'S HANDBOOK OF COMMON STOCKS. Published quarterly.

BANKS, BOOK VALUE PER SHARE, YEARLY (for each of past 18 or so years, for each of about 40 leading banks). VALUE LINE INVESTMENT SURVEY. Part three: published weekly, a few industries each week.

BANKS, CAPITAL FUNDS AS PERCENTAGE OF DEPOSITS, YEARLY (for each of past 18 or so years, for each of about 40 leading banks). VALUE LINE INVESTMENT SURVEY. Part three: published weekly, a few industries each week.

BANKS, CAPITAL FUNDS TOTALS, YEARLY (for each of past 18 or so years, for each of about 40 leading banks). VALUE LINE INVESTMENT SURVEY. Part three: published weekly, a few industries each week.

BANKS, DEPOSIT TOTALS, YEARLY (for each of past eleven years, for each of large banks with active common stock). MOODY'S HANDBOOK OF COMMON STOCKS. Published quarterly.

BANKS, DEPOSIT TOTALS, YEARLY (for each of past 18 or so years, for each of about 40 leading banks). VALUE LINE INVESTMENT SURVEY. Part three: published weekly, a few industries each week.

BANKS, DEPOSITS PER SHARE, YEARLY (for each of past 18 or so years, for each of about 40 leading banks). VALUE LINE INVESTMENT SURVEY. Part three: published weekly, a few industries each week.

BANKS, GOVERNMENT SECURITIES AS PERCENTAGE OF TOTAL INVEST-MENTS, YEARLY (for each of past 18 or so years, for each of about 40 leading banks. Labeled "U.S. Gov'ts. as % Total Inv."). VALUE LINE INVEST-MENT SURVEY. Part three: published weekly, a few industries each week.

BANKS, GOVERNMENT SECURITIES HOLDINGS, VALUE OF, YEARLY (for each of past 18 or so years, for each of about 40 leading banks). VALUE LINE INVESTMENT SURVEY. Part three: published weekly, a few industries each week.

BANKS, GROSS INCOME, YEARLY (for each of past eleven years, for each of large banks with active common stock). MOODY'S HANDBOOK OF COMMON STOCKS. Published quarterly.

BANKS, GROSS INCOME, YEARLY (for each of past 18 or so years, for each of about 40 leading banks). VALUE LINE INVESTMENT SURVEY. Part three: published weekly, a few industries each week.

BANKS, LOAN TOTALS, YEARLY (for each of past eleven years, for each of large banks with active common stock). MOODY'S HANDBOOK OF COMMON STOCKS. Published quarterly.

BANKS, LOAN TOTALS, YEARLY (for each of past 18 or so years, for each of about 40 leading banks. Labeled "Loans & Discounts"). VALUE LINE INVESTMENT SURVEY. Part three: published weekly, a few industries each week.

BANKS, LOANS AS PERCENTAGE OF DEPOSITS, YEARLY (for each of past 18 or so years, for each of about 40 leading banks). VALUE LINE INVEST-MENT SURVEY. Part three: published weekly, a few industries each week.

BANKS, OPERATING EARNINGS TOTALS, YEARLY (for each of past eleven years, for each of large banks with active common stock). MOODY'S HAND-BOOK OF COMMON STOCKS. Published quarterly.

Banks, regulation of investments.

   SEE: Comptroller of the Currency regulations. . .

BANKS FOR COOPERATIVES BONDS, PRICES, DAILY (bid and asked prices for each of about six issues, for previous day. Amount outstanding in millions of dollars shown for each issue). NEW YORK TIMES. Published weekdays.

BANKS FOR COOPERATIVES BONDS, PRICES, DAILY (bid and asked prices for each of about six issues, for previous day). WALL STREET JOURNAL. Published business days.

BANKS FOR COOPERATIVES BONDS, PRICES, MONTHLY, CLOSE (end-of-month bid and asked prices for each of about six issues. Listed under "United States and Municipal Bonds"). BANK AND QUOTATION RECORD. Published monthly.

BANKS FOR COOPERATIVES BONDS, PRICES, WEEKLY, CLOSE (end-of-week bid and asked prices for each of about six issues. Listed under "Obligations of Government Agencies"). COMMERCIAL AND FINANCIAL CHRONICLE. Monday edition.

BANKS FOR COOPERATIVES BONDS, YIELDS TO MATURITY, DAILY (percentage yield for each of about six issues, for previous trading day. Amount outstanding in millions of dollars shown for each issue). NEW YORK TIMES. Published weekdays.

BANKS FOR COOPERATIVES BONDS, YIELDS TO MATURITY, DAILY (per-centage yield for each of about six issues, for previous trading day). WALL STREET JOURNAL. Published business days.

BARRON'S CONFIDENCE INDEX, WEEKLY, CHART (charted weekly for about two years. Reflects investor confidence in medium grade bonds, relative to high grade bonds). TRENDLINE DAILY BASIS STOCK CHARTS. Published weekly.

BARRON'S CONFIDENCE INDEX, WEEKLY, CHART (charted weekly for about six years. Reflects investor confidence in medium grade bonds, relative to high grade bonds). TRENDLINE'S CURRENT MARKET PERSPECTIVES. Published monthly.

BARRON'S CONFIDENCE INDEX, WEEKLY-YEARLY (index for end of week just past, previous week, and same week one year ago. Reflects investor confidence in medium grade bonds, relative to high grade bonds -- a ratio of yield on Barron's ten high-grade bonds average to yield on Dow-Jones composite 40 bonds average). BARRON'S. Published weekly.

BARRON'S 50-STOCK AVERAGE, DIVIDEND YIELD (PERCENT), WEEKLY-YEARLY (for end of week just past, previous week, and same week one year ago. Labeled "Div yield in year ended"). BARRON'S. Published weekly.

BARRON'S 50-STOCK AVERAGE, DIVIDENDS, TOTAL AMOUNT, YEARLY-QUARTERLY (total dividends paid in year just past by stocks in average. Figure changed quarterly as new dividend data become available. Comparable figure given for one year ago. Labeled "Divs paid in year ended"). BARRON'S. Published weekly.

BARRON'S 50-STOCK AVERAGE, EARNINGS, FIVE-YEAR AVERAGE, QUAR-TERLY (figure for five-year average earnings is changed quarterly as new earnings become available . Comparable figure given for one year ago). BARRON'S. Published weekly.

BARRON'S 50-STOCK AVERAGE, EARNINGS, YEARLY-WEEKLY (estimated annual earnings for year ending with current week, previous week, and same week one year ago). BARRON'S. Published weekly.

BARRON'S 50-STOCK AVERAGE, EARNINGS (PROJECTED), QUARTERLY (an estimate of earnings for the next quarter, with a comparable figure for the same period one year ago). BARRON'S. Published weekly.

BARRON'S 50-STOCK AVERAGE, EARNINGS (PROJECTED), YEARLY (estimated earnings for next quarter are multiplied by four to get annual figure, with comparable data for previous year). BARRON'S. Published weekly.

BARRON'S 50-STOCK AVERAGE, EARNINGS YIELD (PERCENT), WEEKLY-YEARLY (for latest week, previous week, and same week one year ago. Labeled "Earn yield yr ended earn"). BARRON'S. Published weekly.

BARRON'S 50-STOCK AVERAGE, PRICE, WEEKLY-YEARLY (for latest week, previous week, and same week one year ago). BARRON'S. Published weekly.

BARRON'S 50-STOCK AVERAGE, PRICE-EARNINGS RATIO, WEEKLY-YEARLY (for latest week, previous week, and same week one year ago. Labeled "Ratio price to yr end earn"). BARRON'S. Published weekly.

BARRON'S 50-STOCK AVERAGE, PRICE-EARNINGS RATIO BASED ON FIVE-YEAR AVERAGE EARNINGS, WEEKLY-YEARLY (for latest week, previous week, and same week one year ago. Labeled "Ratio price to 5-yr av earn"). BARRON'S. Published weekly.

BARRON'S 50-STOCK AVERAGE, PRICE-EARNINGS RATIO (PROJECTED), WEEKLY-YEARLY (projected quarterly earnings are multiplied by four to obtain figure used in computing price-earnings ratio, for week just past, previous week, and same week one year ago. Labeled "Ratio price to proj an earn"). BARRON'S. Published weekly.

Barron's 50-stock average, yield.

> SEE: Barron's 50-stock average, dividend yield. . .
> Barron's 50-stock average, earnings yield. . .

BARRON'S GROUP STOCK AVERAGES, PRICES, NEW HIGHS, WEEKLY (for each of 32 stock groups, including banks, insurance, and closed-end investment companies. New high for current year is indicated by "H" before latest week's closing price). BARRON'S. Published weekly.

BARRON'S GROUP STOCK AVERAGES, PRICES, WEEKLY, CLOSE (for each
of 32 stock groups, including banks, insurance, and closed-end investment
companies, for end of week just past and previous week. Weekly percentage
price change also indicated in each case). BARRON'S. Published weekly.

BARRON'S GROUP STOCK AVERAGES, PRICES, YEAR TO DATE, HIGH-LOW
(current year's price range for each of 32 stock groups, including banks, insurance, and closed-end investment companies). BARRON'S. Published weekly.

BARRON'S HIGH-GRADE BOND INDEX, YIELD (PERCENT), MONTHLY AV-
ERAGE (average yield for latest month, previous month, and same month one
year ago. Under "The Statistical Record, Monthly Average"). BARRON'S.
This date normally appears in first issue of each month.

BARRON'S HIGH-GRADE BOND INDEX, YIELD (PERCENT), WEEKLY-YEARLY
(for end of latest week, week previous, and same period one year ago).
BARRON'S. Published weekly.

BARRON'S LOW-PRICED STOCK INDEX, PRICE, WEEKLY-YEARLY, CLOSE
(for end of latest week, previous week, and same week one year ago. Labeled "20 Low Priced Stocks: Index"). BARRON'S. Published weekly.

BARRON'S LOW-PRICED STOCK INDEX, RATIO OF VOLUME TO DOW-
JONES INDUSTRIAL VOLUME, WEEKLY-YEARLY (volume of 20 low-priced
stocks expressed as percentage of volume of 30 stocks in Dow-Jones industrial
stock average, for latest week, previous week, and same period one year ago.
Labeled "20 Low Priced Stocks, % of vol to D-J Ind vol"). BARRON'S.
Published weekly.

BARRON'S LOW-PRICED STOCK INDEX, VOLUME OF TRADING, WEEKLY-
YEARLY (combined volume in thousands of shares for 20 stocks in index, for
latest week, previous week, and same period one year ago. Labeled "20
Low Priced Stocks: Volume, th shs"). BARRON'S. Published weekly.

Barron's mutual fund averages.

SEE: Mutual fund averages. . .

Barron's stock group averages.

SEE: Barron's group stock averages. . .

Beginning year of dividends.

SEE: Dividends, uninterrupted, year of beginning. . .

Belgian stocks.

SEE: Stock prices on Brussels Stock Exchange. . .
Foreign stock price indexes. . .

Bills, treasury.

SEE: Treasury bills. . .

Block transactions.

> SEE: Large block transactions. . .

Bond average, Barron's.

> SEE: Barron's high-grade bond index. . .

Bond averages, Dow-Jones.

> See entries beginning "Dow-Jones. . . "

Bond averages, Moody's.

> See entries beginning "Moody's. . . "

Bond averages, Standard & Poor's (indexes).

> See entries beginning "Standard & Poor's. . ."

Bond calls.

> SEE: Redemptions. . .

Bond interest charges, "times earned."

> SEE: Earnings to fixed charges ratio. . .

BOND INTEREST PAYMENT DATES (interest periods for about 5,000 individual issues -- industrial, foreign, public utility, railroad, municipal, U.S. government, etc.). BANK AND QUOTATION RECORD. Published monthly.

BOND INTEREST PAYMENT DATES (months of interest period for each bond traded on New York and American Stock Exchanges). COMMERCIAL AND FINANCIAL CHRONICLE. Monday edition.

BOND INTEREST PAYMENT DATES (for about 3,300 individual issues -- corporate, foreign, and convertible). STANDARD & POOR'S EARNINGS AND RATINGS BOND GUIDE. Published monthly.

Bond interest rates.

> SEE ALSO: Bond yields to maturity. . .
> Convertible bonds, yields to maturity. . .
> Foreign bonds, interest rates. . .
> Foreign bonds, yields to maturity. . .
> Government bonds, interest rates. . .
> Government bonds, yields to maturity. . .

> (Also see cross references under "Bond interest yield averages. . .")

BOND INTEREST RATES (stated rates for about 5,000 individual issues -- U.S. government, industrial, foreign, municipal, public utility, railroad, etc.). BANK AND QUOTATION RECORD. Published monthly.

BOND INTEREST RATES (stated rates for about 3,300 individual issues -- corporate, foreign, and convertible). STANDARD & POOR'S EARNINGS AND RATINGS BOND GUIDE. Published monthly.

Bond interest yield average, Barron's.

> SEE: Barron's high-grade bond index, yield. . .

Bond interest yield averages, Moody's.

> See entries beginning "Moody's. . ."

Bond interest yield averages, Standard & Poor's.

> See entries beginning "Standard & Poor's. . ."

Bond issues, new.

> SEE: New issues, bonds. . .

Bond maturity dates.

> SEE: Bonds, due dates. . .

Bond prices.

> Also see specific kinds of bonds, such as "Convertible bonds, prices...,"
> "Government bonds, prices...,"etc.

Bond prices, American Exchange.

> SEE: Bond prices on American Stock Exchange. . .

Bond prices, London.

> SEE: Bond prices on London Stock Exchange. . .

BOND PRICES, MONTHLY, CLOSE (for about 2,600 individual corporate and 200 foreign bonds, for end of month prior to month of publication). STANDARD & POOR'S EARNINGS AND RATINGS BOND GUIDE. Published monthly.

Bond prices, New York.

> SEE: Bond prices on New York Stock Exchange. . .

BOND PRICES, OFFERING (original offering price for each of about 2,600 corporate and 200 foreign bonds. Year of original offering also indicated). STANDARD & POOR'S EARNINGS AND RATINGS BOND GUIDE. Published monthly.

Bond prices, over-the-counter.

> Also see specific kinds of bonds, such as "Railroad bonds (unlisted), prices. . .," "Utility bonds (unlisted), prices. . .," etc.

BOND PRICES, OVER-THE-COUNTER, DAILY (bid-asked prices for each of about 20 unlisted, corporate bonds, for previous day, with former bid). NEW YORK TIMES. Published weekdays.

BOND PRICES, OVER-THE-COUNTER, DAILY (bid-asked prices for previous day for each of about 20 unlisted "Corporation Bonds"). WALL STREET JOURNAL. Published business days.

BOND PRICES, OVER-THE-COUNTER, MONTHLY, CLOSE (bid price for end of month prior to month of publication for each of about 500 unlisted "Industrial and Miscellaneous Bonds"). BANK AND QUOTATION RECORD. Published monthly.

BOND PRICES, OVER-THE-COUNTER, WEEKLY, HIGH-LOW-CLOSE (weekly range and closing bid for each of about 20 unlisted, corporate bonds, for week just past). NEW YORK TIMES. Sunday edition.

BOND PRICES, SEVEN YEAR PERIOD, HIGH-LOW (highest and lowest price reached by each of about 2,600 corporate bonds during recent seven year period). STANDARD & POOR'S EARNINGS AND RATINGS BOND GUIDE. Published monthly.

BOND PRICES, YEARLY, HIGH-LOW (price ranges for current year and previous year for each of about 2,600 corporate bonds). STANDARD & POOR'S EARNINGS AND RATINGS BOND GUIDE. Published monthly.

BOND PRICES ON AMERICAN STOCK EXCHANGE, DAILY, HIGH-LOW-CLOSE (for each bond traded on previous day). NEW YORK TIMES. Published weekdays.

BOND PRICES ON AMERICAN STOCK EXCHANGE, DAILY, HIGH-LOW-CLOSE (for each bond traded on previous day). WALL STREET JOURNAL. Published business days.

BOND PRICES ON AMERICAN STOCK EXCHANGE, MONTHLY, OPEN-HIGH-LOW-CLOSE (for each bond traded on American Stock Exchange, for month prior to month of publication). BANK AND QUOTATION RECORD. Published monthly.

BOND PRICES ON AMERICAN STOCK EXCHANGE, WEEKLY, HIGH-LOW-CLOSE (for each listed bond, for week just past. Under "Listed Bond Quotations -- American Bonds"). BARRON'S. Published weekly.

BOND PRICES ON AMERICAN STOCK EXCHANGE, WEEKLY, HIGH-LOW-CLOSE (for each bond traded during past week). NEW YORK TIMES. Sunday edition.

BOND PRICES ON AMERICAN STOCK EXCHANGE, YEAR TO DATE, HIGH-LOW (current year's range for each listed bond. Under "Listed Bond Quotations -- American Bonds"). BARRON'S. Published weekly.

BOND PRICES ON AMERICAN STOCK EXCHANGE, YEAR TO DATE, HIGH-LOW (current year's range for each listed bond). COMMERCIAL AND FINANCIAL CHRONICLE. Monday edition.

BOND PRICES ON AMERICAN STOCK EXCHANGE, YEAR TO DATE, HIGH-LOW (current year's range for each listed bond traded on previous day). NEW YORK TIMES. Published weekdays.

BOND PRICES ON AMERICAN STOCK EXCHANGE, YEAR TO DATE, HIGH-LOW (current year's range for each listed bond). NEW YORK TIMES. Sunday edition.

BOND PRICES ON AMERICAN STOCK EXCHANGE, YEAR TO DATE, HIGH-LOW (current year's range for each listed bond traded on previous day). WALL STREET JOURNAL. Published business days.

BOND PRICES ON AMERICAN STOCK EXCHANGE, YEAR TO DATE, OPEN-HIGH-LOW (opening price and price range for current year for each bond listed, up to and including month prior to month of publication). BANK AND QUOTATION RECORD. Published monthly.

BOND PRICES ON LONDON STOCK EXCHANGE, DAILY, CLOSE (in pounds, for previous trading day, for each of about six selected bonds). NEW YORK TIMES. Published weekdays.

BOND PRICES ON NEW YORK STOCK EXCHANGE, DAILY, HIGH-LOW-CLOSE (for each bond traded on previous day). NEW YORK TIMES. Published weekdays.

BOND PRICES ON NEW YORK STOCK EXCHANGE, DAILY, HIGH-LOW-CLOSE (for each bond traded on previous day). WALL STREET JOURNAL. Published business days.

BOND PRICES ON NEW YORK STOCK EXCHANGE, MONTHLY, HIGH-LOW (price range for each listed bond, for each of the 12 months of the year just past). COMMERCIAL AND FINANCIAL CHRONICLE. This data published annually around the first of February in a special section of the Thursday edition.

BOND PRICES ON NEW YORK STOCK EXCHANGE, MONTHLY, OPEN-HIGH-LOW-CLOSE (prices for month prior to month of publication, for each listed bond). BANK AND QUOTATION RECORD. Published monthly.

BOND PRICES ON NEW YORK STOCK EXCHANGE, WEEKLY, HIGH-LOW-CLOSE (for each listed bond, for week just past. Under "Listed Bond Quotations -- Corporation"). BARRON'S. Published weekly.

BOND PRICES ON NEW YORK STOCK EXCHANGE, WEEKLY, HIGH-LOW-CLOSE (for each listed bond, for week just past). COMMERCIAL AND FINANCIAL CHRONICLE. Monday edition.

BOND PRICES ON NEW YORK STOCK EXCHANGE, WEEKLY, HIGH-LOW-CLOSE (for each listed bond, for week just past). NEW YORK TIMES. Sunday edition.

BOND PRICES ON NEW YORK STOCK EXCHANGE, YEAR TO DATE, HIGH-LOW (current year's range for each listed bond. Under "Listed Bond Quotations -- Corporation"). BARRON'S. Published weekly.

BOND PRICES ON NEW YORK STOCK EXCHANGE, YEAR TO DATE, HIGH-LOW (current year's price range for each listed bond). COMMERCIAL AND FINANCIAL CHRONICLE. Monday edition.

BOND PRICES ON NEW YORK STOCK EXCHANGE, YEAR TO DATE, HIGH-LOW (current year's price range for each listed bond traded on previous day). NEW YORK TIMES. Published weekdays.

BOND PRICES ON NEW YORK STOCK EXCHANGE, YEAR TO DATE, HIGH-LOW (current year's price range for each listed bond). NEW YORK TIMES. Sunday edition.

BOND PRICES ON NEW YORK STOCK EXCHANGE, YEAR TO DATE, HIGH-LOW (current year's price range for each listed bond traded on previous day). WALL STREET JOURNAL. Published business days.

BOND PRICES ON NEW YORK STOCK EXCHANGE, YEAR TO DATE, OPEN-HIGH-LOW (current year's initial price and price range for each listed bond, up to and including month prior to month of publication). BANK AND QUOTATION RECORD. Published monthly.

Bond quality ratings.

    SEE: Ratings, bonds. . .

Bond redemptions.

    SEE: Redemptions. . .

Bond sales volume.

    SEE: Volume of trading in bonds. . .

Bond-stock ratio, Barron's.

    SEE: Yield spread ratio, Barron's. . .

Bond yield average, Barron's.

    SEE: Barron's high-grade bond index, yield. . .

Bond yield averages, Moody's.

    See entries beginning "Moody's. . ."

Bond yield averages, Standard & Poor's.

    See entries beginning "Standard & Poor's. . ."

Bond yields to maturity.

> SEE ALSO: Convertible bonds, yields to maturity. . .
> Foreign bonds, yields to maturity. . .
> Government bonds, yields to maturity. . .

BOND YIELDS TO MATURITY, MONTHLY (percentage yields for each of about 2,600 corporate and 200 foreign bonds). STANDARD & POOR'S EARNINGS AND RATINGS BOND GUIDE. Published monthly.

Bonds.

> SEE ALSO: Banks for Cooperatives bonds. . .
> Convertible bonds. . .
> Federal Home Loan Bank bonds. . .
> Federal Land Bank bonds. . .
> Federal National Mortgage Association Bonds. . .
> Foreign bonds. . .
> Government bonds. . .
> International Bank. . .bonds. . .
> Municipal bonds. . .
> Public authority bonds. . .
> Railroad bonds. . .
> Railroad equipment trust certificates. . .
> Toll revenue bonds. . .
> Utility bonds. . .

Bonds, amounts outstanding.

> SEE: Bonds, dollar amounts outstanding. . .

Bonds, call prices.

> SEE: Call prices, bonds. . .

Bonds, called for payment.

> SEE: Redemptions. . .

Bonds, Canadian municipal.

> SEE: Municipal bonds, Canadian. . .

Bonds, city and state.

> SEE: Municipal bonds. . .

Bonds, convertible.

> SEE: Convertible bonds. . .

Bonds, coupon form.

> SEE: Bonds, form of. . .

Bonds, coupon rates.

SEE: Bond interest rates. . .

Bonds, debt ratio.

SEE: Funded debt to net property ratio. . .

BONDS, DOLLAR AMOUNTS OUTSTANDING (for each of about 3,000 bonds of various kinds). STANDARD & POOR'S EARNINGS AND RATINGS BOND GUIDE. Published monthly.

BONDS, DUE DATES (maturity years and months for each of about 5,000 bonds of various kinds). BANK AND QUOTATION RECORD. Published monthly.

BONDS, DUE DATES (month and year of maturity indicated for each bond traded on New York and American Stock Exchanges). COMMERCIAL AND FINANCIAL CHRONICLE. Monday edition.

BONDS, DUE DATES (maturity dates for each of about 3,000 bonds of various kinds). STANDARD & POOR'S EARNINGS AND RATINGS BOND GUIDE. Published monthly.

Bonds, earnings to fixed charges ratio.

SEE: Earnings to fixed charges ratio. . .

Bonds, eligibility for bank investment under Comptroller of the Currency regulations.

SEE ALSO: Bonds, legal investment status. . .
Comptroller of the Currency. . .

BONDS, ELIGIBILITY FOR BANK INVESTMENT UNDER COMPTROLLER OF THE CURRENCY REGULATIONS (eligibility indicated for each of about 2,600 corporate issues). STANDARD & POOR'S EARNINGS AND RATINGS BOND GUIDE. Published monthly.

Bonds, fixed charges ratio.

SEE: Earnings to fixed charges ratio. . .

Bonds, foreign.

SEE: Foreign bonds. . .

BONDS, FORM OF (for each of about 2,600 corporate issues, tells if bond is registered or coupon or available either way). STANDARD & POOR'S EARNINGS AND RATINGS BOND GUIDE. Published monthly.

Bonds, funded debt ratio.

SEE: Funded debt to net property ratio. . .

Bonds, government.

>   SEE: Government bonds. . .

Bonds, highway.

>   SEE: Public authority bonds. . .
>   Toll revenue bonds. . .

Bonds, industrial revenue.

>   SEE: Industrial revenue bonds. . .

Bonds, interest periods.

>   SEE: Bond interest payment dates. . .

Bonds, interest rates.

>   SEE: Bond interest rates. . .

Bonds, lease rental.

>   SEE: Industrial revenue bonds. . .

BONDS, LEGAL INVESTMENT STATUS (legality indicated for each of about 2,600 corporate issues for savings bank and trust fund investment in each of six states -- Connecticut, Maine, Massachusetts, New Hampshire, New Jersey, and New York). STANDARD & POOR'S EARNINGS AND RATINGS BOND GUIDE. Published monthly.

Bonds, markets where traded.

>   SEE: Markets where bonds are traded. . .

Bonds, maturity dates.

>   SEE: Bonds, due dates. . .

Bonds, municipal.

>   SEE: Municipal bonds. . .

Bonds, new issues.

>   SEE: New issues, bonds. . .

Bonds, offering prices.

>   SEE: Bond prices, offering. . .

Bonds, outstanding dollar amounts.

>   SEE: Bonds, dollar amounts outstanding. . .

Bonds, payment dates.

>   SEE: Bond interest payment dates. . .

Bonds, prices.

    SEE: Bond prices. . .

Bonds, public authority.

    SEE: Public authority bonds. . .
           Toll revenue bonds. . .

Bonds, public utility.

    SEE: Utility bonds. . .

Bonds, railroad.

    SEE: Railroad bonds. . .
           Railroad equipment trust certificates. . .

Bonds, ratings.

    SEE: Ratings, bonds. . .

BONDS, REFUNDING (refunding call price and year for individual corporate and foreign bonds). STANDARD & POOR'S EARINGS AND RATINGS BOND GUIDE. Published monthly.

Bonds, registered or coupon.

    SEE: Bonds, form of. . .

Bonds, regulations concerning bank investment.

    SEE: Bonds, eligibility for bank investment. . .
           Bonds, legal investment status. . .
           Comptroller of the Currency regulations. . .

Bonds, sinking fund call prices.

    SEE: Call prices, bonds, sinking fund. . .

Bonds, state and city.

    SEE: Municipal bonds. . .
           Public authority bonds. . .

Bonds, tax exempt.

    SEE: Municipal bonds. . .
           Public authority bonds. . .

BONDS, TRANSFER TAXES (currently an explanation that none exist, although rates are given for the federal tax that expired in 1966). STANDARD & POOR'S SECURITY OWNER'S STOCK GUIDE. Published monthly.

Bonds, turnpike.

    SEE: Toll revenue bonds. . .

Bonds, underwriters.

    SEE: Underwriters of bond issues. . .

Bonds, utility.

    SEE: Utility bonds. . .

BONDS, YEAR OF ISSUE (year of original offering for each of about 2,600 corporate and 200 foreign bonds. Original offering price also given). STANDARD & POOR'S EARNINGS AND RATINGS BOND GUIDE. Published monthly.

Bonds, year of maturity.

    SEE: Bonds, due dates. . .

Bonds, yields.

    SEE: Bond yields. . .

"BONDTRADE" INDEX, PRICES AND YIELDS, WEEKLY (yields and prices for medium-term index and long-term index for current week and previous week). NEW YORK TIMES. This data normally appears in Saturday edition.

BOOK VALUE PER SHARE, CURRENT (for each of over 1,200 less actively traded common stocks. Book value not given for major, active stocks). MOODY'S HANDBOOK OF COMMON STOCKS. Published quarterly.

BOOK VALUE PER SHARE, CURRENT (for each of about 960 listed stocks). TRENDLINE'S CURRENT MARKET PERSPECTIVES. Published monthly.

BOOK VALUE PER SHARE, YEARLY (for each of past 18 or so years, for each of about 1,400 leading common stocks). VALUE LINE INVESTMENT SURVEY. Part three: published weekly, a few industries each week.

Boston Stock Exchange.

    SEE: Dividends, amount, indicated annual rate, Boston Stock Exchange. . .
           Earnings per share, interim, Boston Stock Exchange. . .
           Stock prices on Boston Stock Exchange. . .
           Volume of trading in stocks, individual stocks on Boston Stock Exchange. . .
           Volume of trading in stocks, total for Boston Stock Exchange. . .

Bourse, Paris.

    SEE: Stock prices on Paris Stock Exchange (Bourse). . .

Breadth of the market.

    SEE: Advances and declines. . .
           Issues traded. . .
           New highs and new lows. . .

Brokers.

SEE ALSO: Underwriters. . .

BROKERS (names and addresses, including branches, of about 1,600 domestic security dealers). NATIONAL MONTHLY STOCK SUMMARY. This information appears in semiannual, cumulative volumes, April 1 and October 1.

BROKERS' LOANS, CHICAGO, WEEKLY-YEARLY (total in millions of dollars for "large commercial banks in. . .Chicago" for current week, with plus or minus change in amount since previous week, and since same date one year ago. Under "Federal Reserve Statistics -- Assets and Liabilities in Reserve Cities"). NEW YORK TIMES. This data normally appears in Friday edition.

BROKERS' LOANS, NEW YORK CITY, WEEKLY-YEARLY (total in millions of dollars for "N.Y. City, excluding government bond loans," for latest week, previous week, and same week one year ago. Under "Week's Market Statistics"). BARRON'S. Published weekly.

BROKERS' LOANS, NEW YORK CITY, WEEKLY-YEARLY (total in millions of dollars for "large commercial banks in New York" for latest week, with plus or minus change in amount since previous week, and since same date a year ago. Under "Federal Reserve Statistics -- Assets and Liabilities in Reserve Cities"). NEW YORK TIMES. This data normally appears in Friday edition.

Brokers' loans, rates.

SEE: Call loan rates. . .

BROKERS' LOANS, TOTAL, WEEKLY-YEARLY (total in millions of dollars for Federal Reserve member banks. Amount given for end of latest weekly period, with dollar increase or decrease indicated since end of previous week and same week one year ago. Separate figures for U.S. government securities and "other securities." Headed "Condition Statement of Member Banks"). COMMERCIAL AND FINANCIAL CHRONICLE. Thursday edition.

BROKERS' LOANS, TOTAL, WEEKLY-YEARLY (total dollar amount for "large commercial banks" for end of latest weekly period, with dollar increase or decrease indicated since end of previous week and same period a year ago. Separate figures for U.S. securities and others. Headed "The Assets and Liabilities of Banks Reporting Weekly to the Federal Reserve System"). NEW YORK TIMES. This data normally appears in Thursday edition.

Brussels Stock Exchange.

SEE: Stock prices on Brussels Stock Exchange. . .
     Foreign stock price indexes. . .

Buenos Aires Stock Exchange.

SEE: Stock prices on Buenos Aires Stock Exchange. . .

INVESTMENT INFORMATION

Calendar of new issues.

SEE: New issues, corporate offerings, probable. . .

Call loan rates.

SEE ALSO: Brokers' loans. . .

CALL LOAN RATES (PERCENT), DAILY ("Brokers' loan rate, Governments" and "Stock Exchange Collateral" rate for previous day. Under "Money" heading). NEW YORK TIMES. Published weekdays.

CALL LOAN RATES (PERCENT), DAILY (separate rates on stock exchange collateral and government securities for New York City banks and banks outside New York. Under "Money Rates"). WALL STREET JOURNAL. Published business days.

CALL LOAN RATES (PERCENT), NEW YORK STOCK EXCHANGE, DAILY ("Low," "High," and "Renewal" rates for each day of month prior to month of publication). BANK AND QUOTATION RECORD. Published monthly.

CALL LOAN RATES (PERCENT), RENEWAL, WEEKLY-YEARLY (for end of week just past, previous week, and same week one year ago). BARRON'S. Published weekly.

CALL PRICES, BONDS (regular call prices for individual corporate and foreign bonds). STANDARD & POOR'S EARNINGS AND RATINGS BOND GUIDE. Published monthly.

Call prices, bonds, refunding.

SEE: Bonds, refunding. . .

CALL PRICES, BONDS, SINKING FUND (call price for sinking fund for individual corporate and foreign bonds). STANDARD & POOR'S EARNINGS AND RATINGS BOND GUIDE. Published monthly.

Call prices, foreign bonds, refunding.

SEE: Foreign bonds, refunding. . .

CALL PRICES, PREFERRED STOCK (call price information given, if applicable). STANDARD & POOR'S SECURITY OWNER'S STOCK GUIDE. Published monthly.

Calls for redemption.

SEE: Redemptions. . .

Calls (options).

SEE: Puts and calls. . .

Canadian commission rates.

SEE: Commission rates, Canadian stock exchanges. . .

Canadian municipal bonds.

SEE: Municipal bonds, Canadian. . .

Canadian mutual funds.

SEE: Mutual funds, Canadian. . .

Canadian stock prices.

SEE: Stock prices on Montreal Stock Exchange. . .
Stock prices on Toronto Stock Exchange. . .

Canadian stock transfer taxes.

SEE: Stock transfer taxes, Canadian. . .

Capital, senior.

SEE: Senior capital. . .

Capital, working.

SEE: Working capital. . .

Capital earnings rate.

SEE: Earnings rate on total capital. . .

Capital funds.

SEE: Banks, capital funds. . .
Insurance companies, capital funds. . .
Life insurance companies, capital funds. . .
Savings and loan companies, capital funds. . .

Capital gains dividends.

SEE: Closed-end investment companies, dividends from capital gains. . .
Mutual funds, dividends from capital gains. . .

Capital gains tax liability, closed-end investment companies.

SEE: Closed-end investment companies, capital gains tax liability. . .

Capital goods stock index, Standard & Poor's.

SEE: Standard & Poor's capital goods stock index. . .

CAPITAL GROWTH RATIO (PERCENT), YEARLY (for each of past 18 or so years, for each of about 1,400 leading companies. Capital growth ratio represents retained cash flow per share as a percentage of book value per share). VALUE LINE INVESTMENT SURVEY. Part three: published weekly, a few industries each week.

CAPITAL SPENDING PER SHARE, YEARLY (spending for plant and equipment for each of past 18 or so years, for each of about 1,400 leading companies). VALUE LINE INVESTMENT SURVEY. Part three: published weekly, a few industries each week.

CAPITALIZATION STATED AS DOLLAR AMOUNTS (current common stock and surplus, deferred income tax, preferred stock, and long term debt are stated as dollar amounts for each of over 1,000 companies with actively traded common stock). MOODY'S HANDBOOK OF COMMON STOCKS. Published quarterly.

CAPITALIZATION STATED AS PERCENTAGE (current common stock and surplus, deferred income tax, preferred stock, and long term debt are shown as percentages of total capital for each of over 1,000 companies with actively traded common stock). MOODY'S HANDBOOK OF COMMON STOCKS. Published quarterly.

CASH AS CURRENT ASSET (amounts held by individual corporations with bond issues, according to latest available balance sheets). STANDARD & POOR'S EARNINGS AND RATINGS BOND GUIDE. Published monthly.

CASH AS CURRENT ASSET (amounts held by individual corporations with stock issues, according to latest available balance sheets). STANDARD & POOR'S SECURITY OWNER'S STOCK GUIDE. Published monthly.

Cash asset totals.

    SEE: Closed-end investment companies, each asset totals. . .
            Mutual funds, cash asset totals. . .

Cash flow per share, growth rate.

    SEE: Growth rate of cash flow per share (percent). . .

CASH FLOW PER SHARE, YEARLY (for each of past eleven years, for each of over 1,000 companies having actively traded common stock. Cash flow represents amount earned before deducting depreciation and other charges not involving actual outlay of cash). MOODY'S HANDBOOK OF COMMON STOCKS. Published quarterly.

CASH FLOW PER SHARE, YEARLY (for each of past four years, for each of about 960 listed stocks). TRENDLINE'S CURRENT MARKET PERSPECTIVES. Published monthly.

CASH FLOW PER SHARE, YEARLY (for each of past 18 or so years, for each of about 1,400 leading companies with common stock. Labeled "Cash Earnings per Share"). VALUE LINE INVESTMENT SURVEY. Part three: published weekly, a few industries each week.

Cash position of mutual funds.

    SEE: Mutual funds, cash asset totals. . .
            Mutual funds, cash position total (percent). . .

Certificates, treasury.

SEE: Treasury certificates. . .

CERTIFICATES OF DEPOSIT RATES, DAILY (secondary market rates for three months and six months. Under "Money" heading). NEW YORK TIMES. Published weekdays.

CERTIFICATES OF DEPOSIT RATES, DAILY (major New York City bank rates for 30 to 59 days, 60 to 89 days, 90 to 179 days, and 180 to 270 days. Under "Money Rates" heading). WALL STREET JOURNAL. Published business days.

CERTIFICATES OF DEPOSIT RATES, WEEKLY-YEARLY (three months and six months rates shown separately for end of week just past, week before that, and same week one year ago. Under "Economic and Financial Indicators" heading). BARRON'S. Published weekly.

Charts.

See specific subjects, such as "Stock prices, monthly, high-low, charts. . ."

Cincinnati Stock Exchange.

SEE: Dividends, amount, indicated annual rate, Cincinnati Stock Exchange. . .
Earnings per share, interim, Cincinnati Stock Exchange. . .
Stock prices on Cincinnati Stock Exchange. . .
Volume of trading in stocks, individual stocks on Cincinnati Stock Exchange. . .

City bonds.

SEE: Municipal bonds. . .

Classification of stocks by industry.

SEE: Industry classification, stocks. . .

Closed-end investment companies.

SEE ALSO: Dual-purpose funds. . .
Investment companies. . .
Small business investment companies. . .

CLOSED-END INVESTMENT COMPANIES, ASSET TOTALS, YEARLY (for each of past eleven years, for each of large companies with actively traded common stock). MOODY'S HANDBOOK OF COMMON STOCKS. Published quarterly.

CLOSED-END INVESTMENT COMPANIES, ASSET TOTALS, YEARLY (for each of past 18 or so years, for each of about 25 leading companies). VALUE LINE INVESTMENT SURVEY. Part three: published weekly, a few industries each week.

Closed-end investment companies, asset value changes (percent).

SEE: Closed-end investment companies, changes in asset value (percent). . .

Closed-end investment companies, asset value growth.

SEE: Closed-end investment companies, growth of assets. . .

CLOSED-END INVESTMENT COMPANIES, ASSET VALUE PER SHARE (NET), QUARTERLY (for end of current year's quarters and each of quarters for three previous years, for each of large companies with actively traded common stock). MOODY'S HANDBOOK OF COMMON STOCKS. Published quarterly.

CLOSED-END INVESTMENT COMPANIES, ASSET VALUE PER SHARE (NET), WEEKLY (for end of week just past, for each of about 25 leading funds). BARRON'S. Published weekly.

CLOSE-END INVESTMENT COMPANIES, ASSET VALUE PER SHARE (NET), WEEKLY (for end of week just past, for each of about 25 leading funds). NEW YORK TIMES. This data is normally published in Monday edition.

CLOSED-END INVESTMENT COMPANIES, ASSET VALUE PER SHARE (NET), WEEKLY (for end of week just past, for each of about 25 leading funds). WALL STREET JOURNAL. This data normally appears in Monday edition.

CLOSED-END INVESTMENT COMPANIES, ASSET VALUE PER SHARE (NET), YEARLY (for each of past eleven years, for each of large companies with actively traded common stock. End-of-year data). MOODY'S HANDBOOK OF COMMON STOCKS. Published quarterly.

CLOSED-END INVESTMENT COMPANIES, ASSET VALUE PER SHARE (NET), YEARLY (for end of each of past five years, for each of many companies). STANDARD & POOR'S SECURITY OWNER'S STOCK GUIDE. Published monthly.

CLOSED-END INVESTMENT COMPANIES, ASSET VALUE PER SHARE (NET), YEARLY (for end of each of past 18 or so years, for each of about 25 leading companies). VALUE LINE INVESTMENT SURVEY. Part three: published weekly, a few industries each week.

CLOSED-END INVESTMENT COMPANIES, CAPITAL GAINS TAX LIABILITY AS PERCENTAGE OF NET ASSET VALUE, YEARLY (for end of each of past 18 or so years, for each of about 25 leading companies. Shows what tax liability percentage would be if all capital gains were realized. Labeled "C. G. Tax Liability as % NAV"). VALUE LINE INVESTMENT SURVEY. Part three: published weekly, a few industries each week.

CLOSED-END INVESTMENT COMPANIES, CAPITAL GAINS TAX LIABILITY PER SHARE, YEARLY (for end of each of past 18 or so years, for each of about 25 leading companies. Shows what tax amount per share would be if all capital gains were realized). VALUE LINE INVESTMENT SURVEY. Part three: published weekly, a few industries each week.

CLOSED-END INVESTMENT COMPANIES, CASH ASSET TOTALS (NET), QUARTERLY (for each of about 15 companies, for end of latest and previous quarter. Grand totals for combined companies also given). COMMERCIAL AND FINANCIAL CHRONICLE. This data normally appears around the 20th of February, May, August, and November, in Thursday edition.

CLOSED-END INVESTMENT COMPANIES, CASH ASSET TOTALS (NET), YEARLY (for each of past eleven years, for each of large companies with actively traded common stock. Year-end "net cash asset" totals include government securities). MOODY'S HANDBOOK OF COMMON STOCKS. Published quarterly.

CLOSED-END INVESTMENT COMPANIES, CASH ASSETS AS PERCENTAGE OF TOTAL ASSETS, QUARTERLY (for each of about 15 companies, for end of latest quarter and one previous. Grand total average cash percentage for combined companies also given). COMMERCIAL AND FINANCIAL CHRONICLE. This data normally appears around the 20th of February, May, August, and November, in Thursday edition.

CLOSED-END INVESTMENT COMPANIES, CASH ASSETS AS PERCENTAGE OF TOTAL ASSETS, YEARLY (for end of each of past 18 or so years, for each of about 25 leading companies). VALUE LINE INVESTMENT SURVEY. Part three: published weekly, a few industries each week.

CLOSED-END INVESTMENT COMPANIES, CHANGES IN ASSET VALUE (PERCENT), YEAR TO YEAR (percent change for each of past 18 or so years, for each of about 25 leading companies. Labeled "Annual Ch. in NAV"). VALUE LINE INVESTMENT SURVEY. Part three: published weekly, a few industries each week.

CLOSED-END INVESTMENT COMPANIES, COMMON STOCK EQUITY (CAPITALIZATION), YEARLY (for each of past 18 or so years, for each of about 25 leading companies). VALUE LINE INVESTMENT SURVEY. Part three: published weekly, a few industries each week.

CLOSED-END INVESTMENT COMPANIES, COMMON STOCKS AS PERCENT-AGE OF ASSETS, QUARTERLY (for each of about 15 companies, for end of latest and one previous quarter. Grand total average percentage for combined companies also given). COMMERCIAL AND FINANCIAL CHRONICLE. This data normally appears around the 20th of February, May, August, and November, in Thursday edition.

CLOSED-END INVESTMENT COMPANIES, COMMON STOCKS AS PERCENT-AGE OF ASSETS, YEARLY (for end of each of past 18 or so years, for each of about 25 leading companies). VALUE LINE INVESTMENT SURVEY. Part three: published weekly, a few industries each week.

CLOSED-END INVESTMENT COMPANIES, DISCOUNT OR PREMIUM RELATIVE TO NET ASSET VALUE, WEEKLY (market price discount or premium in percent for each of about 25 leading funds, for end of week just past). BARRON'S. Published weekly.

CLOSED-END INVESTMENT COMPANIES, DISCOUNT OR PREMIUM RELATIVE TO NET ASSET VALUE, WEEKLY (market price discount or premium in percent for each of about 25 leading funds, for end of week just past). NEW YORK TIMES. This data normally appears in Monday edition.

CLOSED-END INVESTMENT COMPANIES, DISCOUNT OR PREMIUM RELATIVE TO NET ASSET VALUE, WEEKLY (market price discount or premium in percent for each of about 25 leading funds, for end of week just past). WALL STREET JOURNAL. This data normally appears in Monday edition.

CLOSED-END INVESTMENT COMPANIES, DISCOUNT OR PREMIUM RELATIVE TO NET ASSET VALUE, YEARLY (year-end market price discount or premium in percent, for each of large companies with actively traded common stock, for each of past eleven years). MOODY'S HANDBOOK OF COMMON STOCKS. Published quarterly.

CLOSED-END INVESTMENT COMPANIES, DISCOUNT OR PREMIUM RELATIVE TO NET ASSET VALUE, YEARLY AVERAGE (market price discount or premium in percent, expressed as an average for each of past 18 or so years, for each of about 25 leading companies). VALUE LINE INVESTMENT SURVEY. Part three: published weekly, a few industries each week.

Closed-end investment companies, dividend growth.

SEE: Closed-end investment companies, growth of dividends. . .

CLOSED-END INVESTMENT COMPANIES, DIVIDENDS FROM CAPITAL GAINS, YEARLY (per share payments for each of past eleven years, for each of large companies with actively traded common stock). MOODY'S HANDBOOK OF COMMON STOCKS. Published quarterly.

CLOSED-END INVESTMENT COMPANIES, DIVIDENDS FROM CAPITAL GAINS, YEARLY (per share payments in current year and one year previous, for many individual companies). STANDARD & POOR'S SECURITY OWNER'S STOCK GUIDE. Published monthly.

CLOSED-END INVESTMENT COMPANIES, DIVIDENDS FROM CAPITAL GAINS, YEARLY (per share total for each of past 18 or so years, for each of about 25 leading companies). VALUE LINE INVESTMENT SURVEY. Part three: published weekly, a few industries each week.

CLOSED-END INVESTMENT COMPANIES, DIVIDENDS FROM INVESTMENT INCOME, YEARLY (per share total for each of past 20 or so years, for each of large companies with actively traded common stock. Figures shown below price chart). MOODY'S HANDBOOK OF COMMON STOCKS. Published quarterly.

CLOSED-END INVESTMENT COMPANIES, DIVIDENDS FROM INVESTMENT INCOME, YEARLY (per share payments in current year and one year previous, for many individual companies). STANDARD & POOR'S SECURITY OWNER'S STOCK GUIDE. Published monthly.

CLOSED-END INVESTMENT COMPANIES, DIVIDENDS FROM INVESTMENT INCOME, YEARLY (per share total for each of past 18 or so years, for each of about 25 leading companies). VALUE LINE INVESTMENT SURVEY. Part three: published weekly, a few industries each week.

CLOSED-END INVESTMENT COMPANIES, FUNDED DEBT, YEARLY (for end of each of past 18 or so years, for each of about 25 leading companies). VALUE LINE INVESTMENT SURVEY. Part three: published weekly, a few industries each week.

CLOSED-END INVESTMENT COMPANIES, GROWTH OF ASSETS, YEARLY (for each of past 18 or so years, for each of about 25 leading companies. Shows value at end of each year of $100. invested some years ago, generally in 1945 or 1951. Labeled "$100. Net Assets grew to"). VALUE LINE INVESTMENT SURVEY. Part three: published weekly, a few industries each week.

CLOSED-END INVESTMENT COMPANIES, GROWTH OF DIVIDENDS, YEARLY (for each of past 18 or so years, for each of about 25 leading companies. Shows value at end of each year of dividends on $100. invested some years ago, generally in 1945 or 1951. Labeled "Div'ds on $100. grew to"). VALUE LINE INVESTMENT SURVEY. Part three: published weekly, a few industries each week.

Closed-end investment companies, index.

   SEE: Standard & Poor's stock group indexes. . .

CLOSED-END INVESTMENT COMPANIES, INVESTMENT INCOME PER SHARE (NET), YEARLY (for each of past 20 or so years, for each of large companies with actively traded common stock. Figures shown below price chart). MOODY'S HANDBOOK OF COMMON STOCKS. Published quarterly.

CLOSED-END INVESTMENT COMPANIES, INVESTMENT INCOME TOTAL (NET), YEARLY (annual total net income for each of past eleven years, for each of large companies with actively traded common stock). MOODY'S HANDBOOK OF COMMON STOCKS. Published quarterly.

CLOSED-END INVESTMENT COMPANIES, INVESTMENTS OTHER THAN GOVERNMENT SECURITIES, VALUE OF, YEARLY (for end of each of past eleven years, for each of large companies with actively traded common stock). MOODY'S HANDBOOK OF COMMON STOCKS. Published quarterly.

Closed-end investment companies, net asset value.

   SEE: Closed-end investment companies, asset value per share (net). . .

CLOSED-END INVESTMENT COMPANIES, PREFERRED STOCK CAPITALIZATION, YEARLY (for each of past 18 or so years, for each of about 25 leading companies, where applicable). VALUE LINE INVESTMENT SURVEY. Part three: published weekly, a few industries each week.

INVESTMENT INFORMATION

Closed-end investment companies, premiums over net asset value.

> SEE: Closed-end investment companies, discount or premium relative to net asset value. . .

Closed-end investment companies, price average.

> SEE: Barron's group stock averages. . .
> Standard & Poor's stock group indexes. . .

Closed-end investment companies, prices.

> SEE ALSO: Stock prices. . .

CLOSED-END INVESTMENT COMPANIES, PRICES, MONTHLY (UNLISTED), CLOSE (tabulation of over-the-counter "Investing Companies Stocks and Bonds" includes unlisted closed-end funds. Bid and asked prices are for end of month prior to month of publication). BANK AND QUOTATION RECORD. Published monthly.

CLOSED-END INVESTMENT COMPANIES, PRICES, WEEKLY, CLOSE (price for end of week just past for each of about 25 leading funds). BARRON'S. Published weekly.

CLOSED-END INVESTMENT COMPANIES, PRICES, WEEKLY, CLOSE (price for end of week just past for each of about 25 leading funds). NEW YORK TIMES. This data normally appears in Monday edition.

CLOSED-END INVESTMENT COMPANIES, PRICES, WEEKLY, CLOSE (price for end of week just past for each of about 25 leading funds). WALL STREET JOURNAL. This data normally appears in Monday edition.

Closed-end investment companies, total assets.

> SEE: Closed-end investment companies, asset totals. . .

COLLATERAL, REGISTERED AND EXEMPT, TOTAL FOR NEW YORK STOCK EXCHANGE FIRMS' MARGIN ACCOUNTS, MONTHLY-YEARLY (total in millions of dollars for end of latest month available, previous month, and same month one year ago. Labeled "Registd Col mil"). BARRON'S. Published weekly.

Collateral, stock exchange, interest rates.

> SEE: Call loan rates. . .

COMMERCIAL PAPER RATES, DAILY, DEALERS (percentage rates for 30-270 days. Under "Money" heading). NEW YORK TIMES. Published weekdays.

COMMERCIAL PAPER RATES, DAILY, DEALERS (percentage rates for 30-270 days. Under "Money Rates" heading). WALL STREET JOURNAL. Published business days.

COMMERCIAL PAPER RATES, DAILY, FINANCE COMPANIES (percentage rates for 30-59 days and 60-270 days. Under "Money" heading). NEW YORK

TIMES. Published weekdays.

COMMERCIAL PAPER RATES, DAILY, FINANCE COMPANIES (percentage rates for 30-59 days and 60-270 days. Under "Money Rates" heading). WALL STREET JOURNAL. Published business days.

COMMERCIAL PAPER RATES, WEEKLY-YEARLY (30-270 days rate for end of week just past, previous week, and same week one year ago. Under "Economic and Financial Indicators" heading). BARRON'S. Published weekly.

COMMISSION RATE FORMULA (quick method for computing minimum commissions for both round lot and odd lot transactions on New York and American Stock Exchanges). STANDARD & POOR'S SECURITY OWNER'S STOCK GUIDE. Published monthly.

COMMISSION RATES, BONDS (non-member minimum commission rates on bonds traded on New York or American Stock Exchange, except governmental, short-term or called bonds). STANDARD & POOR'S EARNINGS AND RATINGS BOND GUIDE. Published monthly.

COMMISSION RATES, BONDS (non-member minimum commission rates on bonds traded on New York or American Stock Exchange, except governmental, short-term or called bonds). STANDARD & POOR'S SECURITY OWNER'S STOCK GUIDE. Published monthly.

COMMISSION RATES, CANADIAN STOCK EXCHANGES (current rates for "Montreal-Toronto-Canadian Exchanges"). STANDARD & POOR'S SECURITY OWNER'S STOCK GUIDE. Published monthly.

COMMISSION RATES, MAJOR STOCK EXCHANGES (detailed explanation and table of rates on New York, American, and other major stock exchanges). STANDARD & POOR'S SECURITY OWNER'S STOCK GUIDE. Published monthly.

Commission rates, mutual funds.

SEE: Mutual funds, sales charge. . .

Common stock equity.

SEE: Capitalization stated as dollar amounts. . .
Capitalization stated as percentages. . .
Earnings rate on common stock equity. . .
Airlines, common stock equity. . .
Railroads, common stock equity. . .
Utilities, common stock equity. . .

Common stock prices.

SEE: Stock prices. . .

Common stock shares outstanding.

SEE: Shares outstanding, common stock. . .

Composite bond averages.

> SEE: Dow-Jones composite bond average. . .
> Moody's corporate (composite) bond averages. . .
> New York Times composite bond average. . .
> Standard & Poor's corporate (composite) bond indexes. . .

Composite stock averages.

> SEE: Dow-Jones composite stock average. . .
> Financial Times (London) composite stock index. . .
> Moody's composite stock average. . .
> New York Stock Exchange composite stock index. . .
> New York Times composite stock average. . .
> Standard & Poor's composite 500 stock index. . .
> Value Line composite stock index. . .

COMPTROLLER OF THE CURRENCY REGULATIONS REGARDING INVESTMENTS OF BANKS (regulations are briefly explained). STANDARD & POOR'S EARNINGS AND RATINGS BOND GUIDE. Published monthly.

Confidence index, Barron's.

> SEE: Barron's confidence index. . .

Consumers' goods stock index, Standard & Poor's.

> SEE: Standard & Poor's consumers' goods stock index. . .

Continuous dividends.

> SEE: Dividends, uninterrupted. . .

Conversion.

> SEE: Convertible bonds, conversion. . .

Convertible bonds, bond value of stocks.

> SEE: Convertible bonds, conversion parity. . .

CONVERTIBLE BONDS, CALL PRICE (for each of about 350 issues). MOODY'S BOND SURVEY. This data appears in special supplement, third week of each month.

CONVERTIBLE BONDS, CONVERSION PARITY (for each of about 350 issues, gives price at which stock would have to sell to equal current bond price). MOODY'S BOND SURVEY. This data appears in special supplement, third week of each month.

CONVERTIBLE BONDS, CONVERSION PARITY (for each of about 500 issues, gives price at which stock would have to sell to equal current bond price). STANDARD & POOR'S EARNINGS AND RATINGS BOND GUIDE. Published monthly. Also in supplement to BOND OUTLOOK, second week of each month.

CONVERTIBLE BONDS, CONVERSION PRICE (per share of stock for each of about 350 issues). MOODY'S BOND SURVEY. This data appears in special supplement, third week of each month.

CONVERTIBLE BONDS, CONVERSION PRICE (per share of stock for each of about 500 issues). STANDARD & POOR'S EARNINGS AND RATINGS BOND GUIDE. Published monthly. Also in supplement to BOND OUTLOOK, second week of each month.

CONVERTIBLE BONDS, CONVERSION PRIVILEGE EXPIRATION DATE (year in which conversion privilege is given for each of about 500 issues). STANDARD & POOR'S EARNINGS AND RATINGS BOND GUIDE. Published monthly. Also in supplement to BOND OUTLOOK, second week of each month.

CONVERTIBLE BONDS, CONVERSION PRIVILEGE, RECENT EXPIRATIONS OR CHANGES (list of individual issues having recent conversion privilege expirations or changes, with short explanations). STANDARD & POOR'S EARNINGS AND RATINGS BOND GUIDE. Published monthly. Also in supplement to BOND OUTLOOK, second week of each month.

Convertible bonds, conversion ratio.

    SEE: Convertible bonds, shares per bond. . .

Convertible bonds, conversion value of bond based on price of stock.

    SEE: Convertible bonds, stock value of bond. . .

Convertible bonds, conversion value of stock based on price of bond.

    SEE: Conversion bonds, conversion parity. . .

Convertible bonds, debt value.

    SEE: Convertible bonds, estimated investment worth. . .

Convertible bonds, dividend equivalent.

    SEE: Convertible bonds, equivalent dividend income. . .

CONVERTIBLE BONDS, DOLLAR AMOUNT OUTSTANDING (for each of about 350 issues). MOODY'S BOND SURVEY. This data appears in special supplement, third week of each month.

CONVERTIBLE BONDS, DOLLAR AMOUNT OUTSTANDING (for each of about 500 issues). STANDARD & POOR'S EARNINGS AND RATINGS BOND GUIDE. Published monthly. Also in supplement to BOND OUTLOOK, second week of each month.

CONVERTIBLE BONDS, DUE DATES (maturity dates for each of about 350 issues). MOODY'S BOND SURVEY. This data appears in special supplement, third week of each month.

CONVERTIBLE BONDS, DUE DATES (maturity dates for each of about 500 issues). STANDARD & POOR'S EARNINGS AND RATINGS BOND GUIDE. Published monthly. Also in supplement to BOND OUTLOOK, second week of each month.

CONVERTIBLE BONDS, EQUIVALENT DIVIDEND INCOME (for most of about 500 individual issues, the yearly dividend amount is shown that could be expected after the conversion of one bond into stock). STANDARD & POOR'S EARNINGS AND RATINGS BOND GUIDE. Published monthly. Also in supplement to BOND OUTLOOK, second week of each month.

CONVERTIBLE BONDS, ESTIMATED INVESTMENT WORTH (indicates what most of about 350 individual convertible bonds would currently be worth if they were straight bonds, without conversion privileges). MOODY'S BOND SURVEY. This data appears in special supplement, third week of each month.

CONVERTIBLE BONDS, ESTIMATED INVESTMENT WORTH (indicates what most of about 500 individual convertible bonds would currently be worth if they were straight bonds, without conversion privileges). STANDARD & POOR'S EARNINGS AND RATINGS BOND GUIDE. Published monthly. Also in supplement to BOND OUTLOOK, second week of each month.

CONVERTIBLE BONDS, ESTIMATED INVESTMENT WORTH, YIELD BASIS (indicates what percentage yields of most of about 350 individual convertible bonds would be if they were straight bonds, without conversion privileges). MOODY'S BOND SURVEY. This data appears in special supplement, third week of each month.

Convertible bonds, expiration dates.

> SEE: Convertible bonds, conversion privilege, expiration data. . .

Convertible bonds, expiration of conversion privilege, recent changes.

> SEE: Convertible bonds, conversion privilege, recent expirations or changes. . .

CONVERTIBLE BONDS, INTEREST PAYMENT DATES (for each of about 500 issues). STANDARD & POOR'S EARNINGS AND RATINGS BOND GUIDE. Published monthly. Also in supplement to BOND OUTLOOK, second week of each month.

Convertible bonds, interest yield.

> SEE: Convertible bonds, yield, current. . .
> Convertible bonds, yield to maturity. . .

Convertible bonds, investment worth.

> SEE: Convertible bonds, estimated investment worth. . .

CONVERTIBLE BONDS, MARKETS WHERE TRADED (symbols are used to indicate listing on American or New York Stock Exchange, where applicable, for each of about 500 convertibles. Absence of symbol indicates over-the-counter). STANDARD & POOR'S EARNINGS AND RATINGS BOND GUIDE. Published monthly. Also in supplement to BOND OUTLOOK, second week of each month.

Convertible bonds, maturity dates.
> SEE: Convertible bonds, due dates. . .
Convertible bonds, new issues.

SEE: New issues, convertible bonds. . .

Convertible bonds, outstanding dollar amount.

SEE: Convertible bonds, dollar amount outstanding. . .

Convertible bonds, parity.

SEE: Convertible bonds, conversion parity. . .

CONVERTIBLE BONDS, PRICES, MONTHLY (middle of the month price for each of about 350 issues). MOODY'S BOND SURVEY. This data appears in special supplement, third week of each month.

CONVERTIBLE BONDS, PRICES, MONTHLY ("current" price for each of about 500 issues). STANDARD & POOR'S EARNINGS AND RATINGS BOND GUIDE. Published monthly. Also in supplement to BOND OUTLOOK, second week of each month.

CONVERTIBLE BONDS, PRICES, YEARLY, HIGH-LOW (current year's price range for each of about 500 issues). STANDARD & POOR'S EARNINGS AND RATINGS BOND GUIDE. Published monthly. Also in supplement in BOND OUTLOOK, second week of each month.

Convertible bonds, privileges expiring or changing.

SEE: Convertible bonds, conversion privilege, recent expirations or changes. . .

Convertible bonds, ratings.

SEE: Ratings, bonds. . .
Ratings, convertible bonds. . .

CONVERTIBLE BONDS, SHARES PER BOND (number of shares of stock that would be received from the conversion of one bond is shown for each of about 500 issues). STANDARD & POOR'S EARNINGS AND RATINGS BOND GUIDE. Published monthly. Also in supplement to BOND OUTLOOK, second week of each month.

CONVERTIBLE BONDS, STOCK VALUE OF BOND (for each of about 350 issues, gives the price at which bond would have to sell to equal current stock price). MOODY'S BOND SURVEY. This data appears in special supplement, third week of each month.

CONVERTIBLE BONDS, STOCK VALUE OF BOND (for each of about 500 issues, gives the price at which bond would have to sell to equal current stock price). STANDARD & POOR'S EARNINGS AND RATINGS BOND GUIDE. Published monthly. Also in supplement to BOND OUTLOOK, second week of each month.

Convertible bonds, straight debt value.

SEE: Convertible bonds, estimated investment worth. . .

Convertible bonds, trading markets.

    SEE: Convertible bonds, markets where traded. . .

CONVERTIBLE BONDS, YIELD, CURRENT (percentage return on current basis for each of about 500 issues). STANDARD & POOR'S EARNINGS AND RATINGS BOND GUIDE. Published monthly. Also in supplement to BOND OUTLOOK, second week of each month.

CONVERTIBLE BONDS, YIELD TO MATURITY (based on middle of the month price for each of about 350 issues). MOODY'S BOND SURVEY. This data appears in special supplement, third week of each month.

Convertible debentures.

    SEE: Convertible bonds. . .

Cooperatives, Banks for, bonds.

    SEE: Banks for Cooperatives bonds. . .

Corporate address.

    SEE: Address of principal office. . .

Corporate bond averages.

    SEE: Moody's corporate (composite) bond averages. . .
          Standard & Poor's corporate (composite) bond indexes. . .

Corporate bond ratings.

    SEE: Ratings, bonds. . .
          Ratings, convertible bonds. . .

Corporate founding dates.

    SEE: Founding dates. . .

Corporate income (net).

    SEE: Net income. . .

Corporate officers.

    SEE: Officers, corporate. . .

Corporate revenue.

    SEE: Sales (corporate revenue). . .

Coupon bond form.

    SEE: Bonds, form of. . .

Coupon rates.

    SEE: Bond interest rates. . .

Credit balances, free.

> SEE: Free credit balances. . .

Currency exchange rates.

> SEE: Foreign exchange rates. . .

CURRENT ASSETS (for individual corporations with bond issues, according to latest available balance sheet or report). STANDARD & POOR'S EARNINGS AND RATINGS BOND GUIDE. Published monthly.

CURRENT ASSETS (for individual corporations with stock issues, according to latest available balance sheet or report). STANDARD & POOR'S SECURITY OWNER'S STOCK GUIDE. Published monthly.

Current assets, cash portion.

> SEE: Cash as current asset. . .

CURRENT LIABILITIES (for individual corporations with bond issues, according to latest available balance sheet or report). STANDARD & POOR'S EARNINGS AND RATING BOND GUIDE. Published monthly.

CURRENT LIABILITIES (for individual corporations with stock issues, according to latest available balance sheet or report). STANDARD & POOR'S SECURITY OWNER'S STOCK GUIDE. Published monthly.

Customers under 40% equity (margin accounts).

> SEE: Margin customers having less than 40 per cent equity. . .

Cyclical turning points.

> SEE: Trading swings. . .

Dates.

> SEE: Annual meeting dates. . .
>
> Balance sheets, dates. . .
>
> Bond interest payment dates. . .
>
> Bonds, due dates. . .
>
> Bonds, year of issue. . .
>
> Convertible bonds, due dates. . .
>
> Convertible bonds, interest payment dates. . .
>
> Dividend meeting dates. . .
>
> Dividends, dates of payment. . .

    Dividends, dates of record. . .

    Dividends, uninterrupted, year of beginning. . .

    Ex-dividend dates. . .

    Fiscal year ending month. . .

    Foreign bonds, due dates. . .

    Foreign bonds, interest payment dates. . .

    Founding dates. . .

    Government bonds, due dates. . .

    Government bonds, interest payment dates. . .

    Stock prices, dates of highs and lows. . .

Dealers commercial paper rates.

  SEE: Commercial paper rates, dealers.

DEALINGS SUSPENDED (names of stocks that have recently been delisted from New York or American Stock Exchange). BARRON'S. Published weekly.

Debentures.

  SEE: Bonds. . .
     Convertible bonds. . .

Debit balances (margin accounts).

  SEE: Margin debt. . .

Debt.

  SEE: Funded debt. . .
     Long term debt. . .
     Margin debt. . .
     Senior capital. . .

Declines.

  SEE: Advances and declines. . .
     Trading swings. . .

Decreases in dividends.

  SEE: Dividend decreases. . .

DEFERRED INCOME TAX (where applicable, amount for each of over 1,000 companies with actively traded common stock, according to recent balance sheet). MOODY'S HANDBOOK OF COMMON STOCKS. Published quarterly.

Delistings.
>   SEE: Dealings suspended. . .

Department stores.
>   SEE: Retailers. . .

Deposit totals.
>   SEE: Banks, deposit totals. . .
>   Savings and loan companies, savings totals. . .

Deposits per share (banks).
>   SEE: Banks, deposits per share. . .

DEPRECIATION RATE (PERCENT), YEARLY (for each of past 18 or so years, for each of over 1,200 leading industrial companies. Depreciation rate is annual depreciation charge expressed as percentage of gross plant). VALUE LINE INVESTMENT SURVEY. Part three: published weekly, a few industries each week.

Detroit Stock Exchange.
>   SEE: Dividends, amount, indicated annual rate, Detroit
>   Stock Exchange. . .
>   Earnings per share, interim, Detroit Stock Exchange. . .
>   Stock prices on Detroit Stock Exchange. . .
>   Volume of trading in stocks, individual stocks on
>   Detroit Stock Exchange. . .
>   Volume of trading in stocks, total for Detroit
>   Stock Exchange. . .

DILUTED EARNINGS PER SHARE (for corporations issuing convertible bonds, shows company pro-forma reports of what earnings per common share for recent year would have been if outstanding bonds had been converted to common stock and other stock rights, if any, had been exercised). STANDARD & POOR'S EARNINGS AND RATINGS BOND GUIDE. Published monthly.

Discount bills.
>   SEE: Treasury bills. . .

Discount from net asset value (closed-end investment companies).
>   SEE: Closed-end investment companies, discount or premium
>   relative to net asset value.

DISCOUNT RATE, FEDERAL RESERVE (current percentage rate. Year ago rate also given. Under "Economic and Financial Indicators" heading). BARRON'S. Published weekly.

DISCOUNT RATE, FEDERAL RESERVE (current percentage rate, with date that it became effective. Under "Money" heading). NEW YORK TIMES. Published weekdays.

Dissolutions.

SEE: Mergers and acquisitions. . .

DISTILLERS, EXCISE TAXES AS PERCENTAGE OF SALES, YEARLY (for each of past 18 or so years, for each of about ten leading distillers). VALUE LINE INVESTMENT SURVEY. Part three: published weekly, a few industries each week.

Distributions, secondary.

SEE: Secondary distributions. . .

Dividend amounts.

SEE: Dividends, amount. . .

Dividend announcements.

SEE: Dividends, amount, current, daily list. . .

Dividend averages.

See cross reference under ("Dividends, average. . .")

Dividend dates.

SEE: Dividends, dates. . .

DIVIDEND DECREASES, CURRENT, DAILY ("Dividends Announced" includes separate "Reduced" category). NEW YORK TIMES. Published weekdays.

DIVIDEND INCREASES, CURRENT, DAILY ("Dividends Announced" includes separate "Increased" category). NEW YORK TIMES. Published weekdays.

DIVIDEND INCREASES, CURRENT, WEEKLY (corporations with currently announced dividend increases are listed, with amount of former dividend, amount of increased dividend, date of record, and date of payment). BARRON'S. Published weekly.

DIVIDEND INCREASES, CURRENT, WEEKLY (leading corporations with currently announced dividend increases are listed, with amount of dividend and date of payment). VALUE LINE INVESTMENT SURVEY. Part three: published weekly, a few industries each week.

DIVIDEND MEETING DATES, CURRENT (date of next dividend meeting is given for each of about 1,400 leading corporations). VALUE LINE INVESTMENT SURVEY. Part three: published weekly, a few industries each week.

DIVIDEND MEETINGS, DAILY LIST ("Dividend Meetings Today," alphabetically by company). NEW YORK TIMES. Published weekdays.

DIVIDEND MEETINGS, WEEKLY LIST (under each day of coming week, leading companies having dividend meetings are listed). NEW YORK TIMES. This information normally appears in Monday edition.

DIVIDEND OMISSIONS, CURRENT, DAILY ("Dividends Announced" includes separate "Omitted" category). NEW YORK TIMES. Published weekdays.

Dividend payment dates.

SEE: Dividends, dates of payment. . .

DIVIDEND PAYOUT AS PERCENTAGE OF CASH FLOW (for each of past 18 or so years for each of about 1,400 leading companies with common stock. Labeled "Dividend Payout Ratio"). VALUE LINE INVESTMENT SURVEY. Part three: published weekly, a few industries each week.

DIVIDEND PAYOUT AS PERCENTAGE OF EARNINGS (for each of past eleven years, for each of over 1,000 companies having actively traded common stock). MOODY'S HANDBOOK OF COMMON STOCKS. Published quarterly.

Dividend record dates.

SEE: Dividends, dates of record. . .

Dividend reports.

SEE: Dividends, amount, current, daily list. . .

Dividend yield averages.

SEE: Barron's 50-stock average, dividend yield. . .
Dow-Jones industrial stock average, dividend
yield. . .
Dow-Jones railroad stock average, dividend
yield. . .
Dow-Jones utility stock average, dividend
yield. . .
Moody's fire insurance stock average, dividend
yield. . .
Moody's industrial stock average, dividend
yield. . .
Moody's New York bank stock average, dividend
yield. . .
Moody's preferred stock averages, dividend
yields. . .
Moody's railroad stock average, dividend yield. . .
Moody's utility stock average, dividend yield. . .
Standard & Poor's composite 500 stock index,
dividend yield. . .
Standard & Poor's industrial 425 stock index,
dividend yield. . .
Standard & Poor's preferred stock index, dividend
yield. . .
Standard & Poor's railroad stock index, dividend
yield. . .

Standard & Poor's utility stock index, dividend
yield. . .
Value Line composite stock index, dividend
yield. . .
DIVIDEND YIELDS (PERCENT), CURRENT (for each of over 1,000 actively traded common stocks, and for each of over 1,200 less actively traded common stocks). MOODY'S HANDBOOK OF COMMON STOCKS. Published quarterly.

DIVIDEND YIELDS (PERCENT), CURRENT (for each of about 5,000 common and preferred, listed and unlisted issues). STANDARD & POOR'S SECURITY OWN-ER'S STOCK GUIDE. Published monthly.

DIVIDEND YIELDS (PERCENT), CURRENT (for each of about 1,400 leading com-mon stocks). VALUE LINE INVESTMENT SURVEY. Part one, published weekly. Also in part three: published weekly, a few industries each week.

Dividend yields (percent), high.

SEE: High yielding stocks. . .

DIVIDEND YIELDS (PERCENT), YEARLY AVERAGE (for each of past eleven years, for each of over 1,000 actively traded common stocks). MOODY'S HANDBOOK OF COMMON STOCKS. Published quarterly.

DIVIDEND YIELDS (PERCENT), YEARLY AVERAGE (for each of past four years, for each of about 960 listed stocks). TRENDLINE'S CURRENT MARKET PER-SPECTIVES. Published monthly.

DIVIDEND YIELDS (PERCENT), YEARLY AVERAGE (for each of past 18 or so years, for each of about 1,400 leading common stocks). VALUE LINE IN-VESTMENT SURVEY. Part three: published weekly, a few industries each week.

DIVIDEND YIELDS (PERCENT), 15-YEAR AVERAGE (a 15-year median dividend yield is given for each of about 1,400 leading common stocks). VALUE LINE INVESTMENT SURVEY. Part three: published weekly, a few industries each week.

Dividends, amount, current.

SEE ALSO: Dividends, amount, indicated annual rate. . .

DIVIDENDS, AMOUNT, CURRENT (latest payment per share for each of about 5,000 common and preferred, listed and unlisted issues). STANDARD & POOR'S SECURITY OWNER'S STOCK GUIDE. Published monthly.

DIVIDENDS, AMOUNT, CURRENT (latest payment per share for each of about 700 active, listed stocks). TRENDLINE DAILY BASIS STOCK CHARTS. Pub-lished weekly.

DIVIDENDS, AMOUNT, CURRENT (latest payment per share and corresponding payment for previous year for each of about 960 listed stocks). TRENDLINE'S CURRENT MARKET PERSPECTIVES. Published monthly.

DIVIDENDS, AMOUNT, CURRENT (latest payment per share and corresponding payment for previous year for each of about 1,400 leading common stocks). VALUE LINE INVESTMENT SURVEY. Part three: published weekly, a few industries each week.

DIVIDENDS, AMOUNT, CURRENT, AMERICAN STOCK EXCHANGE (latest declared dividend per share for each listed stock). BARRON'S. Published weekly.

DIVIDENDS, AMOUNT, CURRENT, DAILY LIST (for dividends reported on previous day. Arranged alphabetically by company under "Dividends Announced." Dates of payment and record are included. Dividend into various groups: "Stock" (non-cash), "Increased," "Reduced," "Omitted," "Regular"). NEW YORK TIMES. Published weekdays.

DIVIDENDS, AMOUNT, CURRENT, DAILY LIST (for dividends reported on previous day. Arranged alphabetically by company under "Dividends Reported. . ." Dates of payment and record are included, as well as dividends payable in stock). WALL STREET JOURNAL. Published business days.

DIVIDENDS, AMOUNT, CURRENT, NEW YORK STOCK EXCHANGE (latest declared dividend per share for each listed stock). BARRON'S. Published weekly.

DIVIDENDS, AMOUNT, CURRENT, PREVIOUSLY ANNOUNCED (alphabetical list, by company, of dividends previously announced and to be paid in near future. "When Payable" and "Holders of Record" dates are shown in each case). COMMERCIAL AND FINANCIAL CHRONICLE. Monday edition.

DIVIDENDS, AMOUNT, CURRENT, WEEKLY LIST (under each day of week to come, companies are arranged alphabetically with amount of dividend. Labeled "Dividend Payment Dates This Week"). BARRON'S. Published weekly.

DIVIDENDS, AMOUNT, CURRENT, WEEKLY LIST (includes "all the dividends announced during the current week," alphabetically by company. "When Payable" and "Holders of Record" dates are shown in each case). COMMERCIAL AND FINANCIAL CHRONICLE. Monday edition.

Dividends, amount, indicated annual rate.

SEE ALSO: Dividends, amount, yearly. . .

DIVIDENDS, AMOUNT, INDICATED ANNUAL RATE (probable annual amount to be paid per share for each of over 1,000 actively traded common stocks). MOODY'S HANDBOOK OF COMMON STOCKS. Published quarterly.

DIVIDENDS, AMOUNT, INDICATED ANNUAL RATE (probable annual amount to be paid per share, where applicable, for each of about 30,000 unlisted and listed, common and preferred stock issues). NATIONAL MONTHLY STOCK SUMMARY. Published monthly.

DIVIDENDS, AMOUNT, INDICATED ANNUAL RATE, AMERICAN STOCK

EXCHANGE (probable annual amount to be paid per share for each stock listed).
BARRON'S. Published weekly. NEW YORK TIMES. Published weekdays. NEW
YORK TIMES. Sunday edition. WALL STREET JOURNAL. Published business
days.

DIVIDENDS, AMOUNT, INDICATED ANNUAL RATE, BOSTON STOCK EX-
CHANGE (for each exclusively listed stock). BARRON'S. Published weekly.

DIVIDENDS, AMOUNT, INDICATED ANNUAL RATE, CINCINNATI STOCK
EXCHANGE (for each exclusively listed stock). BARRON'S. Published weekly.

DIVIDENDS, AMOUNT, INDICATED ANNUAL RATE, DETROIT STOCK EX-
CHANGE (for each exclusively listed stock). BARRON'S. Published weekly.

DIVIDENDS, AMOUNT, INDICATED ANNUAL RATE, MIDWEST STOCK EX-
CHANGE (for each exclusively listed stock). BARRON'S. Published weekly.

DIVIDENDS, AMOUNT, INDICATED ANNUAL RATE, MONTREAL STOCK EX-
CHANGE (for each exclusively listed stock). BARRON'S. Published weekly.

DIVIDENDS, AMOUNT, INDICATED ANNUAL RATE, NEW YORK STOCK EX-
CHANGE (probable annual amount to be paid per share for each stock listed).
BARRON'S. Published weekly. NEW YORK TIMES. Published weekdays.
NEW YORK TIMES. Sunday edition. WALL STREET JOURNAL. Published
business days.

DIVIDENDS, AMOUNT, INDICATED ANNUAL RATE, OVER-THE-COUNTER
STOCKS (for each of about 1,500 unlisted industrial, miscellaneous, and utility
stocks. Less-active stocks are labeled "Weekly List"). BARRON'S. Published
weekly.

DIVIDENDS, AMOUNT, INDICATED ANNUAL RATE, OVER-THE-COUNTER
STOCKS (for each of roughly 27,000 unlisted stocks of all kinds). NATIONAL
MONTHLY STOCK SUMMARY. Published monthly.

DIVIDENDS, AMOUNT, INDICATED ANNUAL RATE, OVER-THE-COUNTER
STOCKS (for each of about 1,200 unlisted industrial, miscellaneous, and utility
stocks). NEW YORK TIMES. Published weekdays. Also in Sunday edition.

DIVIDENDS, AMOUNT, INDICATED ANNUAL RATE, OVER-THE-COUNTER
STOCKS (for each of about 1,000 unlisted industrial, miscellaneous, and utility
stocks). WALL STREET JOURNAL. Published business days.

DIVIDENDS, AMOUNT, INDICATED ANNUAL RATE, PACIFIC COAST STOCK
EXCHANGE (for each exclusively listed stock). BARRON'S. Published weekly.

DIVIDENDS, AMOUNT, INDICATED ANNUAL RATE, PHILADELPHIA-BALTI-
MORE-WASHINGTON STOCK EXCHANGE (for each exclusively listed stock).
BARRON'S. Published weekly.

DIVIDENDS, AMOUNT, INDICATED ANNUAL RATE, PITTSBURGH STOCK
EXCHANGE (for each exclusively listed stock). BARRON'S. Published weekly.

DIVIDENDS, AMOUNT, INDICATED ANNUAL RATE, TORONTO STOCK EX-
CHANGE (for each exclusively listed stock. Three lists: industrials, banks,
and mines-oils). BARRON'S. Published weekly.

DIVIDENDS, AMOUNT, QUARTERLY (paid per share in most recent five quarters
for each of over 1,000 actively traded common stocks). MOODY'S HANDBOOK
OF COMMON STOCKS. Published quarterly.

DIVIDENDS, AMOUNT, QUARTERLY (paid per share for each quarter for about
seven years, for each of about 1,400 leading common stocks). VALUE LINE IN-
VESTMENT SURVEY. Part three: published weekly, a few industries each week.

Dividends, amount, yearly.

    SEE: ALSO: Dividends, amount, indicated annual rate. . .

DIVIDENDS, AMOUNT, YEARLY (paid per share for each of past 20 or so years
for each of over 1,000 actively traded common stocks, and for past three years
for over 1,200 less actively traded common stocks). MOODY'S HANDBOOK
OF COMMON STOCKS. Published quarterly.

DIVIDENDS, AMOUNT, YEARLY (paid per share in current year and previous
year, for each of about 5,000 common and preferred, listed and unlisted issues).
STANDARD & POOR'S SECURITY OWNER'S STOCK GUIDE. Published monthly.

DIVIDENDS, AMOUNT, YEARLY (paid per share so far in current year, plus
each of two previous years, for each of about 700 active, listed stocks).
TRENDLINE DAILY BASIS STOCK CHARTS. Published weekly.

DIVIDENDS, AMOUNT, YEARLY (paid per share for each of past four years for
each of about 960 listed stocks). TRENDLINE'S CURRENT MARKET PERSPEC-
TIVES. Published monthly.

DIVIDENDS, AMOUNT, YEARLY (paid per share for each of past 18 or so years
for each of about 1,400 leading common stocks). VALUE LINE INVESTMENT
SURVEY. Part three: published weekly, a few industries each week.

Dividends, annual rate.

    SEE: Dividends, amount, indicated annual rate. . .

Dividends, bank stocks.

    SEE: Bank stocks, dividends. . .

Dividends, continuous.

    SEE: Dividends, uninterrupted. . .

Dividends, current.

    SEE: Dividends, amount, current. . .

Dividends, dates of ex-dividend.

SEE: Ex-dividend dates. . .

Dividends, dates of meetings.

SEE: Dividend meeting dates. . .

DIVIDENDS, DATES OF PAYMENT, DAILY ("Dividend Payment Dates This Week." Under each day of week to come, companies are arranged alphabetically, with amount of dividend). BARRON'S. Published weekly.

DIVIDENDS, DATES OF PAYMENT, DAILY (for dividends reported on previous day. Arranged alphabetically by company under "Dividends Reported"). WALL STREET JOURNAL. Published business days.

DIVIDENDS, DATES OF PAYMENT, LATEST (month-day-year of most recent dividend payment for each of over 1,200 less actively traded common stocks). MOODY'S HANDBOOK OF COMMON STOCKS. Published quarterly.

DIVIDENDS, DATES OF PAYMENT, LATEST (month-day-year of most recent dividend payment for each of about 5,000 common and preferred, listed and unlisted stocks). STANDARD & POOR'S SECURITY OWNER'S STOCK GUIDE. Published monthly.

DIVIDENDS, DATES OF PAYMENT, LATEST, AMERICAN STOCK EXCHANGE (payment date for latest declared dividend for each stock listed). BARRON'S. Published weekly.

DIVIDENDS, DATES OF PAYMENT, LATEST, NEW YORK STOCK EXCHANGE (payment date for latest declared dividend for each stock listed). BARRON'S. Published weekly.

DIVIDENDS, DATES OF PAYMENT, PREVIOUSLY ANNOUNCED (includes amount, date of payment, and date of record for each of all dividends of listed and unlisted stocks previously announced and to be paid in the near future. Arrangement is alphabetical by company name). COMMERCIAL AND FINANCIAL CHRONICLE. Monday edition.

DIVIDENDS, DATES OF PAYMENT, QUARTERLY (month-day-year of five most recent quarterly dividend payments for each of over 1,000 companies with actively traded common stock). MOODY'S HANDBOOK OF COMMON STOCKS. Published quarterly.

DIVIDENDS, DATES OF PAYMENT, WEEKLY (includes amount, date of payment, and date of record for each of "all the dividends announced during the current week," both listed and over-the-counter, alphabetically by company). COMMERCIAL AND FINANCIAL CHRONICLE. Monday edition.

DIVIDENDS, DATES OF RECORD, DAILY (for dividends reported on previous day. Arranged alphabetically by company under "Dividends Reported . . ."). WALL STREET JOURNAL. Published business days.

DIVIDENDS, DATES OF RECORD, LATEST, AMERICAN STOCK EXCHANGE ("Stock of Record" date given for latest declared dividend for each listed stock).

BARRON'S. Published weekly.

DIVIDENDS, DATES OF RECORD, LATEST, NEW YORK STOCK EXCHANGE ("Stock of Record" date given for latest declared dividend for each listed stock). BARRON'S. Published weekly.

DIVIDENDS, DATES OF RECORD, PREVIOUSLY ANNOUNCED (includes amount, date of payment, and date of record for each of all dividends of listed and un-listed stocks previously announced and to be paid in the near future. Arrange-ment is alphabetical by company name). COMMERCIAL AND FINANCIAL CHRONICLE. Monday edition.

DIVIDENDS, DATES OF RECORD, QUARTERLY (month-day-year of record of five most recent quarterly dividends for each of over 1,000 actively traded common stocks). MOODY'S HANDBOOK OF COMMON STOCKS. Published quarterly.

DIVIDENDS, DATES OF RECORD, WEEKLY (includes amount, date of payment, and date of record for each of "all the dividends announced during the current week," both listed and over-the-counter, alphabetically by company). COM-MERCIAL AND FINANCIAL CHRONICLE. Monday edition.

Dividends, decreased.

 SEE: Dividend decreases. . .

Dividends, Dow-Jones stock averages.

 See entries beginning "Dow-Jones. . ."

Dividends, ex-dividend dates.

 SEE: Ex-dividend dates. . .

Dividends, increased.

 SEE: Dividend increases. . .

Dividends, indicated annual rate.

 SEE: Dividends, amount, indicated annual rate. . .

Dividends, insurance stocks.

 SEE: Insurance stocks (unlisted), dividends. . .

Dividends, meeting dates.

 SEE: Dividend meeting dates. . .

Dividends, Moody's stock averages.

 See entries beginning "Moody's. . ."

Dividends, omitted.

 SEE: Dividend omissions. . .

Dividends, over-the-counter stocks.
> SEE: Dividends, amount, indicated annual rate,
> over-the-counter. . .

Dividends, payment dates.
> SEE: Dividends, dates of payment. . .

Dividends, preferred stock, total corporate amount payable annually.
> SEE: Preferred stock, total corporate dollar amount of
> dividends. . .

Dividends, previously announced.
> SEE: Dividends, amount, current, previously
> announced. . .

Dividends, reduced.
> SEE: Dividend decreases. . .

Dividends, skipped.
> SEE: Dividend omissions. . .

Dividends, some each year.
> SEE: Dividends, uninterrupted. . .

Dividends, Standard & Poor's stock indexes.
> See entries beginning "Standard & Poor's. . ."

Dividends, stock.
> SEE: Stock dividends. . .

DIVIDENDS, UNINTERRUPTED, YEAR OF BEGINNING (for each of about
5,000 individual common and preferred, listed and unlisted issues). STANDARD
& POOR'S SECURITY OWNER'S STOCK GUIDE. Published monthly.

DIVIDENDS, UNINTERRUPTED, YEAR OF BEGINNING (for each of over
1,000 active common stocks and 1,200 less active stocks). MOODY'S HAND-
BOOK OF COMMON STOCKS. Published quarterly.

Dividends, weekly list of.
> SEE: Dividends, amount, current, weekly list. . .

Dividends, yields.
> SEE: Dividend yields. . .

Dividends, yields, averages.
> (See cross references under "Dividend yield averages.")

Dividends announced.
> SEE: Dividends, amount, current, daily list. . .

Dividends each year (uninterrupted).
>   SEE: Dividends, uninterrupted. . .

Dividends from capital gains.
>   SEE: Closed-end investment companies, dividends from
>   capital gains. . .
>   Mutual funds, dividends from capital gains. . .

Dividends from investment income.
>   SEE: Closed-end investment companies, dividends from
>   investment. . .
>   Mutual funds, dividends from investment. . .

Dividends paid each year (uninterrupted).
>   SEE: Dividends, uninterrupted. . .

Dividends per share.
>   SEE: Dividends, amount. . .

Dividends reported.
>   SEE: Dividends, amount, current, daily list. . .

DIVISORS FOR DOW-JONES AVERAGES (current numerical divisors used to compile each of daily stock averages: industrials, railroads, utilities, and 65 stock composite). BARRON'S. Published weekly. Also in WALL STREET JOURNAL. Published business days.

DOW-JONES COMPOSITE BOND AVERAGE, PRICE, DAILY, CLOSE (for each day of week just past. Labeled "40 Bonds" under "Bond Averages and NYSE Bond Sales"). BARRON'S. Published weekly.

DOW-JONES COMPOSITE BOND AVERAGE, PRICE, DAILY, CLOSE (for each day of week just past). COMMERCIAL AND FINANCIAL CHRONICLE. Monday edition.

DOW-JONES COMPOSITE BOND AVERAGE, PRICE, DAILY-MONTHLY, CLOSE (final price for each day of previous month. Monthly high-low also indicated. Labeled "Dow-Jones Averages. . .40 Bonds"). BARRON'S. This data normally appears between the 20th and 30th of each month.

DOW-JONES COMPOSITE BOND AVERAGE, PRICE, DAILY-YEARLY, CLOSE (closing price for previous day, as well as corresponding day one year ago and two years ago). WALL STREET JOURNAL. Published business days.

DOW-JONES COMPOSITE BOND AVERAGE, PRICE, WEEKLY, OPEN-HIGH-LOW-CLOSE (for week just past). BARRON'S. Published weekly.

DOW-JONES COMPOSITE BOND AVERAGE, PRICE, YEARLY, HIGH-LOW (price range for each of three latest years). WALL STREET JOURNAL. Published business days.

DOW-JONES COMPOSITE BOND AVERAGE, YIELD (PERCENT), WEEKLY-YEARLY (for end of latest week, previous week, and same week one year ago. Labeled "40 Bonds"). BARRON'S. Published weekly.

DOW-JONES COMPOSITE STOCK AVERAGE, DIVIDENDS, QUARTERLY-YEARLY. Quarterly and yearly composite average dividends appear frequently in BARRON'S.

Dow-Jones composite stock average, divisor.
  SEE: Divisors for Dow-Jones averages. . .

DOW-JONES COMPOSITE STOCK AVERAGE, EARNINGS PER SHARE, QUAR-TERLY-YEARLY. Composite average quarterly earnings for a number of years appear frequently in BARRON'S.

Dow-Jones composite stock average, percentage change.
  SEE: Dow-Jones composite stock average, price, daily,
     percentage change. . .
    Dow-Jones composite stock average, price, year
     to date, percentage change. . .

DOW-JONES COMPOSITE STOCK AVERAGE, PRICE, DAILY, CLOSE (closing price is given for each day of the month prior to month of publication). BANK AND QUOTATION RECORD. Published monthly.

DOW-JONES COMPOSITE STOCK AVERAGE, PRICE, DAILY, CLOSE (for each day of week just past). COMMERCIAL AND FINANCIAL CHRONICLE. Monday edition.

DOW-JONES COMPOSITE STOCK AVERAGE, PRICE, DAILY, HIGH-LOW-CLOSE (for previous trading day--"65 Stocks"). NEW YORK TIMES. Published weekdays.

DOW-JONES COMPOSITE STOCK AVERAGE, PRICE, DAILY, OPEN-HIGH-LOW-CLOSE (for each day of week just past). BARRON'S. Published weekly.

DOW-JONES COMPOSITE STOCK AVERAGE, PRICE, DAILY, OPEN-HIGH-LOW-CLOSE (for each of five previous trading days). WALL STREET JOURNAL. Published business days.

DOW-JONES COMPOSITE STOCK AVERAGE, PRICE, DAILY, PERCENTAGE CHANGE (for each of five previous trading days). WALL STREET JOURNAL. Published business days.

DOW-JONES COMPOSITE STOCK AVERAGE, PRICE, DAILY-YEARLY, CLOSE (closing price for previous day and corresponding day one year ago). WALL STREET JOURNAL. Published business days.

DOW-JONES COMPOSITE STOCK AVERAGE, PRICE, HOURLY (each hour on the hour, for each day of week just past). BARRON'S. Published weekly.

DOW-JONES COMPOSITE STOCK AVERAGE, PRICE, HOURLY (each hour on the hour, for each of five previous trading days). WALL STREET JOURNAL. Published business days.

DOW-JONES COMPOSITE STOCK AVERAGE, PRICE, WEEKLY, HIGH-LOW-CLOSE (for week just past, including dates of high and low for week). NEW YORK TIMES. Sunday edition.

DOW-JONES COMPOSITE STOCK AVERAGE, PRICE, YEAR TO DATE, OPEN-HIGH-LOW-CLOSE (current year so far). BARRON'S. Published weekly.

DOW-JONES COMPOSITE STOCK AVERAGE, PRICE, YEAR TO DATE, PER-CENTAGE CHANGE (from beginning of year). BARRON'S. Published weekly.

DOW-JONES COMPOSITE STOCK AVERAGE, PRICE, YEARLY, HIGH-LOW. Yearly price ranges for a number of years appear frequently in BARRON'S, sometimes with exact dates of annual highs and lows.

DOW-JONES COMPOSITE STOCK AVERAGE, VOLUME OF TRADING, DAILY (number of shares traded each day of week just past, for total stocks in average). BARRON'S. Published weekly.

DOW-JONES COMPOSITE STOCK AVERAGE, VOLUME OF TRADING, DAILY (number of shares traded on each of five previous trading days, for total stocks in average). WALL STREET JOURNAL. Published business days.

DOW-JONES COMPOSITE STOCK AVERAGE, VOLUME OF TRADING, WEEKLY AND YEARLY (combined volume in thousands of shares for latest week, previous week, and same period one year ago). BARRON'S. Published weekly.

Dow-Jones divisors.

SEE: Divisors for Dow-Jones averages. . .

Dow-Jones 40 bonds average.

SEE: Dow-Jones composite bond average. . .

DOW-JONES INDUSTRIAL BOND AVERAGE, PRICE, DAILY, CLOSE (for each day of week just past. Labeled "Bond Averages and NYSE Bond Sales"). BARRON'S. Published weekly.

DOW-JONES INDUSTRIAL BOND AVERAGE, PRICE, DAILY, CLOSE (for each day of week just past). COMMERCIAL AND FINANCIAL CHRONICLE. Monday edition.

DOW-JONES INDUSTRIAL BOND AVERAGE, PRICE, DAILY-YEARLY, CLOSE (closing price for previous day, as well as corresponding day one year ago and two years ago). WALL STREET JOURNAL. Published business days.

DOW-JONES INDUSTRIAL BOND AVERAGE, PRICE, WEEKLY, OPEN-HIGH-LOW-CLOSE (for week just past). BARRON'S. Published weekly.

DOW-JONES INDUSTRIAL BOND AVERAGE, PRICE, YEARLY, HIGH-LOW (price range for each of three latest years). WALL STREET JOURNAL. Published business days.

DOW-JONES INDUSTRIAL BOND AVERAGE, YIELD (PERCENT), WEEKLY-YEARLY (for end of latest week, previous week, and same week one year ago. Labeled "10 Ind"). BARRON'S. Published weekly.

DOW-JONES INDUSTRIAL STOCK AVERAGE, DIVIDEND YIELD (PERCENT), WEEKLY-YEARLY (yield for end of latest week, previous week, and same week one year ago). BARRON'S. Published weekly.

DOW-JONES INDUSTRIAL STOCK AVERAGE, DIVIDENDS, QUARTERLY-YEARLY. Quarterly and yearly industrial average dividends appear frequently in BARRON'S.

Dow-Jones industrial stock average, divisor.

SEE: Divisors for Dow-Jones averages. . .

DOW-JONES INDUSTRIAL STOCK AVERAGE, EARNINGS PER SHARE, QUARTERLY-YEARLY. Industrial average quarterly earnings for a number of years appear frequently in BARRON'S.

DOW-JONES INDUSTRIAL STOCK AVERAGE, EARNINGS PER SHARE, QUARTERLY-YEARLY (figure for latest twelve month earnings is revised quarterly. Comparable figure given for one year ago. Stated in paragraph that includes information on price-earnings ratio). WALL STREET JOURNAL. This data normally appears in Monday edition.

DOW-JONES INDUSTRIAL STOCK AVERAGE, NAMES OF STOCKS COMPRISING (30 stocks are listed). MOODY'S HANDBOOK OF COMMON STOCKS. Published quarterly.

DOW-JONES INDUSTRIAL STOCK AVERAGE, NAMES OF STOCKS COMPRISING (30 stocks are listed). WALL STREET JOURNAL. This data normally appears in Monday edition.

Dow-Jones industrial stock average, percentage change.

SEE: Dow-Jones industrial stock average, price, daily, percentage change. . .
Dow-Jones industrial stock average, price, weekly, percentage change. . .
Dow-Jones industrial stock average, price, year to date, percentage change. . .

DOW-JONES INDUSTRIAL STOCK AVERAGE, PRICE, DAILY, CLOSE (closing price for each day of month prior to month of publication). BANK AND QUOTATION RECORD. Published monthly.

DOW-JONES INDUSTRIAL STOCK AVERAGE, PRICE, DAILY, CLOSE (for each day of week just past). COMMERCIAL AND FINANCIAL CHRONICLE. Monday edition.

DOW-JONES INDUSTRIAL STOCK AVERAGE, PRICE, DAILY, HIGH-LOW-CLOSE (for previous trading day). NEW YORK TIMES. Published weekdays.

DOW-JONES INDUSTRIAL STOCK AVERAGE, PRICE, DAILY, HIGH-LOW-CLOSE, CHART (daily prices are charted for about four years). TRENDLINE DAILY BASIS STOCK CHARTS. Published weekly.

DOW-JONES INDUSTRIAL STOCK AVERAGE, PRICE, DAILY, HIGH-LOW-CLOSE, CHART (daily prices are charted for about four months). WALL STREET JOURNAL. Published business days.

DOW-JONES INDUSTRIAL STOCK AVERAGE, PRICE, DAILY, OPEN-HIGH-LOW-CLOSE (for each day of week just past). BARRON'S. Published weekly.

DOW-JONES INDUSTRIAL STOCK AVERAGE, PRICE, DAILY, OPEN-HIGH-LOW-CLOSE (for each of five previous trading days). WALL STREET JOURNAL. Published business days.

DOW-JONES INDUSTRIAL STOCK AVERAGE, PRICE, DAILY, PERCENTAGE CHANGE (for each of five previous trading days). WALL STREET JOURNAL. Published business days.

DOW-JONES INDUSTRIAL STOCK AVERAGE, PRICE, DAILY-MONTHLY, HIGH-LOW-CLOSE (price range and close for each day of previous month. Monthly high-low also indicated). BARRON'S. This data normally appears between the 20th and 30th of each month.

DOW-JONES INDUSTRIAL STOCK AVERAGE, PRICE, DAILY-YEARLY, CLOSE (closing price for previous day and corresponding day one year ago). WALL STREET JOURNAL. Published business days.

DOW-JONES INDUSTRIAL STOCK AVERAGE, PRICE, HOURLY (each hour on the hour, for each day of week just past). BARRON'S. Published weekly.

DOW-JONES INDUSTRIAL STOCK AVERAGE, PRICE, HOURLY (each hour on the hour, for each of five previous trading days). WALL STREET JOURNAL. Published business days.

DOW-JONES INDUSTRIAL STOCK AVERAGE, PRICE, MONTHLY, HIGH-LOW, CHART (monthly price ranges are charted for about 40 years). MOODY'S HANDBOOK OF COMMON STOCKS. Published quarterly.

DOW-JONES INDUSTRIAL STOCK AVERAGE, PRICE, MONTHLY, HIGH-LOW, CHART (monthly price ranges are charted for about 50 years). TRENDLINE'S CURRENT MARKET PERSPECTIVES. Published monthly.

DOW-JONES INDUSTRIAL STOCK AVERAGE, PRICE, MONTHLY AVERAGE (average daily price for latest month, previous month, and same month one year ago. Labeled "The Statistical Record, Monthly Average"). BARRON'S. This data normally appears in first issue of each month.

DOW-JONES INDUSTRIAL STOCK AVERAGE, PRICE, MOVING AVERAGE, CHART (200-day moving average is shown on daily price chart covering about four years). TRENDLINE DAILY BASIS STOCK CHARTS. Published weekly.

Dow-Jones industrial stock average, price, percentage change.

    SEE: Dow-Jones industrial stock average, price, daily,
            percentage change. . .
          Dow-Jones industrial stock average, price, weekly,
            percentage change. . .
          Dow-Jones industrial stock average, price, year
            to date, percentage change. . .

Dow-Jones industrial stock average, price, rallies and declines.

    SEE: Trading swings, Dow-Jones. . .

DOW-JONES INDUSTRIAL STOCK AVERAGE, PRICE, WEEKLY, CLOSE (for end of each of four previous weeks). MOODY'S STOCK SURVEY. Published weekly.

DOW-JONES INDUSTRIAL STOCK AVERAGE, PRICE, WEEKLY, HIGH-LOW-CLOSE (for week just past, with dates of high and low for week). NEW YORK TIMES. Sunday edition.

DOW-JONES INDUSTRIAL STOCK AVERAGE, PRICE, WEEKLY, HIGH-LOW-CLOSE, CHART (weekly prices are charted for about five years). TRENDLINE'S CURRENT MARKET PERSPECTIVES. Published monthly.

DOW-JONES INDUSTRIAL STOCK AVERAGE, PRICE, WEEKLY, OPEN-HIGH-LOW-CLOSE (for week just past). BARRON'S. Published weekly.

DOW-JONES INDUSTRIAL STOCK AVERAGE, PRICE, WEEKLY, PERCENTAGE CHANGE (for end of week just past. Included with data labeled "Mutual Fund Investment Performance Index"). BARRON'S. Published weekly.

DOW-JONES INDUSTRIAL STOCK AVERAGE, PRICE, WEEKLY, PERCENTAGE CHANGE (for end of week just past. Labeled "Last Week's Markets"). WALL STREET JOURNAL. This data normally appears in Monday edition.

DOW-JONES INDUSTRIAL STOCK AVERAGE, PRICE, WEEKLY-YEARLY, CLOSE (price for end of latest week, week previous, and same week one year ago). BARRON'S. Published weekly.

DOW-JONES INDUSTRIAL AVERAGE, PRICE, YEAR TO DATE, OPEN-HIGH-LOW-CLOSE (current year). BARRON'S. Published weekly.

DOW-JONES INDUSTRIAL STOCK AVERAGE, PRICE, YEAR TO DATE, PER-CENTAGE CHANGE (from beginning of year). BARRON'S. Published weekly.

DOW-JONES INDUSTRIAL STOCK AVERAGE, PRICE, YEARLY, HIGH-LOW.
Yearly ranges for a number of years appear frequently in BARRON'S, sometimes
with exact dates of annual highs and lows.

DOW-JONES INDUSTRIAL STOCK AVERAGE, PRICE, YEARLY, HIGH-LOW
(range for current year and each of two previous years). MOODY'S STOCK
SURVEY. Published weekly.

DOW-JONES INDUSTRIAL STOCK AVERAGE, PRICE, YEARLY, HIGH-LOW,
CHART (annual price range is charted for about twelve years). TRENDLINE
DAILY BASIS STOCK CHARTS. Published weekly.

DOW-JONES INDUSTRIAL STOCK AVERAGE, PRICE-EARNINGS RATIO,
WEEKLY-MONTHLY-YEARLY (for end of week just past, and for same week
a month ago, a year ago, and two years ago). BARRON'S. Published weekly.

DOW-JONES INDUSTRIAL STOCK AVERAGE, PRICE-EARNINGS RATIO,
WEEKLY-YEARLY (for end of week just past, previous week, and same week
one year ago. Stated in paragraph form). WALL STREET JOURNAL. This
data normally appears in Monday edition.

DOW-JONES INDUSTRIAL STOCK AVERAGE, PRICE-EARNINGS RATIO
(ARBITRARY), YEARLY, CHART (arbitrary "24 times earnings" and "9 times
earnings" lines are drawn above and below actual, monthly price ranges.
The arbitrary lines are plotted back to 1926). TRENDLINE'S CURRENT MAR-
KET PERSPECTIVES. Published monthly.

Dow-Jones industrial stock average, rallies and declines.
        SEE: Trading swings, Dow-Jones. . .

DOW-JONES INDUSTRIAL STOCK AVERAGE, VOLUME OF TRADING, DAILY
(number of shares traded each day of week just past, for the total of the 30
stocks in the average). BARRON'S. Published weekly.

DOW-JONES INDUSTRIAL STOCK AVERAGE, VOLUME OF TRADING, DAILY
(number of shares traded on each of the five previous trading days, for the
total of the 30 stocks in the average). WALL STREET JOURNAL. Published
business days.

DOW-JONES INDUSTRIAL STOCK AVERAGE, VOLUME OF TRADING, WEEK-
LY-YEARLY (combined volume in thousands of shares for the 30 stocks in aver-
age, for latest week, previous week, and same week one year ago). BARRON'S.
Published weekly.

Dow-Jones industrial stock average, yield.
        SEE: Dow-Jones industrial stock average, dividend
                yield. . .

DOW-JONES MUNICIPAL BOND AVERAGE, YIELD (PERCENT), WEEKLY-
YEARLY (for end of latest week, previous week, and same week one year ago).
BARRON'S. Published weekly.

Dow-Jones public utility averages.

   SEE: Dow-Jones utility. . .

DOW-JONES RAILROAD BOND AVERAGE (HIGHER GRADE), PRICE, DAILY, CLOSE (for each day of week just past. Labeled "Bond Averages and NYSE Bond Sales"). BARRON'S. Published weekly.

DOW-JONES RAILROAD BOND AVERAGE (HIGHER GRADE), PRICE, DAILY, CLOSE (for each day of week just past). COMMERCIAL AND FINANCIAL CHRONICLE. Monday edition.

DOW-JONES RAILROAD BOND AVERAGE (HIGHER GRADE), PRICE, DAILY-YEARLY, CLOSE (closing price for previous day and corresponding day one year ago and two years ago). WALL STREET JOURNAL. Published business days.

DOW-JONES RAILROAD BOND AVERAGE (HIGHER GRADE), PRICE, WEEKLY, OPEN-HIGH-LOW-CLOSE (for week just past). BARRON'S. Published weekly.

DOW-JONES RAILROAD BOND AVERAGE (HIGHER GRADE), PRICE, YEARLY, HIGH-LOW (price range for each of three latest years). WALL STREET JOURNAL. Published business days.

DOW-JONES RAILROAD BOND AVERAGE (HIGHER GRADE), YIELD (PERCENT), WEEKLY-YEARLY (for end of latest week, previous week, and same week one year ago. Labeled "10 Hi Gr"). BARRON'S. Published weekly.

DOW-JONES RAILROAD BOND AVERAGE (INCOME BONDS), PRICE, DAILY, CLOSE (for each day of week just past. Under "Bond Averages and NYSE Bond Sales"). BARRON'S. Published weekly.

DOW-JONES RAILROAD BOND AVERAGE (INCOME BONDS), PRICE, DAILY-YEARLY, CLOSE (closing price for previous day, and corresponding day one year ago and two years ago). WALL STREET JOURNAL. Published business days.

DOW-JONES RAILROAD BOND AVERAGE (INCOME BONDS), PRICE, WEEKLY, OPEN-HIGH-LOW-CLOSE (for week just past). BARRON'S. Published weekly.

DOW-JONES RAILROAD BOND AVERAGE (INCOME BONDS), PRICE, YEARLY, HIGH-LOW (price range for each of three latest years). WALL STREET JOURNAL. Published business days.

DOW-JONES RAILROAD BOND AVERAGE (SECOND GRADE), PRICE, DAILY, CLOSE (for each day of week just past. Labeled "Bond Averages and NYSE Bond Sales"). BARRON'S. Published weekly.

DOW-JONES RAILROAD BOND AVERAGE (SECOND GRADE), PRICE, DAILY, CLOSE (for each day of week just past). COMMERCIAL AND FINANCIAL CHRONICLE. Monday edition.

DOW-JONES RAILROAD BOND AVERAGE (SECOND GRADE), PRICE, DAILY, YEARLY, CLOSE (closing price for previous day, as well as corresponding day one year ago and two years ago). WALL STREET JOURNAL. Published business days.

DOW-JONES RAILROAD BOND AVERAGE (SECOND GRADE), PRICE, WEEKLY, OPEN-HIGH-LOW-CLOSE (for week just past). BARRON'S. Published weekly.

DOW-JONES RAILROAD BOND AVERAGE (SECOND GRADE), PRICE, YEARLY, HIGH-LOW (price range for each of three latest years). WALL STREET JOURNAL. Published business days.

DOW-JONES RAILROAD BOND AVERAGE (SECOND GRADE), YIELD (PERCENT), WEEKLY-YEARLY (for end of latest week, previous week, and same week one year ago. Labeled "10 2nd Gr"). BARRON'S. Published weekly.

DOW-JONES RAILROAD STOCK AVERAGE, DIVIDEND YIELD (PERCENT), WEEKLY-YEARLY (yield for end of latest week, previous week, and same week one year ago). BARRON'S. Published weekly.

DOW-JONES RAILROAD STOCK AVERAGE, DIVIDENDS, QUARTERLY-YEARLY. Quarterly and yearly railroad average dividends appear frequently in BARRON'S.

Dow-Jones railroad stock average, divisor.

    SEE: Divisors for Dow-Jones averages. . .

DOW-JONES RAILROAD STOCK AVERAGE, EARNINGS PER SHARE, QUARTERLY-YEARLY. Railroad average quarterly earnings for a number of years appear frequently in BARRON'S.

DOW-JONES RAILROAD STOCK AVERAGE, NAMES OF STOCKS COMPRISING (20 stocks are listed). WALL STREET JOURNAL. This information normally appears in Monday edition.

Dow-Jones railroad stock average, percentage change.

    SEE: Dow-Jones railroad stock average, price, daily,
           percentage change. . .
        Dow-Jones railroad stock average, price, weekly,
           percentage change. . .
        Dow-Jones railroad stock average, price, year
           to date, percentage change. . .

DOW-JONES RAILROAD STOCK AVERAGE, PRICE, DAILY, CLOSE (closing price is given for each day of month prior to month of publication). BANK AND QUOTATION RECORD. Published monthly.

DOW-JONES RAILROAD STOCK AVERAGE, PRICE, DAILY, CLOSE (for each day of week just past). COMMERCIAL AND FINANCIAL CHRONICLE. Monday edition.

DOW-JONES RAILROAD STOCK AVERAGE, PRICE, DAILY, HIGH-LOW-CLOSE (for previous trading day). NEW YORK TIMES. Published weekdays.

DOW-JONES RAILROAD STOCK AVERAGE, PRICE, DAILY, HIGH-LOW-CLOSE, CHART (daily prices charted for about four months). WALL STREET JOURNAL. Published business days.

DOW-JONES RAILROAD STOCK AVERAGE, PRICE, DAILY, OPEN-HIGH-LOW-CLOSE (for each day of week just past). BARRON'S. Published weekly.

DOW-JONES RAILROAD STOCK AVERAGE, PRICE, DAILY, OPEN-HIGH-LOW-CLOSE (for each of five previous trading days). WALL STREET JOURNAL. Published business days.

DOW-JONES RAILROAD STOCK AVERAGE, PRICE, DAILY, PERCENTAGE CHANGE (for each of five previous trading days). WALL STREET JOURNAL. Published business days.

DOW-JONES RAILROAD STOCK AVERAGE, PRICE, DAILY-MONTHLY, HIGH-LOW-CLOSE (price range and close for each day of previous month. Monthly high-low also indicated). BARRON'S. This data normally appears between the 20th and 30th of each month.

DOW-JONES RAILROAD STOCK AVERAGE, PRICE, DAILY-YEARLY, CLOSE (closing price for previous day, as well as corresponding day one year ago). WALL STREET JOURNAL. Published business days.

DOW-JONES RAILROAD STOCK AVERAGE, PRICE, HOURLY (each hour on the hour, for each day of week just past). BARRON'S. Published weekly.

DOW-JONES RAILROAD STOCK AVERAGE, PRICE, HOURLY (each hour on the hour for each of five previous trading days). WALL STREET JOURNAL. Published business days.

DOW-JONES RAILROAD STOCK AVERAGE, PRICE, MONTHLY AVERAGE (average daily price for latest month, previous month, and same month one year ago. Labeled "The Statistical Record, Monthly Average"). BARRON'S. This data normally appears in first issue of each month.

DOW-JONES RAILROAD STOCK AVERAGE, PRICE, MOVING AVERAGE, CHART (200-day moving average charted weekly for about two years). TREND-LINE DAILY BASIS STOCK CHARTS. Published weekly.

Dow-Jones railroad stock average, price, percentage change.

> SEE: Dow-Jones railroad stock average, price, daily,
>   percentage change. . .
>   Dow-Jones railroad stock average, price, weekly,
>   percentage change. . .
>   Dow-Jones railroad stock average, price, year
>   to date, percentage change. . .

DOW-JONES RAILROAD STOCK AVERAGE, PRICE, WEEKLY, CLOSE (for end of each of previous four weeks). MOODY'S STOCK SURVEY. Published weekly.

DOW-JONES RAILROAD STOCK AVERAGE, PRICE, WEEKLY, HIGH-LOW-CLOSE (for week just past, with dates of high and low for week). NEW YORK TIMES. Sunday edition.

DOW-JONES RAILROAD STOCK AVERAGE, PRICE, WEEKLY, HIGH-LOW-CLOSE, CHART (weekly prices are charted for about two years). TRENDLINE DAILY BASIS STOCK CHARTS. Published weekly.

DOW-JONES RAILROAD STOCK AVERAGE, PRICE, WEEKLY, OPEN-HIGH-LOW-CLOSE (for week just past). BARRON'S. Published weekly.

DOW-JONES RAILROAD STOCK AVERAGE, PRICE, WEEKLY, PERCENTAGE CHANGE (for end of week just past. Labeled "Last Week's Markets"). WALL STREET JOURNAL. This data normally appears in Monday edition.

DOW-JONES RAILROAD STOCK AVERAGE, PRICE, WEEKLY-YEARLY, CLOSE (price for end of latest week, previous week, and same week one year ago). BARRON'S. Published weekly.

DOW-JONES RAILROAD STOCK AVERAGE, PRICE, YEAR TO DATE, OPEN-HIGH-LOW-CLOSE (current year). BARRON'S. Published weekly.

DOW-JONES RAILROAD STOCK AVERAGE, PRICE, YEAR TO DATE, PERCENTAGE CHANGE (from beginning of year). BARRON'S. Published weekly.

DOW-JONES RAILROAD STOCK AVERAGE, PRICE, YEARLY, HIGH-LOW. Yearly ranges for a number of years appear frequently in BARRON'S, sometimes with exact dates of annual highs and lows.

DOW-JONES RAILROAD STOCK AVERAGE, PRICE, YEARLY, HIGH-LOW (range for current year and each of two previous years). MOODY'S STOCK SURVEY. Published weekly.

DOW-JONES RAILROAD STOCK AVERAGE, PRICE-EARNINGS RATIO, WEEKLY-MONTHLY-YEARLY (for end of week just past, and for same period a month ago, one year ago, and two years ago). BARRON'S. Published weekly.

DOW-JONES RAILROAD STOCK AVERAGE, VOLUME OF TRADING, DAILY (total number of shares traded each day of week just past, for the combined 20 stocks). BARRON'S. Published weekly.

DOW-JONES RAILROAD STOCK AVERAGE, VOLUME OF TRADING, DAILY (total number of shares traded on each of five previous days, for the combined 20 stocks). WALL STREET JOURNAL. Published business days.

DOW-JONES RAILROAD STOCK AVERAGE, VOLUME OF TRADING, WEEKLY-YEARLY (combined volume in thousands of shares for the 20 stocks, for latest week, previous week, and same week one year ago). BARRON'S. Published weekly.

Dow-Jones 65 stocks average.

SEE: Dow-Jones composite stock average. . .

Dow-Jones trading swings.

SEE: Trading swings, Dow-Jones. . .

DOW-JONES UTILITY BOND AVERAGE, PRICE, DAILY, CLOSE (for each day of week just past. Labeled "Bond Averages and NYSE Bond Sales"). BARRON'S. Published weekly.

DOW-JONES UTILITY BOND AVERAGE, PRICE, DAILY, CLOSE (for each day of week just past). COMMERCIAL AND FINANCIAL CHRONICLE. Monday edition.

DOW-JONES UTILITY BOND AVERAGE, PRICE, DAILY-YEARLY, CLOSE (closing price for previous day, as well as corresponding day one year ago and two years ago). WALL STREET JOURNAL. Published business days.

DOW-JONES UTILITY BOND AVERAGE, PRICE, WEEKLY, OPEN-HIGH-LOW-CLOSE (for week just past). BARRON'S. Published weekly.

DOW-JONES UTILITY BOND AVERAGE, PRICE, YEARLY, HIGH-LOW (range for each of three latest years, including current year). WALL STREET JOURNAL. Published business days.

DOW-JONES UTILITY BOND AVERAGE, YIELD (PERCENT), WEEKLY-YEARLY (for end of latest week, previous week, and same week one year ago. Labeled "10 Util"). BARRON'S. Published weekly.

DOW-JONES UTILITY STOCK AVERAGE, DIVIDEND YIELD (PERCENT), WEEKLY-YEARLY (yield for end of latest week, previous week, and same week one year ago). BARRON'S. Published weekly.

DOW-JONES UTILITY STOCK AVERAGE, DIVIDENDS, QUARTERLY-YEARLY. Quarterly and yearly utility average dividends appear frequently in BARRON'S.

Dow-Jones utility stock average, divisor.

SEE: Divisors for Dow-Jones averages. . .

DOW-JONES UTILITY STOCK AVERAGE, EARNINGS PER SHARE, QUARTERLY-YEARLY. Utility average quarterly earnings for a number of years appear frequently in BARRON'S.

DOW-JONES UTILITY STOCK AVERAGE, NAMES OF STOCKS COMPRISING (15 stocks are listed). WALL STREET JOURNAL. This information normally appears in Monday edition.

Dow-Jones utility stock average, percentage change.

SEE: Dow-Jones utility stock average, price, daily, percentage change. . .

Dow-Jones utility stock average, price, weekly, percentage change. . .

Dow-Jones utility stock average, price, year to date, percentage change. . .

DOW-JONES UTILITY STOCK AVERAGE, PRICE, DAILY, CLOSE (closing price is given for each day of month prior to month of publication). BANK AND QUOTATION RECORD. Published monthly.

DOW-JONES UTILITY STOCK AVERAGE, PRICE, DAILY, CLOSE (for each day of week just past). COMMERCIAL AND FINANCIAL CHRONICLE. Monday edition.

DOW-JONES UTILITY STOCK AVERAGE, PRICE, DAILY, HIGH-LOW-CLOSE (for previous trading day). NEW YORK TIMES. Published weekdays.

DOW-JONES UTILITY STOCK AVERAGE, PRICE, DAILY, HIGH-LOW-CLOSE, CHART (daily prices charted for about four months). WALL STREET JOURNAL. Published business days.

DOW-JONES UTILITY STOCK AVERAGE, PRICE, DAILY, OPEN-HIGH-LOW-CLOSE (for each day of week just past). BARRON'S. Published weekly.

DOW-JONES UTILITY STOCK AVERAGE, PRICE, DAILY, OPEN-HIGH-LOW-CLOSE (for each of five previous trading days). WALL STREET JOURNAL. Published business days.

DOW-JONES UTILITY STOCK AVERAGE, PRICE, DAILY, PERCENTAGE CHANGE (for each of five previous trading days). WALL STREET JOURNAL. Published business days.

DOW-JONES UTILITY STOCK AVERAGE, PRICE, DAILY-MONTHLY, HIGH-LOW-CLOSE (price range and close for each day of previous month. Monthly high-low also indicated). BARRON'S. This data normally appears between the 20th and 30th of each month.

DOW-JONES UTILITY STOCK AVERAGE, PRICE, DAILY-YEARLY, CLOSE (closing price for previous day, as well as corresponding day one year ago). WALL STREET JOURNAL. Published business days.

DOW-JONES UTILITY STOCK AVERAGE, PRICE, HOURLY (each hour on the hour for each day of week just past). BARRON'S. Published weekly.

DOW-JONES UTILITY STOCK AVERAGE, PRICE, HOURLY (each hour on the hour for each of five previous trading days). WALL STREET JOURNAL. Published business days.

DOW-JONES UTILITY STOCK AVERAGE, PRICE, MONTHLY AVERAGE (average daily price for latest month, previous month, and same month one year ago. Labeled "The Statistical Record, Monthly Average"). BARRON'S. This data normally appears in first issue of each month.

DOW-JONES UTILITY STOCK AVERAGE, PRICE, MOVING AVERAGE, CHART (200-day moving average charted weekly for about two years). TRENDLINE DAILY BASIS STOCK CHARTS. Published weekly.

Dow-Jones utility stock average, price, percentage change.

SEE: Dow-Jones utility stock average, price, daily,
        percentage change. . .
     Dow-Jones utility stock average, price, weekly,
        percentage change. . .
     Dow-Jones utility stock average, price, year to
        date, percentage change. . .

DOW-JONES UTILITY STOCK AVERAGE, PRICE, WEEKLY, HIGH-LOW-CLOSE (for week just past, with dates of high and low for week). NEW YORK TIMES. Sunday edition.

DOW-JONES UTILITY STOCK AVERAGE, PRICE, WEEKLY, HIGH-LOW-CLOSE, CHART (about two years are charted on a weekly basis). TRENDLINE DAILY BASIS STOCK CHARTS. Published weekly.

DOW-JONES UTILITY STOCK AVERAGE, PRICE, WEEKLY, OPEN-HIGH-LOW -CLOSE (for week just past). BARRON'S. Published weekly.

DOW-JONES UTILITY STOCK AVERAGE, PRICE, WEEKLY, PERCENTAGE CHANGE (for end of week just past. Labeled "Last Week's Markets"). WALL STREET JOURNAL. This data normally appears in Monday edition.

DOW-JONES UTILITY STOCK AVERAGE, PRICE, WEEKLY-YEARLY, CLOSE (price for end of latest week, previous week, and same week one year ago). BARRON'S. Published weekly.

DOW-JONES UTILITY STOCK AVERAGE, PRICE, YEAR TO DATE, OPEN-HIGH -LOW-CLOSE (current year). BARRON'S. Published weekly.

DOW-JONES UTILITY STOCK AVERAGE, PRICE, YEAR TO DATE, PERCENT-AGE CHANGE (from beginning of year). BARRON'S. Published weekly.

DOW-JONES UTILITY STOCK AVERAGE, PRICE, YEARLY, HIGH-LOW. Yearly ranges for a number of years appear frequently in BARRON'S, sometimes with exact dates of annual highs and lows.

DOW-JONES UTILITY STOCK AVERAGE, PRICE-EARNINGS RATIO, WEEKLY-MONTHLY-YEARLY (for end of week just past, and for same period a month ago, one year ago, and two years ago). BARRON'S. Published weekly.

DOW-JONES UTILITY STOCK AVERAGE, VOLUME OF TRADING, DAILY (total number of shares traded on each day of week just past). BARRON'S. Published weekly.

DOW-JONES UTILITY STOCK AVERAGE, VOLUME OF TRADING, DAILY (total number of shares traded on each of past five trading days). WALL STREET JOURNAL. Published business days.

DOW-JONES UTILITY STOCK AVERAGE, VOLUME OF TRADING, WEEKLY-YEARLY (combined volume in thousands of shares for latest week, previous week, and same week one year ago). BARRON'S. Published weekly.

Downside volume.

> SEE: Upside-downside volume. . .

Drilling and exploration costs.

> SEE: Petroleum companies, drilling and exploration costs per share. . .

DUAL-PURPOSE FUNDS, ASSET VALUE PER SHARE (NET), WEEKLY (for capital shares of each of about seven funds, for end of week just past). BARRON'S. Published weekly.

DUAL-PURPOSE FUNDS, ASSET VALUE PER SHARE (NET), WEEKLY (for capital shares of each of about seven funds, for end of week just past). NEW YORK TIMES. This data normally appears in Monday edition.

DUAL-PURPOSE FUNDS, ASSET VALUE PER SHARE (NET), WEEKLY (for capital shares of each of about seven funds, for end of week just past). WALL STREET JOURNAL. This data normally appears in Monday edition.

DUAL-PURPOSE FUNDS, DISCOUNT OR PREMIUM RELATIVE TO NET ASSET VALUE, WEEKLY (price discount or premium in percentage, for capital shares of each of about seven funds, for end of week just past). This data normally appears in each issue of BARRON'S, as well as in the Monday editions of both the NEW YORK TIMES and the WALL STREET JOURNAL.

DUAL-PURPOSE FUNDS, PRICES, WEEKLY, CLOSE (closing prices for each of about seven funds, for end of week just past). This data normally appears in each issue of BARRON'S, as well as in the Monday editions of both the NEW YORK TIMES and the WALL STREET JOURNAL.

Due dates of bonds.

> SEE: Bonds, due dates. . .
> Convertible bonds, due dates. . .
> Foreign bonds, due dates. . .
> Government bonds, due dates. . .

Earnings, annual.

> SEE: Earnings per share, yearly. . .

Earnings, average.

> SEE: Barron's 50-stock average, earnings. . .
> Dow-Jones industrial stock average, earnings. . .
> Moody's fire insurance stock average, earnings. . .
> Moody's industrial stock average, earnings. . .
> Moody's New York bank stock average, earnings. . .
> Moody's railroad stock average, earnings. . .

Moody's utility stock average, earnings. . .

Earnings, bank stocks.

SEE: Bank stocks, earnings. . .

Earnings, diluted.

SEE: Diluted earnings per share. . .

Earnings, insurance stocks.

SEE: Insurance stocks (unlisted), earnings. . .

Earnings, interim.

SEE: Earnings per share, interim. . .

Earnings, quarterly.

SEE: Earnings per share, interim. . .

Earnings and dividend rankings.

SEE: Ratings, stocks. . .

Earnings averages.

(See cross references under "Earnings, average. . .")

Earnings per share, annual.

SEE: Earnings per share, yearly. . .

EARNINGS PER SHARE, AVERAGE (INDIVIDUAL STOCKS), CHARTS (a line chart of five year averaged "cash earnings" is fitted onto monthly price charts for each of about 1,400 leading common stocks. Time period covered is about 18 years). VALUE LINE INVESTMENT SURVEY. Part three: published weekly, a few industries each week.

Earnings per share, daily list.

SEE: Earnings per share, interim, daily list. . .

Earnings per share, diluted.

SEE: Diluted earnings per share. . .

EARNINGS PER SHARE, INTERIM (shown for each quarter for about four years, for each of about 1,000 actively traded common stocks). MOODY'S HANDBOOK OF COMMON STOCKS. Published quarterly.

EARNINGS PER SHARE, INTERIM (latest interim and same period one year earlier for each of over 1,200 less active common stocks). MOODY'S HANDBOOK OF COMMON STOCKS. Published quarterly.

EARNINGS PER SHARE, INTERIM (latest interim and same period one year earlier for each of about 5,000 common and preferred, listed and unlisted stocks).

STANDARD & POOR'S SECURITY OWNER'S STOCK GUIDE. Published monthly.

EARNINGS PER SHARE, INTERIM (shown for each quarter for two years, for each of about 700 active, listed stocks). TRENDLINE DAILY BASIS STOCK CHARTS. Published weekly.

EARNINGS PER SHARE, INTERIM (latest interim and same period one year earlier for each of about 960 listed stocks). TRENDLINE'S CURRENT MARKET PERSPECTIVES. Published monthly.

EARNINGS PER SHARE, INTERIM (latest quarter and same period one year earlier for each of about 1,400 leading common stocks). VALUE LINE INVESTMENT SURVEY. Part one, published weekly.

EARNINGS PER SHARE, INTERIM (shown for each quarter for about seven years, for each of about 1,400 leading common stocks). VALUE LINE INVESTMENT SURVEY. Part three: published weekly, a few industries each week.

EARNINGS PER SHARE, INTERIM, AMERICAN STOCK EXCHANGE (latest interim and same period one year earlier for each listed stock). BARRON'S. Published weekly.

EARNINGS PER SHARE, INTERIM, BOSTON STOCK EXCHANGE (latest interim for each exclusively listed stock). BARRON'S. Published weekly.

EARNINGS PER SHARE, INTERIM, CINCINNATI STOCK EXCHANGE (latest interim for each exclusively listed stock). BARRON'S. Published weekly.

EARNINGS PER SHARE, INTERIM, DAILY LIST (short summaries each day for individual companies having new earnings reports. Includes sales -- corporate revenue -- and net income for latest period and same period a year ago. Labeled "Other Company Reports"). NEW YORK TIMES. Published weekdays.

EARNINGS PER SHARE, INTERIM, DAILY LIST (short summaries each day for individual companies having new earnings reports. Includes sales -- corporate revenue -- and net income for latest period and same period a year ago. Labeled "Digest of Earnings Reports"). WALL STREET JOURNAL. Published business days.

EARNINGS PER SHARE, INTERIM, DETROIT STOCK EXCHANGE (latest interim for each exclusively listed stock). BARRON'S. Published weekly.

EARNINGS PER SHARE, INTERIM, MIDWEST STOCK EXCHANGE (latest interim for each exclusively listed stock). BARRON'S. Published weekly.

EARNINGS PER SHARE, INTERIM, MONTREAL STOCK EXCHANGE (latest interim for each exclusively listed stock). BARRON'S. Published weekly.

EARNINGS PER SHARE, INTERIM, NEW YORK STOCK EXCHANGE (latest interim and same period one year earlier for each listed stock). BARRON'S. Published weekly.

EARNINGS PER SHARE, INTERIM, OVER-THE-COUNTER STOCKS (latest available interim for each of about 1,500 unlisted industrial and utility stocks. Less-active stocks are labeled "Weekly List"). BARRON'S. Published weekly.

EARNINGS PER SHARE, INTERIM, PACIFIC COAST STOCK EXCHANGE (latest interim for each exclusively listed stock). BARRON'S. Published weekly.

EARNINGS PER SHARE, INTERIM, PHILADELPHIA-BALTIMORE-WASHINGTON STOCK EXCHANGE (latest interim for each exclusively listed stock). BARRON'S. Published weekly.

EARNINGS PER SHARE, INTERIM, PITTSBURGH STOCK EXCHANGE (latest interim for each exclusively listed stock). BARRON'S. Published weekly.

EARNINGS PER SHARE, INTERIM, TORONTO STOCK EXCHANGE (latest interim for each exclusively listed stock). BARRON'S. Published weekly.

Earnings per share, quarterly.

SEE: Earnings per share, interim. . .

EARNINGS PER SHARE, YEARLY (for each of past 20 or so years for each of over 1,000 actively traded common stocks, and for each of past three years for each of over 1,200 less actively traded common stocks). MOODY'S HANDBOOK OF COMMON STOCKS. Published quarterly.

EARNINGS PER SHARE, YEARLY (for each of about 5,000 common and preferred, listed and unlisted stocks, for most recent 12 month period, and for each of most recent five years). STANDARD & POOR'S SECURITY OWNER'S STOCK GUIDE. Published monthly.

EARNINGS PER SHARE, YEARLY (earned so far this year, plus total for each of two previous years, for each of about 700 active, listed stocks). TRENDLINE DAILY BASIS STOCK CHARTS. Published weekly.

EARNINGS PER SHARE, YEARLY (for each of past four years, for each of about 960 listed stocks). TRENDLINE'S CURRENT MARKET PERSPECTIVES. Published monthly.

EARNINGS PER SHARE, YEARLY (for each of past 18 or so years, for each of about 1,400 leading common stocks. Labeled "Reported Earnings"). VALUE LINE INVESTMENT SURVEY. Part three: published weekly.

Earnings rate on common stock equity.

SEE ALSO: Profit margin. . .

EARNINGS RATE ON COMMON STOCK EQUITY (PERCENT), YEARLY (for each of past 18 or so years, for each of about 1,400 leading companies). VALUE LINE INVESTMENT SURVEY. Part three: published weekly, a few industries each week.

EARNINGS RATE ON TOTAL CAPITAL (PERCENT), YEARLY (for each of past 18 or so years, for each of over 1,200 leading industrial companies). VALUE LINE INVESTMENT SURVEY. Part three: published weekly, a few industries each week.

INVESTMENT INFORMATION

English stock prices.

    SEE: Financial Times (London) composite stock index. . .
        Financial Times (London) industrial stock index. . .
        Foreign stock price indexes. . .
        Stock prices on London Stock Exchange. . .

Equity less than 40 percent in margin accounts.

    SEE: Margin customers having less than 40 percent equity. . .

Equity ratio.

    SEE: Railroads, common stock equity. . .
        Utilities, common stock equity. . .

Equivalent dividend income.

    SEE: Convertible bonds, equivalent dividend income. . .

Estimates investment worth.

    SEE: Convertible bonds, estimated investment worth. . .

EUROBONDS, PRICES AND YIELDS, WEEKLY (original price, recent asked price, and yield for each of about ten "Straight Debt" issues, plus bid-asked prices for each of about seven "Convertibles"). NEW YORK TIMES. This data normally appears in Saturday edition.

EURODOLLAR RATES (percentage rates for one, three, and six months. Labeled "Money"). NEW YORK TIMES. Published weekdays.

EURODOLLAR RATE (percentage rates for one, two, and three to six months. Labeled "Money Rates"). WALL STREET JOURNAL. Published business days.

Excess margin.

    SEE: Margin purchasing power. . .

EXCHANGE FUNDS, ASSET VALUES (data regarding total, cash, and per share assets for each of about 30 funds. Percentage changes indicated over five year period). STANDARD & POOR'S SECURITY OWNER'S STOCK GUIDE. Published monthly.

EXCHANGE FUNDS, DATE OF EXCHANGE (for each of about 30 funds). STANDARD & POOR'S SECURITY OWNER'S STOCK GUIDE. Published monthly.

EXCHANGE FUNDS, DIVIDEND YIELD FROM INVESTMENT INCOME, MONTHLY (as of end of month prior to month of publication, for each of about 30 funds). STANDARD & POOR'S SECURITY OWNER'S STOCK GUIDE. Published monthly.

EXCHANGE FUNDS, DIVIDENDS (data on recent dividends from investment income and security profits). STANDARD & POOR'S SECURITY OWNER'S STOCK GUIDE. Published monthly.

EXCHANGE FUNDS, PRICES, MONTHLY, CLOSE (net asset value price per share for each of about 30 funds, for a date near end of month prior to month of publication). STANDARD & POOR'S SECURITY OWNER'S STOCK GUIDE. Published monthly.

EXCHANGE FUNDS, PRICES, WEEKLY, CLOSE (bid price -- net asset value per share -- for each of about 30 funds, for end of week just past and previous week). BARRON'S. Published weekly.

EXCHANGE FUNDS, PRICES, WEEKLY, CLOSE (bid price -- net asset value per share -- for each of about 30 funds, for end of week just past). COMMERCIAL AND FINANCIAL CHRONICLE. Monday edition.

EXCHANGE FUNDS, PRICES, YEAR TO DATE, HIGH-LOW (range for current year for each of about 30 funds). STANDARD & POOR'S SECURITY OWNER'S STOCK GUIDE. Published monthly.

EXCHANGE FUNDS, PRICES, YEARLY (FIVE YEAR) RANGE (high and low over five year period for each of about 30 funds). STANDARD & POOR'S SECURITY OWNER'S STOCK GUIDE. Published monthly.

EXCHANGE FUNDS, TAX PAID, AMOUNT PER SHARE ("Represents applicable 25% tax on retained capital gains paid on behalf of stockholders," for each of last two years, for each of about 30 funds). STANDARD & POOR'S SECURITY OWNER'S STOCK GUIDE. Published monthly.

Exchange listings, new.

SEE: New listings, stocks. . .

Exchange rates, foreign.

SEE: Foreign exchange rates. . .

EXCHANGE SEATS, NUMBER OF (membership totals are indicated for each of 27 stock and commodity exchanges). BANK AND QUOTATION RECORD. Published monthly.

EXCHANGE SEATS, PRICES, MONTHLY (bid and asked, as well as last sale prices are indicated for seats on each of 27 stock and commodity exchanges in the United States and Canada, as of end of latest month). BANK AND QUOTATION RECORD. Published monthly.

EXCHANGE SEATS ON NEW YORK STOCK EXCHANGE, PRICE, WEEKLY-YEARLY (sale price of seat as of middle of latest available week, previous week, and same week one year ago. Labeled "NYSE seat sls th $," under "N.Y. Exchange Monthly Figures"). BARRON'S. Published weekly.

Exchanges where bonds are traded.

SEE: Markets where bonds are traded. . .

Exchanges where stocks are traded.

SEE: Markets where stocks are traded. . .

Excise taxes as percentage of sales.

SEE: Distillers, excise taxes as percentage of sales. . .

EX-DIVIDEND DATES, DAILY ("Stocks Ex-dividend" tomorrow or next trading day, listed alphabetically by company, with dividend amounts). WALL STREET JOURNAL. Published business days.

EX-DIVIDEND DATES, LATEST (for about 5,000 individual common and preferred, listed and unlisted issues). STANDARD & POOR'S SECURITY OWNER'S STOCK GUIDE. Published monthly.

Expense ratio.

SEE: Insurance companies, expense ratio. . .

Expiration dates of conversion privileges.

SEE: Convertible bonds, conversion privileges, expiration dates. . .

Exploration costs per share.

SEE: Petroleum companies, drilling and exploration costs per share. . .

EXPORT-IMPORT BANK PARTICIPATING CERTIFICATES, PRICES, MONTHLY, CLOSE (end-of-month bid and asked prices given for each of about five issues. Labeled "United States and Municipal Bonds"). BANK AND QUOTATION RECORD. Published monthly.

FIC Bank bonds.

SEE: Federal Intermediate Credit Bank bonds. . .

FNMA bonds ("Fannie Mae").

SEE: Federal National Mortgage Association bonds. . .

Farm Loan bonds.

SEE: Federal Land Bank bonds. . .

Federal Bank for Cooperatives bonds.

SEE: Bank for Cooperatives bonds. . .

FEDERAL FUNDS OPEN MARKET RATE, DAILY (opening, high, low, and closing percentage rates for previous day. Labeled "Money"). NEW YORK TIMES. Published weekdays.

FEDERAL FUNDS OPEN MARKET RATE, DAILY (previous day's high and low bid percentage rate, with closing bid and asked. Labeled "Money Rates"). WALL STREET JOURNAL. Published business days.

FEDERAL HOME LOAN BANK BONDS, PRICES, DAILY (bid and asked prices for each of about 15 issues, for previous trading day. Amount outstanding in millions of dollars is shown for each issue). NEW YORK TIMES. Published weekdays.

FEDERAL HOME LOAN BANK BONDS, PRICES, DAILY (bid and asked prices for each of about 15 issues, for previous trading day). WALL STREET JOURNAL. Published business days.

FEDERAL HOME LOAN BANK BONDS, PRICES, MONTHLY, CLOSE (end-of-month bid and asked prices given for each of about 15 issues. Labeled "United States and Municipal Bonds"). BANK AND QUOTATION RECORD. Published monthly.

FEDERAL HOME LOAN BANK BONDS, PRICES, WEEKLY, CLOSE (end-of-week bid and asked prices for each of about 15 issues. Labeled "Obligations of Government Agencies"). COMMERCIAL AND FINANCIAL CHRONICLE. Monday edition.

FEDERAL HOME LOAN BANK BONDS, YIELDS TO MATURITY, DAILY (percentage yield for each of about 15 issues, for previous trading day. Amount outstanding in millions of dollars shown for each issue). NEW YORK TIMES. Published weekdays.

FEDERAL HOME LOAN BANK BONDS, YIELDS TO MATURITY, DAILY (percentage yield for each of about 15 issues, for previous day). WALL STREET JOURNAL. Published business days.

FEDERAL INTERMEDIATE CREDIT BANK BONDS, PRICES, DAILY (bid and asked prices for each of about ten issues, for previous trading day. Amount outstanding in millions of dollars shown for each issue). NEW YORK TIMES. Published weekdays.

FEDERAL INTERMEDIATE CREDIT BANK BONDS, PRICES, DAILY (bid and asked prices for each of about ten issues, for previous day. Labeled "FIC Bank Debs"). WALL STREET JOURNAL. Published business days.

FEDERAL INTERMEDIATE CREDIT BANK BONDS, PRICES, MONTHLY, CLOSE (end-of-month bid and asked prices for each of about ten issues. Labeled "United States and Municipal Bonds"). BANK AND QUOTATION RECORD. Published monthly.

FEDERAL INTERMEDIATE CREDIT BANK BONDS, PRICES, WEEKLY, CLOSE (end-of-week bid and asked prices for each of about ten issues). COMMERCIAL AND FINANCIAL CHRONICLE. Monday edition.

FEDERAL INTERMEDIATE CREDIT BANK BONDS, YIELDS TO MATURITY, DAILY (percentage yield for each of about ten issues, for previous trading day. Amount outstanding in millions of dollars shown for each issue). NEW YORK TIMES. Published weekdays.

FEDERAL INTERMEDIATE CREDIT BANK BONDS, YIELDS TO MATURITY, DAILY (percentage yield for each of about ten issues, for previous day. Labeled "FIC

Bank Debs"). WALL STREET JOURNAL. Published business days.

FEDERAL LAND BANK BONDS, PRICES, DAILY (bid and asked prices for each of about 30 issues, for previous trading day. Amount outstanding in millions of dollars shown for each issue). NEW YORK TIMES. Published weekdays.

FEDERAL LAND BANK BONDS, PRICES, DAILY (bid and asked prices for each of about 30 issues, for previous trading day). WALL STREET JOURNAL. Published business days.

FEDERAL LAND BANK BONDS, PRICES, MONTHLY, CLOSE (end-of-month bid and asked prices for each of about 30 issues. Labeled "United States and Municipal Bonds"). BANK AND QUOTATION RECORD. Published monthly.

FEDERAL LAND BANK BONDS, PRICES, WEEKLY, CLOSE (end-of-week prices for each of about 30 issues. Labeled "Obligations of Government Agencies"). COMMERCIAL AND FINANCIAL CHRONICLE. Monday edition.

FEDERAL LAND BANK BONDS, YIELDS TO MATURITY, DAILY (percentage yield for each of about 30 issues, for previous trading day. Amount outstanding in millions of dollars shown for each issue). NEW YORK TIMES. Published weekdays.

FEDERAL LAND BANK BONDS, YIELDS TO MATURITY, DAILY (percentage yield for each of about 30 issues, for previous day). WALL STREET JOURNAL. Published business days.

FEDERAL NATIONAL MORTGAGE ASSOCIATION BONDS, PRICES, DAILY (bid and asked prices for each of about 20 issues, for previous trading day. Amount outstanding in millions of dollars shown for each issue). NEW YORK TIMES. Published weekdays.

FEDERAL NATIONAL MORTGAGE ASSOCIATION BONDS, PRICES, DAILY (bid and asked prices for each of about 20 issues, for previous trading day. Labeled "FNMA Notes & Debs"). WALL STREET JOURNAL. Published business days.

FEDERAL NATIONAL MORTGAGE ASSOCIATION BONDS, PRICES, MONTHLY, CLOSE (end-of-month bid and asked prices for each of about 20 issues. Labeled "United States and Municipal Bonds"). BANK AND QUOTATION RECORD. Published monthly.

FEDERAL NATIONAL MORTGAGE ASSOCIATION BONDS, PRICES, WEEKLY, CLOSE (end-of-week bid and asked prices for each of about 20 issues. Labeled "Obligations of Government Agencies"). COMMERCIAL AND FINANCIAL CHRONICLE. Monday edition.

FEDERAL NATIONAL MORTGAGE ASSOCIATION BONDS, YIELDS TO MATURITY, DAILY (percentage yield for each of about 20 issues, for previous trading day. Amount outstanding in millions of dollars shown for each issue). NEW YORK TIMES. Published weekdays.

FEDERAL NATIONAL MORTGAGE ASSOCIATION BONDS, YIELDS TO MATU-
RITY, DAILY (percentage yield for each of about 20 issues, for previous day.
Labeled "FNMA Notes & Debs"). WALL STREET JOURNAL. Published business
days.

FEDERAL NATIONAL MORTGAGE ASSOCIATION PARTICIPATING CERTIFI-
CATES, PRICES, MONTHLY, CLOSE (end-of-month bid and asked prices for
each of about 70 issues. Labeled "United States and Municipal Bonds").
BANK AND QUOTATION RECORD. Published monthly.

Federal Reserve discount rate.

    SEE: Discount rate, Federal Reserve. . .

Fee, S. E. C.

    SEE: Securities and Exchange Commission fee. . .

Fees, commission.

    SEE: Commission rates. . .

FINANCE COMPANIES, INTEREST CHARGE DOLLAR AMOUNT TOTALS, YEAR-
LY (for each of past eleven years, for each of large companies with actively
traded common stock). MOODY'S HANDBOOK OF COMMON STOCKS. Published quarterly.

FINANCE COMPANIES, INTEREST RATE PAID, YEARLY AVERAGE (for each of
past 18 or so years, for each of about 15 leading companies, shows average interest rate paid by company on outstanding debt). VALUE LINE INVESTMENT
SURVEY. Part three: published weekly, a few industries each week.

FINANCE COMPANIES, INTEREST RATIO (PERCENT), YEARLY (for each of
past 18 or so years, for each of about 15 leading companies. Interest ratio
equals interest paid, divided by pretax income plus interest paid). VALUE
LINE INVESTMENT SURVEY. Part three: published weekly, a few industries
each week.

Finance companies, loan totals.

    SEE: Finance companies, receivables. . .

FINANCE COMPANIES, OPERATING MARGIN (PERCENT), YEARLY (for each
of past eleven years, for each of large companies with actively traded common
stock. Labeled "Operating Profit Margin"). MOODY'S HANDBOOK OF
COMMON STOCKS. Published quarterly.

FINANCE COMPANIES, OPERATING MARGIN (PERCENT), YEARLY (for each
of past four years, for each of about ten listed companies. Operating margin
represents gross income minus expenses and loss provisions, divided by total gross
income). TRENDLINE'S CURRENT MARKET PERSPECTIVES. Published monthly.

FINANCE COMPANIES, OPERATING MARGIN (PERCENT), YEARLY (for each
of past 18 or so years, for each of about 15 leading companies). VALUE LINE

INVESTMENT SURVEY. Part three: published weekly, a few industries each week.

FINANCE COMPANIES, RECEIVABLES, YEARLY (for each of past eleven years, for each of large companies with actively traded common stock). MOODY'S HANDBOOK OF COMMON STOCKS. Published quarterly.

FINANCE COMPANIES, RECEIVABLES, YEARLY (for each of past four years, for each of about ten listed companies). TRENDLINE'S CURRENT MARKET PERSPECTIVES. Published monthly.

FINANCE COMPANIES, RECEIVABLES PER SHARE, YEARLY (for each of past 18 or so years, for each of about 15 leading companies). VALUE LINE IN-VESTMENT SURVEY. Part three: published weekly, a few industries each week.

FINANCE COMPANIES, SHORT TERM DEBT AS PERCENTAGE OF TOTAL DEBT, YEARLY (for each of past 18 or so years, for each of about 15 leading companies). VALUE LINE INVESTMENT SURVEY. Part three: published weekly, a few industries each week.

Finance stock index, New York Stock Exchange.

SEE: New York Stock Exchange finance stock index. . .

Financial institution stock holdings.

SEE: Institutional holdings. . .
Investment company transactions. . .

Financial position of corporations.

SEE: Cash as current asset. . .
Current assets. . .
Current liabilities. . .
Long term debt. . .
Working capital. . .

FINANCIAL TIMES (LONDON) COMPOSITE STOCK INDEX, PRICE, DAILY, CLOSE (500 stock index quoted for each of two previous trading days. Label-ed "Foreign Stock Indexes"). NEW YORK TIMES. Published weekdays.

FINANCIAL TIMES (LONDON) COMPOSITE STOCK INDEX, PRICE, YEAR TO DATE, HIGH–LOW (500 stock index price range for current year. Labeled "Foreign Stock Indexes"). NEW YORK TIMES. Published weekdays.

FINANCIAL TIMES (LONDON) INDUSTRIAL STOCK INDEX, PRICE, DAILY, CLOSE (30 industrials index quoted for each of two previous trading days. Labeled "Foreign Stock Indexes"). NEW YORK TIMES. Published weekdays.

FINANCIAL TIMES (LONDON) INDUSTRIAL STOCK INDEX, PRICE, YEAR TO DATE, HIGH–LOW (30 industrials index price range for current year. Labeled "Foreign Stock Indexes"). NEW YORK TIMES. Published weekdays.

Fire insurance companies.

    SEE: Insurance companies. . .

Fire insurance stock average, Moody's.

    SEE: Moody's fire insurance stock average. . .

Fiscal year ending month.

    SEE ALSO: Balance sheets, dates. . .

FISCAL YEAR ENDING MONTH (month in which fiscal year ends for each of about 2,000 corporations with bond issues). STANDARD & POOR'S EARNINGS AND RATINGS BOND GUIDE. Published monthly.

FISCAL YEAR ENDING MONTH (month in which fiscal year ends is indicated for each of about 960 listed corporations). TRENDLINE'S CURRENT MARKET PERSPECTIVES. Published monthly.

Fixed charges.

    SEE: Long term debt, total corporate dollar amount of interest payable annually. . .

Fixed charges ratio.

    SEE: Earnings to fixed charges ratio. . .

FLOOR TRADERS' VOLUME, NEW YORK STOCK EXCHANGE, WEEKLY-MONTHLY-YEARLY (total round-lot purchases, sales, and short sales by floor traders, in number of shares, for latest week, previous week, a month ago, and same week one year ago). COMMERCIAL AND FINANCIAL CHRONICLE. Thursday edition.

Fluctuations in stock prices.

    SEE: Trading swings. . .

FOREIGN BANKNOTE RATES, DAILY ("selling prices in United States dollars and cents for banknotes at New York," for each of 25 countries, for each of previous two days). NEW YORK TIMES. Published weekdays.

Foreign basis (foreign bonds).

    SEE: Foreign bonds, foreign basis. . .

Foreign bonds, amount outstanding.

    SEE: Foreign bonds, dollar amount outstanding. . .

Foreign bonds, call prices.

    SEE: Call prices, foreign bonds. . .

Foreign bonds, dates of interest payment.

SEE: Foreign bonds, interest payment dates. . .

Foreign bonds, dates of maturity.

SEE: Foreign bonds, due dates. . .

FOREIGN BONDS, DOLLAR AMOUNT OUTSTANDING (for each of about 200 issues). STANDARD & POOR'S EARNINGS AND RATINGS BOND GUIDE. Published monthly.

FOREIGN BONDS, DUE DATES (month and year of maturity given for each of about 250 foreign issues traded over-the-counter or on the New York Stock Exchange). BANK AND QUOTATION RECORD. Published monthly.

FOREIGN BONDS, DUE DATES (month and year of maturity indicated for each foreign bond traded on the New York Stock Exchange). COMMERCIAL AND FINANCIAL CHRONICLE. Monday edition.

FOREIGN BONDS, DUE DATES (maturity dates for each of about 200 issues). STANDARD & POOR'S EARNINGS AND RATINGS BOND GUIDE. Published monthly.

FOREIGN BONDS, FOREIGN BASIS PRICES, MONTHLY, CLOSE (end of the month prices for individual issues, adjusted for effect of interest equalization tax). STANDARD & POOR'S EARNINGS AND RATINGS BOND GUIDE. Published monthly.

FOREIGN BONDS, FOREIGN BASIS YIELDS TO MATURITY (percentage yields for individual bonds, adjusted for effect of interest equalization tax). STANDARD & POOR'S EARNINGS AND RATINGS BOND GUIDE. Published monthly.

FOREIGN BONDS, INTEREST PAYMENT DATES (months of interest period given for each of about 250 foreign bonds traded over-the-counter or on the New York Stock Exchange). BANK AND QUOTATION RECORD. Published monthly.

FOREIGN BONDS, INTEREST PAYMENT DATES (months of interest period given for each foreign bond traded on the New York Stock Exchange). COMMERCIAL AND FINANCIAL CHRONICLE. Monday edition.

FOREIGN BONDS, INTEREST PAYMENT DATES (for each of about 200 issues). STANDARD & POOR'S EARNINGS AND RATINGS BOND GUIDE. Published monthly.

FOREIGN BONDS, INTEREST RATES ("coupon rate" shown for each of about 250 foreign bonds traded over-the-counter or on the New York Stock Exchange). BANK AND QUOTATION RECORD. Published monthly.

FOREIGN BONDS, INTEREST RATES ("coupon rate" shown for each of foreign bonds traded on New York Stock Exchange). COMMERCIAL AND FINANCIAL CHRONICLE. Monday edition.

FOREIGN BONDS, INTEREST RATES ("coupon rate" for each of about 200 foreign issues). STANDARD & POOR'S EARNINGS AND RATINGS BOND GUIDE. Published monthly.

Foreign bonds, maturity dates.

SEE: Foreign bonds, due dates. . .

Foreign bonds, offering prices.

SEE: Foreign bonds, prices, offering. . .

Foreign bonds, outstanding dollar amount.

SEE: Foreign bonds, dollar amount outstanding. . .

Foreign bonds, payment dates.

SEE: Foreign bonds, interest payment dates. . .

FOREIGN BONDS, PRICES, DAILY, HIGH-LOW-CLOSE (for each foreign bond traded on New York Stock Exchange on previous day). NEW YORK TIMES. Published weekdays.

FOREIGN BONDS, PRICES, DAILY, HIGH-LOW-CLOSE (for each foreian bond traded on New York Stock Exchange on previous day). WALL STREET JOURNAL. Published business days.

FOREIGN BONDS, PRICES, MONTHLY, CLOSE (for each of about 200 issues for end of month previous to month of publication). STANDARD & POOR'S EARNINGS AND RATINGS BOND GUIDE. Published monthly.

FOREIGN BONDS, PRICES, MONTHLY, OPEN-HIGH-LOW-CLOSE (for each of about 230 issues, for month prior to month of publication. Labeled "New York Stock Exchange Bonds"). BANK AND QUOTATION RECORD. Published monthly.

FOREIGN BONDS, PRICES, OFFERING (original offering price for each of about 200 foreign bonds). STANDARD & POOR'S EARNINGS AND RATINGS BOND GUIDE. Published monthly.

FOREIGN BONDS, PRICES, WEEKLY, HIGH-LOW-CLOSE (for each of about 230 foreign issues, for week just past. Labeled "New York Stock Exchange Bond Record"). COMMERCIAL AND FINANCIAL CHRONICLE. Monday edition.

FOREIGN BONDS, PRICES, WEEKLY, HIGH-LOW-CLOSE (for each foreign bond traded on the New York Stock Exchange, for week just past). NEW YORK TIMES. Sunday edition.

FOREIGN BONDS, PRICES, YEAR TO DATE, HIGH-LOW (current year's price range for each foreign bond traded on New York Stock Exchange on previous day). NEW YORK TIMES. Published weekdays.

FOREIGN BONDS, PRICES, YEAR TO DATE, HIGH-LOW (price range for current year for each foreign bond traded on New York Stock Exchange during previous week). NEW YORK TIMES. Sunday edition.

FOREIGN BONDS, PRICES, YEAR TO DATE, HIGH-LOW (current year's price range for each of about 200 foreign issues). STANDARD & POOR'S EARNINGS AND RATINGS BOND GUIDE. Published monthly.

FOREIGN BONDS, PRICES, YEAR TO DATE, HIGH-LOW (price range for current year for each foreign bond traded on New York Stock Exchange on previous day). WALL STREET JOURNAL. Published business days.

FOREIGN BONDS, PRICES, YEAR TO DATE, OPEN-HIGH-LOW (initial price and price range for current year for each of about 250 foreign issues. Labeled "New York Stock Exchange Bonds"). BANK AND QUOTATION RECORD. Published monthly.

FOREIGN BONDS, PRICES, YEARLY (EIGHT YEAR PERIOD), HIGH-LOW (highest and lowest price reached by each of about 200 foreign issues during recent eight year period). STANDARD & POOR'S EARNINGS AND RATINGS BOND GUIDE. Published monthly.

FOREIGN BONDS, REFUNDING (refunding call price and year for individual foreign issues). STANDARD & POOR'S EARNINGS AND RATINGS BOND GUIDE. Published monthly.

Foreign bonds, sales volume (New York Stock Exchange).

SEE: Volume of trading in bonds, individual bonds on
New York Stock Exchange. . .
Volume of trading in bonds, total for New York
Stock Exchange. . .

FOREIGN BONDS, YEAR OF ISSUE (year of original offering for each of about 200 foreign issues. Original offering price also quoted). STANDARD & POOR'S EARNINGS AND RATINGS BOND GUIDE. Published monthly.

FOREIGN BONDS, YIELDS TO MATURITY (percentage yields for individual bonds). STANDARD & POOR'S EARNINGS AND RATINGS BOND GUIDE. Published monthly.

FOREIGN EXCHANGE RATES, DAILY (for each of two previous days, U.S. dollar rate is shown for each of about 35 foreign currencies). WALL STREET JOURNAL. Published business days.

FOREIGN EXCHANGE RATES, DAILY-MONTHLY (for each day of the month prior to month of publication, U.S. dollar rate is shown for each of about 45 foreign currencies). BANK AND QUOTATION RECORD. Published monthly.

FOREIGN EXCHANGE RATES, DAILY-WEEKLY (for each day of week just past, U.S. dollar rate is shown for each of about 25 foreign currencies). COMMERCIAL AND FINANCIAL CHRONICLE. Monday edition.

FOREIGN EXCHANGE RATES, DAILY-WEEKLY-YEARLY (for each of about 30 foreign currencies, U.S. dollar rate is shown for previous day, day before that, same day a week ago, and same day one year ago. "High and low support levels" are quoted in many cases). NEW YORK TIMES. Published weekdays.

FOREIGN MUTUAL FUNDS, PRICES, DAILY (a price is indicated in German marks for each of about seven funds in Frankfurt, in French francs for each of about five funds in Paris, in Swiss francs for each of about nine funds in Zurich, and in U.S. dollars for each of about ten funds in Geneva). NEW YORK TIMES. Published weekdays.

FOREIGN STOCK PRICE INDEXES, DAILY, CLOSE (indexes for each of ten major foreign cities, for previous trading day and day before that). NEW YORK TIMES. Published weekdays.

FOREIGN STOCK PRICE INDEXES, WEEKLY, CLOSE (indexes for each of twelve major countries, for end of week just past). BARRON'S. Published weekly.

FOREIGN STOCK PRICE INDEXES, YEAR TO DATE, HIGH-LOW (range for each of twelve major countries, for current year). BARRON'S. Published weekly.

FOREIGN STOCK PRICE INDEXES, YEAR TO DATE, HIGH-LOW (indexes for each of ten major foreign cities, showing price range for current year). NEW YORK TIMES. Published weekdays.

Foreign stock prices.

> SEE ALSO: Stock prices on Amsterdam Stock Exchange. . .
> Stock prices on Brussels Stock Exchange. . .
> Stock prices on Buenos Aires Stock Exchange. . .
> Stock prices on Frankfurt Stock Exchange. . .
> Stock prices on Johannesburg Stock Exchange. . .
> Stock prices on London Stock Exchange. . .
> Stock prices on Mexico City Stock Exchange. . .
> Stock prices on Milan Stock Exchange. . .
> Stock prices on Montreal Stock Exchange. . .
> Stock prices on Paris Stock Exchange (Bourse). . .
> Stock prices on Sydney Stock Exchange. . .
> Stock prices on Tokyo Stock Exchange. . .
> Stock prices on Toronto Stock Exchange. . .
> Stock prices on Zurich Stock Exchange. . .

FOREIGN STOCK PRICES, DAILY (bid and asked prices for previous day, with former bid, for each of about 50 foreign stocks. Mainly "ADR" -- American Depository Receipt issues). NEW YORK TIMES. Published weekdays.

FOREIGN STOCK PRICES, DAILY (bid and asked prices as of 3 P.M. on previous day for each of about 50 foreign stocks, classified by country. Mainly "ADR" -- American Depository Receipt issues). WALL STREET JOURNAL. Published business days.

FOREIGN STOCK PRICES, WEEKLY, CLOSE (final weekly prices for each of about 50 foreign stocks. Mainly "ADR" -- American Depository Receipt issues).

BARRON'S. Published weekly.

FOREIGN STOCK PRICES, WEEKLY, HIGH-LOW-CLOSE (range and close of bid prices for each of about 50 foreign stocks, for week just past. Mainly "ADR" -- American Depository Receipt issues). NEW YORK TIMES. Sunday edition.

FOREIGN STOCK PRICES, YEAR TO DATE, HIGH-LOW (range of current year's bid prices for each of about 50 foreign stocks. Mainly "ADR" -- American Depository Receipt issues). BARRON'S. Published weekly.

Form of bonds.

> SEE: Bonds, form of. . .

Former names of companies.

> SEE: Name changes. . .

FOUNDING DATES (month-day-year and state of incorporation for each of over 1,000 companies with actively traded common stock). MOODY'S HANDBOOK OF COMMON STOCKS. Published quarterly.

FOUNDING DATES, MUTUAL FUNDS (formation date for each of about 300 mutual funds). STANDARD & POOR'S SECURITY OWNER'S STOCK GUIDE. Published monthly.

Frankfurt Stock Exchange prices.

> SEE: Foreign stock price indexes. . .
> Stock prices on Frankfurt Stock Exchange. . .

Free credit balances.

> SEE ALSO: Margin purchasing power. . .

FREE CREDIT BALANCES, MONTHLY-YEARLY (total amount in millions of dollars in free credit balances in New York Stock Exchange firms' margin accounts, for end of latest month, month previous, and same month one year ago. Labeled "Free Cr Bal mil"). BARRON'S. Published weekly.

French stock prices.

> SEE: Foreign stock price indexes. . .
> Stock prices on Paris Stock Exchange (Bourse). . .

FUNDED DEBT TO NET PROPERTY RATIO (percentage proportion of total long term debt to net property for individual corporations with bond issues). STANDARD & POOR'S EARNINGS AND RATINGS BOND GUIDE. Published monthly.

Funds, investment.

> SEE: Closed-end investment companies. . .
> Dual-purpose funds. . .

Exchange funds. . .
Investment companies. . .
Mutual funds. . .
Small business investment companies. . .

Gas utilities.

SEE: Utilities. . .

German stock prices.

SEE: Foreign stock price indexes. . .
Stock prices on Frankfurt Stock Exchange. . .

Government bond average, Moody's.

SEE: Moody's government bond average. . .
Moody's government bond indexes. . .

Government bond average, Standard & Poor's.

SEE: Standard & Poor's government bond index. . .

Government bonds.

SEE ALSO: Treasury bills. . .
Treasury certificates. . .
Treasury notes. . .
(Also see entries beginning "Federal. . .," such as "Federal
National Mortgage Association. . .").

Government bonds, distribution by maturity.

SEE: Government bonds, maturity distribution. . .

GOVERNMENT BONDS, DUE DATES (month, day, and year of maturity for
individual U.S. government bonds listed on New York Stock Exchange). BANK
AND QUOTATION RECORD. Published monthly.

GOVERNMENT BONDS, DUE DATES (month and year of maturity for about 35
individual U.S. government bonds. Labeled "Listed Bond Quotations -- U.S.
Treasury"). BARRON'S. Published weekly.

GOVERNMENT BONDS, DUE DATES (month, day, and year of maturity for
individual U.S. government bonds listed on New York Stock Exchange). COM-
MERCIAL AND FINANCIAL CHRONICLE. Monday edition.

GOVERNMENT BONDS, DUE DATES (month and year of maturity for about 35
individual U.S. government bonds. Labeled "Treasury Bonds"). WALL STREET
JOURNAL. Published business days.

GOVERNMENT BONDS, INTEREST PAYMENT DATES (months of interest periods
for individual U.S. government bonds listed on New York Stock Exchange).
BANK AND QUOTATION RECORD. Published monthly.

GOVERNMENT BONDS, INTEREST RATES ("coupon rate" for individual U.S. government bonds listed on New York Stock Exchange). BANK AND QUOTATION RECORD. Published monthly.

GOVERNMENT BONDS, INTEREST RATES ("coupon rate" for about 35 individual U.S. government bonds. Labeled "Listed Bond Quotations -- U.S. Treasury"). BARRON'S. Published weekly.

GOVERNMENT BONDS, INTEREST RATES ("coupon rate" for individual U.S. government bonds listed on New York Stock Exchange). COMMERCIAL AND FINANCIAL CHRONICLE. Monday edition.

GOVERNMENT BONDS, INTEREST RATES ("coupon rate" for about 35 individual government bonds. Labeled "Treasury Bonds"). WALL STREET JOURNAL. Published business days.

Government bonds, maturity dates.

> SEE: Government bonds, due dates. . .

GOVERNMENT BONDS, MATURITY DISTRIBUTION, WEEKLY ("Callable government securities classified according to maturity date," with amount of "Holdings" for each of six classes ranging from "Within 15 days" to "Over 10 years." Dollar amount "Changes during week" also shown). NEW YORK TIMES. This data normally appears in Friday edition.

GOVERNMENT BONDS, PRICES, DAILY (bid and asked prices for each of about 50 U.S. "Bonds, Notes and Certificates," for previous trading day). NEW YORK TIMES. Published weekdays.

GOVERNMENT BONDS, PRICES, DAILY (bid and asked prices for each of about 35 U.S. government bonds, for previous day. Labeled "Treasury Bonds"). WALL STREET JOURNAL. Published business days.

GOVERNMENT BONDS, PRICES, DAILY-WEEKLY (bid and asked prices for each of about 35 U.S. government bonds, for each day of week just past. Labeled "Bond Record from the New York Stock Exchange"). COMMERCIAL AND FINANCIAL CHRONICLE. Monday edition.

GOVERNMENT BONDS, PRICES, MONTHLY, OPEN-CLOSE (bid and asked prices for each of about 35 U.S. government bonds, for beginning and end of month prior to month of publication. Labeled "New York Stock Exchange Bonds"). BANK AND QUOTATION RECORD. Published monthly.

GOVERNMENT BONDS, PRICES, WEEKLY, CLOSE (bid and asked prices for each of about 35 U.S. government bonds, for end of week just past. Labeled "Listed Bond Quotations -- U.S. Treasury"). BARRON'S. Published weekly.

Government bonds, yield average.

> SEE: Moody's government bond average. . .
> Moody's government bond indexes. . .
> Standard & Poor's government bond index. . .

GOVERNMENT BONDS, YIELDS TO MATURITY, DAILY (percentage yield for each of about 50 U.S. "Bonds, Notes and Certificates," for previous trading day). NEW YORK TIMES. Published weekdays.

GOVERNMENT BONDS, YIELDS TO MATURITY, DAILY (percentage yield for each of about 35 U.S. government bonds, for previous trading day. Labeled "Treasury Bonds"). WALL STREET JOURNAL. Published business days.

GOVERNMENT BONDS, YIELDS TO MATURITY, WEEKLY (percentage yield for each of about 35 U.S. government bonds, for end of week just past. Labeled "Listed Bond Quotations -- U.S. Treasury"). BARRON'S. Published weekly.

Government securities as percentage of total investments of banks.

    SEE: Banks, government securities as percentage of total investments. . .

Government securities holdings of banks.

    SEE: Banks, government securities holdings. . .

Gross for common (utilities).

    SEE: Utilities, gross for common. . .

Gross income or revenue.

    SEE: Banks, gross income. . .
         Sales (corporate revenue). . .
         Savings and loan companies, gross income. . .

Gross sales.

    SEE: Sales (corporate revenue). . .

Group classification of stocks.

    SEE: Industry classification, stocks. . .

Group price averages, stocks.

    SEE: Barron's group stock averages. . .
         Moody's industry group stock averages. . .
         Standard & Poor's stock group indexes. . .
         Value Line industry group indexes. . .

Growth of assets, closed-end investment companies.

    SEE: Closed-end investment companies, growth of assets. . .

Growth of dividends, closed-end investment companies.

    SEE: Closed-end investment companies, growth of dividends. . .

GROWTH RATE OF CASH FLOW PER SHARE (PERCENT), YEARLY (cash flow or "cash earnings" equals regular earnings plus expenses not actually paid in cash, such as depreciation. Growth rate is "the change in cash earnings per share over the previous 5 years expressed as a compounded annual figure." This figure is stated for each of the past 18 or so years for each of about 1,400 leading corporations. Labeled "5 Year Growth Rate"). VALUE LINE INVEST- MENT SURVEY. Part three: published weekly, a few industries each week.

Growth rates, Moody's industrial stock average.

SEE: Moody's industrial stock average, growth rates. . .

Growth ratio, capital.

SEE: Capital growth ratio. . .

Guaranteed railroad stocks.

SEE: Railroad stocks (unlisted). . .

High-grade bond average, Barron's.

SEE: Barron's high-grade bond index. . .

High-grade common stock index, Standard & Poor's.

SEE: Standard & Poor's high-grade common stock index. . .

High-grade preferred stock average, Moody's.

SEE: Moody's preferred stock averages. . .

High-low dates.

SEE: Stock prices, dates of highs and lows. . .

High-low index.

SEE: New highs and new lows. . .

High volume stocks.

SEE ALSO: Most active stocks. . .

HIGH VOLUME STOCKS, CHARTS (prices of "Selected High Volume-Velocity Stocks" are charted daily for about nine months). TRENDLINE DAILY BASIS STOCK CHARTS. Published weekly.

HIGH VOLUME STOCKS, LIST OF, WEEKLY ("Selected High Volume-Velocity Stocks" are listed each week). TRENDLINE DAILY BASIS STOCK CHARTS. Published weekly.

HIGH YIELDING STOCKS (about 100 leading common stocks with high dividend yields are listed. Quality ratings and current percentage yields are indicated). VALUE LINE INVESTMENT SURVEY. Part one, published weekly.

Highs and lows, dates of.

SEE: Stock prices, dates of highs and lows. . .

Highs and lows, new.

SEE: New highs and new lows. . .

Highs and lows of stock averages (rallies and declines).

SEE: Trading swings. . .
        (Also see entries under names of various averages, such as Dow-
        Jones, for daily, weekly, monthly, and yearly highs and lows.)

Highway bonds.

SEE: Public authority bonds. . .
        Toll revenue bonds. . .

Holders of record, dates for dividends.

SEE: Dividends, dates of record. . .

Holdings, insider.

SEE: Insider transactions. . .

Holdings, institutional.

SEE: Institutional holdings. . .

Holdings, mutual funds, changes.

SEE: Investment company transactions. . .

Home Loan Bank bonds.

SEE: Federal Home Loan Bank bonds. . .

Honolulu Stock Exchange.

SEE: Stock prices on Honolulu Stock Exchange. . .
        Volume of trading in stocks, individual stocks on
            Honolulu Stock Exchange. . .
        Volume of trading in stocks, total for Honolulu
            Stock Exchange. . .

Hourly trading volume.

SEE: Volume of trading in stocks, total for New York
            Stock Exchange, hourly. . .

Income, gross.

SEE: Banks, gross income. . .
        Sales (corporate revenue). . .
        Savings and loan companies, gross income. . .

Income, net.

SEE: Net income. . .

Income bond average (railroads), Dow-Jones.

SEE: Dow-Jones railroad bond average (income bonds). . .

Income tax, deferred.

> SEE: Deferred income tax. . .

Income tax exempt vs. taxable yields.

> SEE: Tax exempt vs. taxable yields. . .

Incorporation, date of.

> SEE: Founding dates. . .

Incorporation, state of.

> SEE: State of incorporation. . .

Incorporation, year of.

> SEE: Founding dates. . .

Increased dividends.

> SEE: Dividend increases. . .

Indexes.

> (For list of various stock and bond indexes, see cross references beginning "Average. . ." or "Averages. . .," as well as cross references for specific kinds of averages, such as "Industrial stock averages . . .")

Indicated annual rate (dividends).

> SEE: Dividends, amount, indicated annual rate. . .

Industrial bond averages.

> SEE: Dow-Jones industrial bond average. . .
> Moody's industrial bond average. . .
> New York Times industrial bond average. . .
> Standard & Poor's industrial bond indexes. . .

Industrial groupings.

> SEE: Industry classification. . .

Industrial preferred stock average, Moody's.

> SEE: Moody's preferred stock averages. . .

INDUSTRIAL REVENUE BONDS (a list of about 75 bonds, arranged geographically by state, with Standard & Poor's rating for each bond. Name of corporation paying "lease rental" given in each case). STANDARD & POOR'S EARNINGS AND RATINGS BOND GUIDE. Published monthly.

Industrial stock averages.

> SEE: Dow-Jones industrial stock average. . .

Financial Times (London) industrial stock index. . .
Moody's industrial stock average. . .
National Quotation Bureau over-the-counter industrial
     stock average. . .
New York Stock Exchange industrial stock average. . .
New York Times industrial stock average. . .
Standard & Poor's industrial 425 stock index. . .
Value Line industrial stock index. . .

INDUSTRIES, PRICE PERFORMANCE ("Relative Price Performance" in percentage for "Last Six Weeks" for each of "12 Best Performing Industries" and "12 Worst Performing Industries"). VALUE LINE INVESTMENT SURVEY. Part two, published weekly.

INDUSTRY CLASSIFICATION, STOCKS (approximately 960 listed stocks are grouped by industry into about 96 classifications). TRENDLINE'S CURRENT MARKET PERSPECTIVES. Published monthly.

INDUSTRY CLASSIFICATION, STOCKS (approximately 1,400 leading common stocks are grouped by industry into about 66 classifications). VALUE LINE IN-VESTMENT SURVEY. Part three: published weekly, a few industries each week.

Industry group stock averages.

SEE: Barron's group stock averages. . .
     Moody's industry group stock averages. . .
     Standard & Poor's stock group indexes. . .
     Value Line industry group stock indexes. . .

Industry groups.

SEE: Industry classification, stocks. . .

Industry price performance.

SEE: Industries, price performance. . .

Initial public offerings.

SEE: New issues. . .

INSIDER TRANSACTIONS, MONTHLY (for latest month, for individual companies within each of about 60 industry groups, shows names of insiders buying or selling during month, relationship to company, number of shares bought or sold by each insider, and each insider's remaining holdings at month-end). VALUE LINE INVESTMENT SURVEY. Part four, "Special Report on Officer-Director Transactions." Published monthly as special part of weekly service.

INSIDER TRANSACTIONS, WEEKLY (insider trading involving at least 10,000 shares or $100,000. is shown for individual companies, in three categories: New York Stock Exchange, American Stock Exchange, and over-the-counter. Individuals are named and details are given, including balance of holdings. Labeled "Changes in Stockholdings"). WALL STREET JOURNAL. This data normally appears in Thursday edition.

INSIDER TRANSACTIONS, QUARTERLY (for latest quarter, for individual companies within each of about 60 industry groups, shows number of shares of common stock bought and sold on balance -- major transactions -- by combined officers, directors, and large stockholders). VALUE LINE INVESTMENT SURVEY. Part three: published weekly, a few industries each week.

Institutional holdings.

    SEE ALSO: Investment company transactions. . .

INSTITUTIONAL HOLDINGS, NUMBER OF INSTITUTIONS (number of institutions holding each of over 1,000 actively traded common stocks and over 1,200 less actively traded common stocks). MOODY'S HANDBOOK OF COMMON STOCKS. Published quarterly.

INSTITUTIONAL HOLDINGS, NUMBER OF INSTITUTIONS (number of institutions holding each of about 5,000 stocks). STANDARD & POOR'S SECURITY OWNER'S STOCK GUIDE. Published monthly.

INSTITUTIONAL HOLDINGS, SHARES OF STOCK (number of shares of each of over 1,000 actively traded common stocks and over 1,200 less actively traded common stocks held by institutions). MOODY'S HANDBOOK OF COMMON STOCKS. Published quarterly.

INSTITUTIONAL HOLDINGS, SHARES OF STOCK (number of shares of each of about 5,000 stocks held by institutions). STANDARD & POOR'S SECURITY OWNER'S STOCK GUIDE. Published monthly.

Insurance companies.

    SEE ALSO: Life insurance companies. . .

INSURANCE COMPANIES, ADJUSTED EARNINGS PER SHARE, YEARLY (for each of past eleven years, for each of large insurance companies with actively traded common stock. Adjusted earnings take into account underwriting results, investment results, and other factors). MOODY'S HANDBOOK OF COMMON STOCKS. Published quarterly.

INSURANCE COMPANIES, ADJUSTED EARNINGS PER SHARE, YEARLY (for each of past 18 or so years, for each of about eleven major life insurance companies). VALUE LINE INVESTMENT SURVEY. Part three: published weekly, a few industries each week.

INSURANCE COMPANIES, ASSET TOTALS, YEARLY (for end of each of past eleven years, for each of large insurance companies with actively traded common stock). MOODY'S HANDBOOK OF COMMON STOCKS. Published quarterly.

INSURANCE COMPANIES, ASSET TOTALS, YEARLY (for end of each of past 18 or so years, for each of about eleven major life companies). VALUE LINE INVESTMENT SURVEY. Part three: published weekly, a few industries each week.

Insurance companies, bond investment ratio.

   SEE: Insurance companies, senior securities as percent of total assets. . .

INSURANCE COMPANIES, CAPITAL FUNDS TOTALS, YEARLY (for each of past eleven years for each of large insurance companies with actively traded common stock). MOODY'S HANDBOOK OF COMMON STOCKS. Published quarterly.

INSURANCE COMPANIES, CAPITAL FUNDS TOTALS, YEARLY (for each of past 18 or so years for each of about 15 leading casualty companies). VALUE LINE INVESTMENT SURVEY. Part three: published weekly, a few industries each week.

INSURANCE COMPANIES, COMBINED RATIO (PERCENT), YEARLY (for each of past eleven years for each of large insurance companies with actively traded common stock. "Combined ratio" is a combination of loss ratio and expense ratio: over 100% indicates loss, less than 100% indicates profit). MOODY'S HANDBOOK OF COMMON STOCKS. Published quarterly.

Insurance companies, common stock investment ratio.

   SEE: Insurance companies, equities as percent of total assets. . .

INSURANCE COMPANIES, EQUITIES AS PERCENT OF TOTAL ASSETS, YEARLY (for each of past 18 or so years, for each of about 15 leading casualty companies. Shows common stock investment ratio). VALUE LINE INVESTMENT SURVEY. Part three: published weekly, a few industries each week.

Insurance companies, equity per share for stockholders.

   SEE ALSO: Insurance companies, liquidating value. . .

INSURANCE COMPANIES, EQUITY PER SHARE FOR STOCKHOLDERS, LATEST (individual insurance companies). STANDARD & POOR'S SECURITY OWNER'S STOCK GUIDE. Published monthly.

INSURANCE COMPANIES, EXPENSE RATIO (PERCENT), YEARLY (for each of past 18 or so years, for each of about 15 leading casualty companies. Expense ratio represents expenses as percent of premiums written). VALUE LINE INVESTMENT SURVEY. Part three: published weekly, a few industries each week.

INSURANCE COMPANIES, INVESTMENT INCOME PER SHARE, YEARLY (for each of past eleven years, for each of large insurance companies with actively traded common stock). MOODY'S HANDBOOK OF COMMON STOCKS. Published quarterly.

INSURANCE COMPANIES, INVESTMENT INCOME PER SHARE, YEARLY (for each of past 18 or so years, for each of about 15 leading casualty and eleven life companies). VALUE LINE INVESTMENT SURVEY. Part three: published weekly, a few industries each week.

Insurance companies, liquidating value per share.

SEE ALSO: Insurance companies, equity per share. . .

INSURANCE COMPANIES, LIQUIDATING VALUE PER SHARE, YEARLY (for each of past eleven years, for each of large insurance companies with actively traded common stock). MOODY'S HANDBOOK OF COMMON STOCKS. Published quarterly.

INSURANCE COMPANIES, LIQUIDATING VALUE PER SHARE, YEARLY (for each of past 18 or so years, for each of about 15 leading casualty and eleven life company stocks). VALUE LINE INVESTMENT SURVEY. Part three: published weekly, a few industries each week.

INSURANCE COMPANIES, LOSS RATIO (PERCENT), YEARLY (for each of past 18 or so years, for each of about 15 leading casualty companies. Loss ratio represents losses as percent of premiums earned). VALUE LINE INVESTMENT SURVEY. Part three: published weekly, a few industries each week.

INSURANCE COMPANIES, PREMIUMS WRITTEN, YEARLY (for each of past eleven years for each of large insurance companies with actively traded common stock). MOODY'S HANDBOOK OF COMMON STOCKS. Published quarterly.

INSURANCE COMPANIES, PREMIUMS WRITTEN, YEARLY (for each of past 18 or so years, for each of about 15 leading casualty companies). VALUE LINE INVESTMENT SURVEY. Part three: published weekly, a few industries each week.

INSURANCE COMPANIES, PREMIUMS WRITTEN AS PERCENTAGE OF CAPITAL FUNDS, YEARLY (for each of past 18 or so years for each of about 15 leading casualty companies). VALUE LINE INVESTMENT SURVEY. Part three: published weekly, a few industries each week.

INSURANCE COMPANIES, PREMIUMS WRITTEN PER SHARE, YEARLY (for each of past 18 or so years, for each of about 15 leading casualty company stocks). VALUE LINE INVESTMENT SURVEY. Part three: published weekly, a few industries each week.

INSURANCE COMPANIES, PRICE-INVESTMENT INCOME RATIO, YEARLY (for each of past 18 or so years, for each of about 15 leading casualty companies). VALUE LINE INVESTMENT SURVEY. Part three: published weekly, a few industries each week.

INSURANCE COMPANIES, PRICE PER SHARE AS PERCENTAGE OF LIQUIDATING VALUE PER SHARE, YEARLY (for each of past 18 or so years, for each of about 15 leading casualty company stocks). VALUE LINE INVESTMENT SURVEY. Part three: published weekly, a few industries each week.

Insurance companies, prices of stocks.

SEE: Insurance stocks (unlisted), prices. . .

INSURANCE COMPANIES, SENIOR SECURITIES AS PERCENT OF TOTAL ASSETS, YEARLY (for each of past 18 or so years, for each of about 15 leading casualty companies. "Senior securities" are generally bonds and preferred stock). VALUE LINE INVESTMENT SURVEY. Part three: published weekly, a few industries each week.

INSURANCE COMPANIES, UNDERWRITING INCOME PER SHARE, YEARLY (for each of past 18 or so years, for each of about 15 leading casualty company stocks). VALUE LINE INVESTMENT SURVEY. Part three: published weekly, a few industries each week.

INSURANCE COMPANIES, UNDERWRITING PROFIT MARGIN (PERCENT), YEARLY (for each of past 18 or so years, for each of about 15 leading casualty companies). VALUE LINE INVESTMENT SURVEY. Part three: published weekly, a few industries each week.

INSURANCE COMPANIES, UNEARNED PREMIUM TOTALS, YEARLY (for each of past eleven years for each of large insurance companies with actively traded common stock. Unearned premiums represent premiums that would be due policyholders if all policies were canceled). MOODY'S HANDBOOK OF COMMON STOCKS. Published quarterly.

Insurance in force.

> SEE: Life insurance companies, insurance in force. . .

Insurance stock average, Moody's.

> SEE: Moody's fire insurance stock average. . .

Insurance stock average, National Quotation Bureau.

> SEE: National Quotation Bureau over-the-counter insurance stock average. . .

Insurance stock averages, Standard & Poor's.

> SEE: Standard & Poor's stock group indexes. . .

INSURANCE STOCKS (UNLISTED), DIVIDENDS, AMOUNT, INDICATED ANNUAL RATE (for each of about 200 over-the-counter insurance stocks). BARRON'S. Published weekly. Also NEW YORK TIMES. Published weekdays. Also NEW YORK TIMES. Sunday edition. Also WALL STREET JOURNAL. Published business days.

INSURANCE STOCKS (UNLISTED), EARNINGS PER SHARE, INTERIM (latest interim earnings given for each of about 200 over-the-counter insurance stocks). BARRON'S. Published weekly.

INSURANCE STOCKS (UNLISTED), PRICES, DAILY (bid and asked prices for previous day for each of about 200 over-the-counter insurance stocks, with former bid). NEW YORK TIMES. Published weekdays.

INSURANCE STOCKS (UNLISTED), PRICES, DAILY (bid and asked prices for previous day for each of about 200 over-the-counter insurance stocks, with net change in bid). WALL STREET JOURNAL. Published business days.

INSURANCE STOCKS (UNLISTED), PRICES, MONTHLY, CLOSE (bid and asked prices for end of month prior to month of publication for each of about 320 over-the-counter insurance stocks). BANK AND QUOTATION RECORD. Published monthly.

INSURANCE STOCKS (UNLISTED), PRICES, WEEKLY, CLOSE (bid and asked prices for end of week just past, and bid price for end of previous week, are quoted for each of about 200 over-the-counter insurance stocks). BARRON'S. Published weekly.

INSURANCE STOCKS (UNLISTED), PRICES, WEEKLY, CLOSE (bid and asked prices for end of week just past for each of about 200 over-the-counter insurance stocks). COMMERCIAL AND FINANCIAL CHRONICLE. Monday edition.

INSURANCE STOCKS (UNLISTED), PRICES, WEEKLY, HIGH-LOW-CLOSE (range and close of bid price for each of about 200 over-the-counter insurance stocks, for week just past). NEW YORK TIMES. Sunday edition.

INSURANCE STOCKS (UNLISTED), PRICES, YEAR TO DATE, HIGH-LOW (range of bid price for current year for each of about 200 over-the-counter insurance stocks). BARRON'S. Published weekly.

INTER-AMERICAN DEVELOPMENT BANK BONDS, PRICES, DAILY (bid and asked prices for each of about six issues, for previous trading day. Amount outstanding in millions of dollars shown for each issue). NEW YORK TIMES. Published weekdays.

INTER-AMERICAN DEVELOPMENT BANK BONDS, PRICES, DAILY (bid and asked prices for each of about six issues, for previous trading day). WALL STREET JOURNAL. Published business days.

INTER-AMERICAN DEVELOPMENT BANK BONDS, PRICES, DAILY-WEEKLY, CLOSE (bid and asked prices for each of about six issues, for each day of week just past. Labeled "Bond Record from the New York Stock Exchange"). COMMERCIAL AND FINANCIAL CHRONICLE. Monday edition.

INTER-AMERICAN DEVELOPMENT BANK BONDS, PRICES, MONTHLY, OPEN-CLOSE (bid and asked prices for each of about six issues, for beginning and end of month prior to month of publication. Labeled "New York Stock Exchange Bonds"). BANK AND QUOTATION RECORD. Published monthly.

INTER-AMERICAN DEVELOPMENT BANK BONDS, YIELDS TO MATURITY, DAILY (percentage yield for each of about six issues, for previous trading day. Amount outstanding in millions of dollars shown for each issue). NEW YORK TIMES. Published weekdays.

INTER-AMERICAN DEVELOPMENT BANK BONDS, YIELDS TO MATURITY, DAILY (percentage yield for each of about six issues, for previous trading day). WALL STREET JOURNAL. Published business days.

Interest charge totals, finance companies.

SEE: Finance companies, interest charge dollar amount
       totals. . .

Interest charges, "times earned."

SEE: Earnings to fixed charges ratio. . .

Interest earned, life insurance companies.

SEE: Life insurance companies, interest earned. . .

Interest equalization tax, effect of.

SEE: Foreign bonds, foreign basis. . .

Interest expense, savings and loan companies.

SEE: Savings and loan companies, interest expense. . .

INTEREST PAYABLE ANNUALLY ON LONG TERM DEBT (for present long term
debt, for each of about 1,400 leading corporations, shows total dollar amount
of interest due annually).   VALUE LINE INVESTMENT SURVEY.   Part three:
published weekly, a few industries each week.

Interest payment dates (bonds).

SEE: Bond interest payment dates. . .
       Convertible bonds, interest payment dates. . .
       Foreign bonds, interest payment dates. . .
       Government bonds, interest payment dates. . .

Interest rates.

SEE: Bankers' acceptance rates. . .
       Bond interest rates. . .
       Bond yields to maturity. . .
       Call loan rates. . .
       Certificates of deposit rates. . .
       Commercial paper rates. . .
       Convertible bonds, yields to maturity. . .
       Discount rate, Federal Reserve. . .
       Eurodollar rates. . .
       Federal funds open market rate. . .
       Foreign bonds, interest rates. . .
       Foreign bonds, yields to maturity. . .
       Government bonds, interest rates. . .
       Government bonds, yields to maturity. . .
       Prime rate. . .
       Time loan rates. . .
       Treasury bills, yields to maturity. . .
       Treasury certificates, yields to maturity. . .
       Treasury notes, yields to maturity. . .
       (Also see cross references under "Bond interest yield averages. . .")

Interest ratio, finance companies.

SEE: Finance companies, interest ratio. . .

Interim earnings.

    SEE: Earnings per share, interim. . .

Intermediate Credit Bank bonds.

    SEE: Federal Intermediate Credit Bank bonds. . .

INTERNATIONAL BANK FOR RECONSTRUCTION AND DEVELOPMENT BONDS, PRICES, DAILY (bid and asked prices for each of about 20 issues, for previous trading day. Amount outstanding in millions of dollars shown for each issue). NEW YORK TIMES. Published weekdays.

INTERNATIONAL BANK FOR RECONSTRUCTION AND DEVELOPMENT BONDS, PRICES, DAILY (bid and asked prices for each of about 20 issues, for previous trading day. Labeled "World Bank Bonds"). WALL STREET JOURNAL. Published business days.

INTERNATIONAL BANK FOR RECONSTRUCTION AND DEVELOPMENT BONDS, PRICES, DAILY-WEEKLY (bid and asked prices for each of about 20 issues, for each day of week just past. Under "Bond Record from the New York Stock Exchange"). COMMERCIAL AND FINANCIAL CHRONICLE. Monday edition.

INTERNATIONAL BANK FOR RECONSTRUCTION AND DEVELOPMENT BONDS, PRICES, MONTHLY, CLOSE (end-of-month bid and asked prices for each of about 20 issues. Labeled "United States and Municipal Bonds"). BANK AND QUOTATION RECORD. Published monthly.

INTERNATIONAL BANK FOR RECONSTRUCTION AND DEVELOPMENT BONDS, PRICES, MONTHLY, OPEN-CLOSE (bid and asked prices given for each of about 20 issues, for beginning and end of month prior to month of publication. Labeled "New York Stock Exchange Bonds"). BANK AND QUOTATION RECORD. Published monthly.

INTERNATIONAL BANK FOR RECONSTRUCTION AND DEVELOPMENT BONDS, YIELDS TO MATURITY, DAILY (percentage yields for each of about 20 issues, for previous trading day. Amount outstanding in millions of dollars shown for each issue). NEW YORK TIMES. Published weekdays.

INTERNATIONAL BANK FOR RECONSTRUCTION AND DEVELOPMENT BONDS, YIELDS TO MATURITY, DAILY (percentage yield for each of about 20 issues, for previous day. Labeled "World Bank Bonds"). WALL STREET JOURNAL. Published business days.

Inventory turnover, retailers.

    SEE: Retailers, inventory turnover. . .

Investment companies.

    SEE ALSO: Closed-end investment companies. . .
                  Dual-purpose funds. . .
                  Exchange funds. . .
                  Mutual fund industry totals. . .
                  Mutual funds. . .
                  Small business investment companies. . .

INVESTMENT COMPANIES, CASH POSITION CHANGES, QUARTERLY (in millions of dollars and also in percent, shows increase or decrease in cash held by 83 major investment companies combined. Separate totals also given for balanced funds, stock funds, and closed-end companies. Labeled "Summary of. . .Transactions of 83 Investment Companies"). BARRON'S. This data is normally published around the 15th of February, May, August, and November.

Investment companies, closed-end.

    SEE: Closed-end investment companies. . .

INVESTMENT COMPANIES, COMMON STOCK PURCHASES, QUARTERLY (in millions of dollars, shows total amount bought and total sold by 83 major investment companies combined, for latest quarter and previous quarter. Also, separate totals are given for balanced funds, stock funds, and closed-end companies. Labeled "Summary of. . .Transactions of 83 Investment Companies"). BARRON'S. This data is normally published around the 15th of February, May, August, and November.

Investment companies, open-end.

    SEE: Mutual funds. . .

Investment company transactions.

    SEE ALSO: Institutional holdings. . .

INVESTMENT COMPANY TRANSACTIONS, QUARTERLY (tabulation lists individual stocks having "Transactions in which buyers exceed sellers--or sellers exceed buyers--by two or more management groups." A few hundred stocks are normally listed, divided into about 30 industry groups, with number of funds and number of shares shown under "Bought" and "Sold" for each stock. New initial purchases and eliminations are also indicated. 83 major investment companies are surveyed). BARRON'S. This data is normally published around the 15th of February, May, August, and November.

INVESTMENT COMPANY TRANSACTIONS, QUARTERLY (tabulation lists individual common stocks bought or sold by more than one of about a hundred funds during latest available quarter. A few hundred stocks are normally listed, divided into about 30 industry groups, with number of funds and number of shares shown under "Bought" and "Sold" for each stock. New eliminations and initial purchases are also indicated). COMMERCIAL AND FINANCIAL CHRONICLE. Thursday edition. This data is normally published in the Thursday edition around the 20th of February, May, August, and November.

INVESTMENT COMPANY TRANSACTIONS, QUARTERLY (major transactions within latest available quarter indicated for a combination of over 100 investment companies. About 50 common stocks are individually listed, with number of funds buying each stock, number of funds selling, total number of shares bought, and total number of shares sold). THE OUTLOOK. This data is normally published around the middle of February, May, August, and November.

INVESTMENT COMPANY TRANSACTIONS, QUARTERLY (for individual corporations within each of about 60 industry groups, for latest available quarter, shows dollar value of common stock bought and sold on balance by a combination of investment companies). VALUE LINE INVESTMENT SURVEY. Part three: pub-lished weekly, a few industries each week.

INVESTMENT COMPANY TRANSACTIONS, QUARTERLY (individual common stocks are arranged alphabetically in two lists: "Stocks Bought on Balance" and "Stocks Sold on Balance." The following data for latest quarter is given for each stock: number of funds holding, number of funds buying or selling, shares bought or sold, dollar value of net purchases or sales, consecutive quarters bought or sold on balance, shares held now by funds, percentage of stock held, and dollar value of shares held. 55 major investment companies are sur-veyed). VALUE LINE INVESTMENT SURVEY. Part four: "Special Report on Investment Company Transactions." Published around the 20th of February, May, August, and November.

Investment dealers.

> SEE: Brokers. . .
> Underwriters. . .

Investment income dividends.

> SEE: Closed-end investment companies, dividends from
> investment income. . .
> Mutual funds, dividends from investment income. . .

Investment income per share.

> SEE: Closed-end investment companies, investment income
> per share. . .
> Insurance companies, investment income per share. . .
> Mutual funds, investment income per share. . .

Investment trusts.

> SEE: Closed-end investment companies. . .
> Mutual funds. . .

Investment worth of convertible bonds.

> SEE: Convertible bonds, estimated investment worth. . .

ISSUES TRADED, BONDS ON AMERICAN STOCK EXCHANGE, DAILY (total number of separate bond issues traded on each of last four trading days). WALL STREET JOURNAL. Published business days.

ISSUES TRADED, BONDS ON NEW YORK STOCK EXCHANGE, DAILY (total number of separate bond issues traded on each of last three trading days). NEW YORK TIMES. Published weekdays.

ISSUES TRADED, BONDS ON NEW YORK STOCK EXCHANGE, DAILY (total number of separate bond issues traded on each of last two trading days, in each of three following categories: foreign, domestic, all issues). WALL STREET JOURNAL. Published business days.

ISSUES TRADED, STOCKS ON AMERICAN STOCK EXCHANGE, DAILY (total number of separate stock issues traded on each day of week just past). BAR-

RON'S. Published weekly.

ISSUES TRADED, STOCKS ON AMERICAN STOCK EXCHANGE, DAILY (total number of separate stock issues traded on each of last six trading days). WALL STREET JOURNAL. Published business days.

ISSUES TRADED, STOCKS ON AMERICAN STOCK EXCHANGE, WEEKLY (total number of separate stock issues traded during each of last two weeks. Labeled "Market Breadth"). NEW YORK TIMES. Sunday edition.

ISSUES TRADED, STOCKS ON NEW YORK STOCK EXCHANGE, DAILY (total number of separate stock issues traded on each day of week just past). BAR-RON'S. Published weekly.

ISSUES TRADED, STOCKS ON NEW YORK STOCK EXCHANGE, DAILY (total number of separate stock issues traded on each of last two trading days. Labeled "Market Summary"). NEW YORK TIMES. Published weekdays.

ISSUES TRADED, STOCKS ON NEW YORK STOCK EXCHANGE, DAILY (total number of separate stock issues traded on each of last six trading days. Labeled "Market Diary"). WALL STREET JOURNAL. Published business days.

ISSUES TRADED, STOCKS ON NEW YORK STOCK EXCHANGE, WEEKLY (total number of separate stock issues traded during week just past). BARRON'S. Published weekly.

ISSUES TRADED, STOCKS ON NEW YORK STOCK EXCHANGE, WEEKLY (total number of separate stock issues traded during each of last two weeks. Labeled "Market Breadth"). NEW YORK TIMES. Sunday edition.

Italian stock prices.

SEE: Foreign stock price indexes. . .
Stock prices on Milan Stock Exchange. . .

Japanese stock prices.

SEE: Foreign stock price indexes. . .
Stock prices on Tokyo Stock Exchange. . .

Johannesburg Stock Exchange prices.

SEE: Stock prices on Johannesburg Stock Exchange. . .

Land Bank bonds.

SEE: Federal Land Bank bonds. . .

LARGE BLOCK TRANSACTIONS (list of individual block sales of 20,000 shares or more of New York Stock Exchange stocks, for week just past. Name of stock, price of transaction, number of shares, and price of sale previous are given in each case). BARRON'S. Published weekly.

LARGE BLOCK TRANSACTIONS, NUMBER OF (total number of large block transactions--trades of 10,000 shares or more--for New York Stock Exchange during week just past). BARRON'S. Published weekly.

Lease rental bonds.

    SEE: Industrial revenue bonds. . .

Legality of bond investments.

    SEE: Bonds, eligibility for bank investment. . .
            Bonds, legal investment status. . .

Liabilities, current.

    SEE: Current liabilities. . .

Liabilities, long term.

    SEE: Long term debt. . .

Life insurance companies.

    SEE ALSO: Insurance companies. . .

LIFE INSURANCE COMPANIES, BOOK VALUE PER SHARE, YEARLY (for each of past 18 or so years, for each of about eleven leading stocks). VALUE LINE INVESTMENT SURVEY. Part three: published weekly, a few industries each week.

LIFE INSURANCE COMPANIES, CAPITAL FUNDS PER SHARE, YEARLY (for each of past eleven years, for each of large life insurance companies with actively traded common stock. "Capital funds" refers to total capital from various sources). MOODY'S HANDBOOK OF COMMON STOCKS. Published quarterly.

LIFE INSURANCE COMPANIES, CURRENT CHARGES, YEARLY (for each of past 18 or so years, for each of about eleven major life stock companies. Current charges are expenses, taxes, and payments of insurance benefits). VALUE LINE INVESTMENT SURVEY. Part three: published weekly, a few industries each week.

LIFE INSURANCE COMPANIES, INSURANCE IN FORCE, YEARLY (for each of past eleven years, for each of large life insurance companies with actively traded common stock). MOODY'S HANDBOOK OF COMMON STOCKS. Published quarterly.

LIFE INSURANCE COMPANIES, INTEREST EARNED (PERCENT), YEARLY (for each of past eleven years, for each of large life insurance companies with actively traded common stock). MOODY'S HANDBOOK OF COMMON STOCKS. Published quarterly.

LIFE INSURANCE COMPANIES, SALES OF INSURANCE, YEARLY (for each of past eleven years, for each of large life companies with actively traded common stock). MOODY'S HANDBOOK OF COMMON STOCKS. Published quarterly.

LIFE INSURANCE COMPANIES, TOTAL INCOME, YEARLY, (for each of past eleven years, for each of large life companies with actively traded common stock). MOODY'S HANDBOOK OF COMMON STOCKS. Published quarterly.

Lipper, Arthur, mutual fund averages.

 SEE: Mutual fund averages. . .

Liquidating value per share, insurance companies.

 SEE: Insurance companies, liquidating value per share. . .

Liquor companies.

 SEE: Distillers. . .

Listed shares, total value, New York Stock Exchange.

 SEE: Market value total of all shares listed on New York . Stock Exchange. . .

Listed stock prices.

 SEE: Stock prices. . .

Listing applications.

 SEE: New listings, stocks, pending. . .

Listings.

 SEE: Markets where bonds are traded. . . Markets where stocks are traded. . . New listings, stocks. . .

Load factor, airlines.

 SEE: Airlines, passenger load factor. . .

Loan rates.

 SEE: Call loan rates. . . Time loan rates. . .

Loan totals.

 SEE: Banks, loan totals. . . Finance companies, receivables. . . Savings and loan companies, loan totals. . .

Loans, brokers'.

 SEE: Brokers' loans. . .

Loans as percentage of deposits.

 SEE: Banks, loans as percentage of deposits. . .

London Financial Times stock averages.

 SEE: Financial Times (London) composite stock index. . . Financial Times (London) industrial stock index. . .

London Stock Exchange prices.

> SEE: Foreign stock price indexes. . .
> Stock prices on London Stock Exchange. . .

Long term debt.

> SEE ALSO: Funded debt. . .
> Senior capital. . .

LONG TERM DEBT (for each of about 1,000 corporations with actively traded common stock, shows total amount of long term debt outstanding, according to latest available balance sheet or report). MOODY'S HANDBOOK OF COMMON STOCKS. Published quarterly.

LONG TERM DEBT (for each of about 2,000 corporations with bond issues, shows total amount of long term debt outstanding, according to latest available balance sheet or report). STANDARD & POOR'S EARNINGS AND RATINGS BOND GUIDE. Published monthly.

LONG TERM DEBT (for each of about 4,300 corporations with stock issues, shows total amount of long term debt outstanding, according to latest available balance sheet or report). STANDARD & POOR'S SECURITY OWNER'S STOCK GUIDE. Published monthly.

LONG TERM DEBT (for each of about 700 active, listed corporations, shows total amount of long term debt outstanding, according to latest available balance sheet or report). TRENDLINE DAILY BASIS STOCK CHARTS. Published weekly.

LONG TERM DEBT (for each of about 960 listed corporations, shows total amount of long term debt outstanding, according to latest available balance sheet or report). TRENDLINE'S CURRENT MARKET PERSPECTIVES. Published monthly.

LONG TERM DEBT (for each of about 1,400 corporations with common stock issues, shows total amount of long term debt outstanding, according to latest available balance sheet or report). VALUE LINE INVESTMENT SURVEY. Part three: published weekly, a few industries each week.

Long term debt, interest payable.

> SEE: Interest payable annually on long term debt. . .

LONG TERM DEBT AS PERCENT OF TOTAL CAPITAL (percent of total capital that is currently represented by long term debt is shown for each of 1,000 companies with actively traded common stock). MOODY'S HANDBOOK OF COMMON STOCKS. Published quarterly.

Loss ratio, insurance companies.

> SEE: Insurance companies, loss ratio. . .

Low-priced stock average.

SEE: Barron's low-priced stock index. . .
Standard & Poor's low-priced common stock index. . .

Maintenance ratio, railroads.

SEE: Railroads, maintenance ratio. . .

Margin account collateral.

SEE: Collateral, registered and exempt. . .

MARGIN ACCOUNTS, NUMBER OF, MONTHLY-YEARLY (number of individual margin accounts with New York Stock Exchange firms, for end of latest month available, previous month, and same period one year ago. Number is given in thousands of accounts. Labeled "Margin Accts, th"). BARRON'S. Published weekly.

MARGIN CUSTOMERS HAVING LESS THAN 40 PERCENT EQUITY, MONTHLY-YEARLY (for New York Stock Exchange firms' margin accounts, shows percentage of customers having equity of less than 40%, for end of latest month available, previous month, and same period one year ago. Labeled "Equity Under 40%"). BARRON'S. Published weekly.

Margin debt.

SEE ALSO: Brokers' loans. . .

MARGIN DEBT, MONTHLY, CHART (total "money owed brokers by margin customers" charted monthly for about four years). TRENDLINE'S CURRENT MARKET PERSPECTIVES. Published monthly.

MARGIN DEBT, MONTHLY-YEARLY (total customers' margin debt at New York Stock Exchange firms, for end of latest month available, previous month, and same period one year ago). BARRON'S. Published weekly.

Margin excess.

SEE: Margin purchasing power. . .

Margin free credit balances.

SEE: Free credit balances. . .

MARGIN 100% (names of stocks listed on New York and American Stock Exchanges for which 100% margin is required). BARRON'S. Published weekly.

Margin purchasing power.

SEE ALSO: Free credit balances. . .

MARGIN PURCHASING POWER, MONTHLY, CHART ("An estimate of the funds currently available in margin accounts to purchase additional securities" is charted monthly for about four years. Labeled "Potential Purchasing Power"). TRENDLINE'S CURRENT MARKET PERSPECTIVES. Published monthly.

Margin requirement of 100%

    SEE: Margin 100%. . .

Market breadth.

    SEE: Advances and declines. . .
           Issues traded. . .
           New highs and new lows. . .

MARKET VALUE TOTAL OF ALL SHARES LISTED ON NEW YORK STOCK EX-
CHANGE, MONTHLY-YEARLY (total value of all shares listed, in billions of
dollars, for end of latest month, previous month, and same period one year ago.
Labeled "Val lstd stks, bil"). BARRON'S. Published weekly.

MARKET VALUE TOTAL OF SHARE SALES ON ALL REGISTERED EXCHANGES,
MONTHLY-YEARLY (value of sales on all registered security exchanges in U.S.,
in millions of dollars, for latest month, previous month, and same period one
year ago. Labeled "All reg exch, mil $"). BARRON'S. Published weekly.

MARKET VALUE TOTAL OF SHARE SALES ON NEW YORK STOCK EXCHANGE,
MONTHLY-YEARLY (value of total share sales in millions of dollars, for latest
month, previous month, and same period one year ago. Labeled "Mkt lstd sls,
mil"). BARRON'S. Published weekly.

MARKETS WHERE BONDS ARE TRADED (tells where each of about 2,600 corporate, 200 foreign, and 500 convertible bonds is traded--name of exchange
indicated where applicable). STANDARD & POOR'S EARNINGS AND RAT-
INGS BOND GUIDE. Published monthly.

MARKETS WHERE STOCKS ARE TRADED (tells where each of over 2,200 listed
common stocks is traded). MOODY'S HANDBOOK OF COMMON STOCKS.
Published quarterly.

MARKETS WHERE STOCKS ARE TRADED (in addition to data on about 27,000
unlisted stocks, shows name of exchange for each of about 3,000 listed issues--
U.S. and Canadian, common and preferred). NATIONAL MONTHLY STOCK
SUMMARY. Published monthly.

MARKETS WHERE STOCKS ARE TRADED (tells where each of approximately 5,000
U.S. and Canadian, common and preferred issues is traded--name of exchange
indicated for each listed stock). STANDARD & POOR'S SECURITY OWNER'S
STOCK GUIDE. Published monthly.

Maturity, yields to.

    SEE: Bond yields to maturity. . .

Maturity dates of bonds.

    SEE: Bonds, due dates. . .
           Convertible bonds, due dates. . .
           Foreign bonds, due dates. . .
           Government bonds, due dates. . .

Maturity distribution of government securities.

    SEE: Government bonds, maturity distribution. . .

Medium-grade preferred stock average, Moody's.

    SEE: Moody's preferred stock averages. . .

Meeting dates, annual.

    SEE: Annual meeting dates. . .

Meeting dates, dividend.

    SEE: Dividend meeting dates. . .

Meetings, dividend.

    SEE: Dividend meetings. . .

MEMBER TRADING, NEW YORK STOCK EXCHANGE, PERCENTAGE OF TOTAL TRADING, WEEKLY-YEARLY (trading volume for members' accounts is expressed as a percentage of total volume, for latest week, previous week, and same week one year ago). BARRON'S. Published weekly.

MEMBER TRADING, NEW YORK STOCK EXCHANGE, WEEKLY-MONTHLY-YEARLY (round-lot purchases, sales, and short sales, in number of shares, for account of members, for latest week, previous week, month ago, and same week one year ago). COMMERCIAL AND FINANCIAL CHRONICLE. Thursday edition.

MEMBER TRADING, NEW YORK STOCK EXCHANGE, WEEKLY-YEARLY (round-lot purchases, sales, and short sales, in thousands of shares, for account of members, for latest week, previous week, and same week one year ago). BARRON'S. Published weekly.

Mergers and acquisitions.

    SEE ALSO: Name changes. . .

MERGERS AND ACQUISITIONS (brief merger information included, where currently applicable, with monthly price and listing information for approximately 30,000 stocks). NATIONAL MONTHLY STOCK SUMMARY. Published monthly.

MERGERS AND ACQUISITIONS, OVER-THE-COUNTER (current and pending mergers, acquisitions, redemptions, and dissolutions are shown alphabetically by unlisted company name under label "Securities Called for Redemption." Basis of exchanges of shares, etc., usually given, but dates usually not given). BANK AND QUOTATION RECORD. Published monthly.

Mexico City Stock Exchange prices.

    SEE: Stock prices on Mexico City Stock Exchange. . .

Midwest Stock Exchange.

SEE: Dividends, amount, indicated annual rate, Midwest
    Stock Exchange. . .
Earnings per share, interim, Midwest Stock
    Exchange. . .
Stock prices on Midwest Stock Exchange. . .
Volume of trading in stocks, individual stocks on
    Midwest Stock Exchange. . .
Volume of trading in stocks, total for Midwest
    Stock Exchange. . .

Milan Stock Exchange prices.
SEE: Foreign stock price indexes. . .
Stock prices on Milan Stock Exchange. . .

Money exchange rates.
SEE: Foreign exchange rates. . .

Money rates (interest).
(See cross references under "Interest rates. . .").

Montreal Stock Exchange.
SEE: Commission rates, Canadian stock exchanges. . .
Dividends, amount, indicated annual rate,
    Montreal Stock Exchange. . .
Earnings per share, interim, Montreal Stock
    Exchange. . .
Stock prices on Montreal Stock Exchange. . .
Volume of trading in stocks, individual stocks
    on Montreal Stock Exchange. . .
Volume of trading in stocks, total for Montreal
    Stock Exchange. . .

Moody's bank stock average.
SEE: Moody's New York bank stock average. . .

Moody's bill averages.
SEE: Moody's treasury bill averages. . .

Moody's composite bond averages.
SEE: Moody's corporate (composite) bond averages. . .

MOODY'S COMPOSITE STOCK AVERAGE, DIVIDEND YIELD (PERCENT),
MONTHLY (yield at end of each of last 13 or 14 months). MOODY'S
STOCK SURVEY. This data normally appears in second issue of each month.

MOODY'S COMPOSITE STOCK AVERAGE, DIVIDENDS, MONTHLY (dividend
dollar average per share as of end of each of last 13 or 14 months). MOODY'S
STOCK SURVEY. This data normally appears in second issue of each month.

MOODY'S COMPOSITE STOCK AVERAGE, EARNINGS PER SHARE, YEARLY
(annual figure for each of two previous years). MOODY'S STOCK SURVEY.
This data normally appears in second issue of each month.

MOODY'S COMPOSITE STOCK AVERAGE, PRICE, MONTHLY, CLOSE (for end of each of last 13 or 14 months). MOODY'S STOCK SURVEY. This data normally appears in second issue of each month.

MOODY'S COMPOSITE STOCK AVERAGE, PRICE-EARNINGS RATIO, MONTHLY (for end of each of last 14 months). MOODY'S STOCK SURVEY. This data normally appears in second issue of each month.

MOODY'S COMPOSITE STOCK AVERAGE, PRICE-EARNINGS RATIO, YEARLY, HIGH-LOW (range for each of previous three years). MOODY'S STOCK SURVEY. This data normally appears in second issue of each month.

MOODY'S CORPORATE (COMPOSITE) BOND AVERAGE, YIELD (PERCENT), WEEKLY (average yield for combined corporate bonds for each of last five weeks. Labeled "Moody's Yield Averages"). MOODY'S STOCK SURVEY. This data normally appears in second issue of each month.

MOODY'S CORPORATE (COMPOSITE) BOND AVERAGE, YIELD (PERCENT), YEARLY, HIGH-LOW (yield range for combined corporate bonds for current year and each of two previous years. Labeled "Moody's Yield Averages"). MOODY'S STOCK SURVEY. This data normally appears in second issue of each month.

MOODY'S CORPORATE (COMPOSITE) BOND AVERAGES, PRICES, WEEKLY-MONTHLY-YEARLY (daily average price for latest week, previous week, month ago, and same week one year ago. Separate price averages given for Aaa, Aa, A, Baa, and combined corporate). COMMERCIAL AND FINANCIAL CHRONICLE. Thursday edition.

MOODY'S CORPORATE (COMPOSITE) BOND AVERAGES, YIELDS (PERCENT), DAILY (yield based on closing price of average for each of previous five days. Separate yields for Aaa, Aa, A, Baa, and combined corporate). MOODY'S BOND SURVEY. Published weekly.

MOODY'S CORPORATE (COMPOSITE) BOND AVERAGES, YIELDS (PERCENT), WEEKLY-MONTHLY-YEARLY (average yields for latest week, previous week, month ago, and same week one year ago. Separate yields for Aaa, Aa, A, Baa, and combined corporate). COMMERCIAL AND FINANCIAL CHRONICLE. Thursday edition.

MOODY'S CORPORATE (COMPOSITE) BOND AVERAGES, YIELDS (PERCENT), YEARLY, HIGH-LOW (yield ranges for current year and one year previous are shown separately for Aaa, Aa, A, Baa, and combined corporates). MOODY'S BOND SURVEY. Published weekly.

MOODY'S FIRE INSURANCE STOCK AVERAGE, DIVIDEND YIELD (PERCENT), MONTHLY (yield at end of each of last 13 or 14 months). MOODY'S STOCK SURVEY. This data normally appears in second issue of each month.

MOODY'S FIRE INSURANCE STOCK AVERAGE, DIVIDENDS, MONTHLY (dividend dollar average per share as of end of each of last 13 or 14 months). MOODY'S STOCK SURVEY. This data normally appears in second issue of each month.

MOODY'S FIRE INSURANCE STOCK AVERAGE, EARNINGS PER SHARE, YEARLY (annual figure for each of two previous years). MOODY'S STOCK SURVEY. This data normally appears in second issue of each month.

MOODY'S FIRE INSURANCE STOCK AVERAGE, PRICE, MONTHLY, CLOSE (for each of last 13 or 14 months). MOODY'S STOCK SURVEY. This data appears in second issue of each month.

MOODY'S GOVERNMENT BOND AVERAGE, YIELD (PERCENT), WEEKLY-MONTHLY-YEARLY (average yield for latest week, previous week, month ago, and same week one year ago). COMMERCIAL AND FINANCIAL CHRONICLE.

MOODY'S GOVERNMENT BOND AVERAGE (LONG-TERM), YIELD (PERCENT), DAILY (yield based on closing price, for each of previous five days). MOODY'S BOND SURVEY. Published weekly.

MOODY'S GOVERNMENT BOND AVERAGE (LONG-TERM), YIELD (PERCENT), YEARLY, HIGH-LOW (yield range for current year and one year previous). MOODY'S BOND SURVEY. Published weekly.

MOODY'S GOVERNMENT BOND AVERAGE (THREE TO FIVE YEARS MATURITY), YIELD (PERCENT), DAILY (yield based on closing price, for each of previous five days). MOODY'S BOND SURVEY. Published weekly.

MOODY'S GOVERNMENT BOND AVERAGE (THREE TO FIVE YEARS MATURITY), YIELD (PERCENT), YEARLY, HIGH-LOW (yield range for current year and one year previous). MOODY'S BOND SURVEY. Published weekly.

MOODY'S GOVERNMENT BOND INDEXES (THREE, FIVE, AND TEN YEAR MATURITIES), YIELDS (PERCENT), MONTHLY ("Indicated yield for an issue of the given maturity, taken from a market yield curve," for each of previous two months). MOODY'S BOND SURVEY. Published weekly.

MOODY'S GOVERNMENT BOND INDEXES (THREE, FIVE, AND TEN YEAR MATURITIES), YIELDS (PERCENT), WEEKLY ("Indicated yield for an issue of the given maturity, taken from a market yield curve," for each of previous four weeks). MOODY'S BOND SURVEY. Published weekly.

MOODY'S GOVERNMENT BOND INDEXES (THREE, FIVE, AND TEN YEAR MATURITIES), YIELDS (PERCENT), YEAR TO DATE, HIGH-LOW (range of yield for each maturity for current year). MOODY'S BOND SURVEY. Published weekly.

Moody's group averages.

SEE: Moody's industry group stock averages. . .

Moody's high grade preferred stock averages.

SEE: Moody's preferred stock averages. . .

MOODY'S INDUSTRIAL BOND AVERAGE, PRICE, WEEKLY-MONTHLY-YEAR-LY (average price for latest week, previous week, month ago, and same week one year ago). COMMERCIAL AND FINANCIAL CHRONICLE. Thursday edition.

MOODY'S INDUSTRIAL BOND AVERAGE, YIELD (PERCENT), WEEKLY-MONTHLY-YEARLY (average yield for latest week, previous week, month ago, and same week one year ago). COMMERCIAL AND FINANCIAL CHRONICLE. Thursday edition.

MOODY'S INDUSTRIAL BOND AVERAGES, YIELDS (PERCENT), DAILY (yield based on closing price for each of previous five days. Separate yields for Aaa, Aa, A, Baa, and combined industrials). MOODY'S BOND SURVEY. Published weekly.

MOODY'S INDUSTRIAL BOND AVERAGES, YIELDS (PERCENT), YEARLY, HIGH-LOW (yield ranges for current year and one year previous shown separately for Aaa, Aa, A, Baa, and combined industrials). MOODY'S BOND SURVEY. Published weekly.

Moody's industrial preferred stock averages.

SEE: Moody's preferred stock averages. . .

MOODY'S INDUSTRIAL STOCK AVERAGE, DIVIDEND YIELD (PERCENT), MONTHLY (yield at end of each of last 13 or 14 months). MOODY'S STOCK SURVEY. This data normally appears in second issue of each month.

MOODY'S INDUSTRIAL STOCK AVERAGE, DIVIDEND YIELD (PERCENT), WEEKLY (yield for end of each of last five weeks). MOODY'S STOCK SURVEY. Published weekly.

MOODY'S INDUSTRIAL STOCK AVERAGE, DIVIDEND YIELD (PERCENT), YEARLY, HIGH-LOW (yield range during current year and each of two previous years). MOODY'S STOCK SURVEY. Published weekly.

Moody's industrial stock average, dividends, growth rate.

SEE: Moody's industrial stock average, growth rates. . .

MOODY'S INDUSTRIAL STOCK AVERAGE, DIVIDENDS, MONTHLY (dividend dollar average per share as of end of each of last 13 or 14 months). MOODY'S STOCK SURVEY. This data normally appears in second issue of each month.

MOODY'S INDUSTRIAL STOCK AVERAGE, DIVIDENDS, WEEKLY (dividend dollar average per share for each of last five weeks). MOODY'S STOCK SURVEY. Published weekly.

MOODY'S INDUSTRIAL STOCK AVERAGE, DIVIDENDS, YEARLY (dividend dollar average per share as of close of each of two previous years). MOODY'S STOCK SURVEY. Published weekly.

MOODY'S INDUSTRIAL STOCK AVERAGE, DIVIDENDS, YEARLY, CHART (dividend dollar average per share charted on annual rate basis for about 40 years). MOODY'S HANDBOOK OF COMMON STOCKS. Published quarterly.

Moody's industrial stock average, earnings per share, growth rate.

SEE: Moody's industrial stock average, growth rates. . .

MOODY'S INDUSTRIAL STOCK AVERAGE, EARNINGS PER SHARE, QUARTER-LY (for each of nine previous quarters). MOODY'S STOCK SURVEY. This data normally appears in second issue of each month.

MOODY'S INDUSTRIAL STOCK AVERAGE, EARNINGS PER SHARE, QUARTER-LY, CHART (earnings average per share is charted quarterly on annual rate basis for about 40 years). MOODY'S HANDBOOK OF COMMON STOCKS. Published quarterly.

MOODY'S INDUSTRIAL STOCK AVERAGE, EARNINGS PER SHARE, YEARLY (estimated figure for current year and actual figure for each of two previous years). MOODY'S STOCK SURVEY. This data normally appears in second issue of each month.

MOODY'S INDUSTRIAL STOCK AVERAGE, GROWTH RATES (separate, "compound five-year" growth rates in percent for the Average's revenues, earnings, dividends, and prices. Labeled "Explanation of Tables"). MOODY'S STOCK SURVEY. Published weekly.

MOODY'S INDUSTRIAL STOCK AVERAGE, NAMES OF STOCKS COMPRISING (125 stocks are listed). MOODY'S HANDBOOK OF COMMON STOCKS. Published quarterly.

Moody's industrial stock average, percentage change in price.

SEE: Moody's industrial stock average, price, monthly-yearly, close, percentage change. . .

Moody's industrial stock average, price, growth rate.

SEE: Moody's industrial stock average, growth rates. . .

MOODY'S INDUSTRIAL STOCK AVERAGE, PRICE, MONTHLY, CHART (a simple line chart representing Moody's industrial stock average is fitted onto each of over 1,000 charts for major common stocks. In most cases, time span is around 20 years). MOODY'S HANDBOOK OF COMMON STOCKS. Published quarterly.

MOODY'S INDUSTRIAL STOCK AVERAGE, PRICE, MONTHLY, CLOSE (for end of each of last 13 or 14 months). MOODY'S STOCK SURVEY. This data normally appears in second issue of each month.

MOODY'S INDUSTRIAL STOCK AVERAGE, PRICE, MONTHLY, CLOSE, CHART (end-of-month price charted for about 40 years). MOODY'S HANDBOOK OF COMMON STOCKS. Published quarterly.

MOODY'S INDUSTRIAL STOCK AVERAGE, PRICE, MONTHLY-YEARLY, CLOSE, PERCENTAGE CHANGE (month-end to month-end percentage change in price for each of last three months, and for latest month compared with same month one year earlier. Labeled "Industry Groups: Market Movements"). MOODY'S

STOCK SURVEY. This data normally appears in second issue of each month.

Moody's industrial stock average, price, percentage change.

    SEE: Moody's industrial stock average, price, monthly-yearly, close, percentage change. . .

MOODY'S INDUSTRIAL STOCK AVERAGE, PRICE, WEEKLY, CLOSE (for end of each of last five weeks). MOODY'S STOCK SURVEY. Published weekly.

MOODY'S INDUSTRIAL STOCK AVERAGE, PRICE, YEARLY, HIGH-LOW (price range for current year and each of two previous years). MOODY'S STOCK SURVEY. Published weekly.

MOODY'S INDUSTRIAL STOCK AVERAGE, PRICE-EARNINGS RATIO, MONTHLY (for end of each of last 13 or 14 months). MOODY'S STOCK SURVEY. This data normally appears in second issue of each month.

MOODY'S INDUSTRIAL STOCK AVERAGE, PRICE-EARNINGS RATIO, WEEKLY (for end of each of last five weeks). MOODY'S STOCK SURVEY. Published weekly.

MOODY'S INDUSTRIAL STOCK AVERAGE, PRICE-EARNINGS RATIO, YEARLY, HIGH-LOW (range of price-earnings ratio during each of two previous years). MOODY'S STOCK SURVEY. Published weekly. (Note: the same data for each of three previous years appears in second issue of each month.)

MOODY'S INDUSTRY GROUP STOCK AVERAGES, PRICES, CHARTS (simple line charts representing appropriate selections from about 55 industry group stock price averages are fitted onto most of over 1,000 price charts for major common stocks. In most cases, time span is about 20 years). MOODY'S HANDBOOK OF COMMON STOCKS. Published quarterly.

MOODY'S INDUSTRY GROUP STOCK AVERAGES, PRICES, MONTHLY-YEARLY, CLOSE, PERCENTAGE CHANGES (month-end to month-end "percentage changes in market prices" for each of about 55 industry groups, for each of last three months, and for latest month compared with same month one year earlier. Labeled "Industry Groups: Market Movements"). MOODY'S STOCK SURVEY. This data normally appears in second issue of each month.

Moody's insurance stock average.

    SEE: Moody's fire insurance stock average. . .

Moody's medium grade preferred stock averages.

    SEE: Moody's preferred stock averages. . .

MOODY'S MUNICIPAL BOND AVERAGES, YIELDS (PERCENT), MONTHLY (average yield for each of "Composite" municipal Aaa, Aa, A, and Baa groups, and for "Ten-Year State" Aaa and Aa groups, for each of last two months). MOODY'S BOND SURVEY. Published weekly.

MOODY'S MUNICIPAL BOND AVERAGES, YIELDS (PERCENT), WEEKLY

(average yield for each of "Composite" municipal Aaa, Aa, A, and Baa groups, and for "Ten-Year State" Aaa and Aa groups, for each of last four weeks). MOODY'S BOND SURVEY. Published weekly.

MOODY'S MUNICIPAL BOND AVERAGES, YIELDS (PERCENT), YEAR TO DATE, HIGH-LOW (yield range for current year for each of "Composite" municipal Aaa, Aa, A, and Baa groups, and for "Ten-Year State" Aaa and Aa groups). MOODY'S BOND SURVEY. Published weekly.

MOODY'S NEW YORK BANK STOCK AVERAGE, DIVIDEND YIELD (PERCENT), MONTHLY (yield at end of each of last 13 or 14 months). MOODY'S STOCK SURVEY. This data normally appears in second issue of each month.

MOODY'S NEW YORK BANK STOCK AVERAGE, DIVIDENDS, MONTHLY (dividend dollar average per share as of end of each of last 13 or 14 months). MOODY'S STOCK SURVEY. This data normally appears in second issue of each month.

MOODY'S NEW YORK BANK STOCK AVERAGE, EARNINGS PER SHARE, YEARLY (annual figure for each of two previous years). MOODY'S STOCK SURVEY. This data normally appears in second issue of each month.

MOODY'S NEW YORK BANK STOCK AVERAGE, PRICE, MONTHLY, CLOSE (for end of each of last 13 or 14 months). MOODY'S STOCK SURVEY. This data normally appears in second issue of each month.

MOODY'S NEW YORK BANK STOCK AVERAGE, PRICE-EARNINGS RATIO, MONTHLY (for end of each of last 13 or 14 months). MOODY'S STOCK SURVEY. This data normally appears in second issue of each month.

MOODY'S NEW YORK BANK STOCK AVERAGE, PRICE-EARNINGS RATIO, YEARLY, HIGH-LOW (range for each of previous three years). MOODY'S STOCK SURVEY. This data normally appears in second issue of each month.

MOODY'S PREFERRED STOCK AVERAGES, DIVIDEND YIELDS (PERCENT), WEEKLY (separate figures for high grade industrial preferreds, medium grade industrial preferreds, high grade utility preferreds, and medium grade utility perferreds, for each of last five weeks. Labeled "Moody's Yield Averages"). MOODY'S STOCK SURVEY. This data normally appears in second issue of each month.

MOODY'S PREFERRED STOCK AVERAGES, DIVIDEND YIELDS (PERCENT), YEARLY, HIGH-LOW (yield ranges for current year and each of two previous years. Separate figures for high grade industrial preferreds, medium

Moody's public utility.

    SEE: Moody's utility. . .

INVESTMENT INFORMATION

MOODY'S RAILROAD BOND AVERAGE, PRICE, WEEKLY-MONTHLY-YEARLY (average price for latest week, previous week, month ago, and same week one year ago). COMMERCIAL AND FINANCIAL CHRONICLE. Thursday edition.

MOODY'S RAILROAD BOND AVERAGE, YIELD (PERCENT), WEEKLY-MONTH-LY-YEARLY (average yield for latest week, previous week, month ago, and same week one year ago). COMMERCIAL AND FINANCIAL CHRONICLE. Thursday edition.

MOODY'S RAILROAD BOND AVERAGES, YIELDS (PERCENT), DAILY (yield based on closing price for each of previous five days. Separate yields for Aa, A, Baa, and combined railroads). MOODY'S BOND SURVEY. Published weekly.

MOODY'S RAILROAD BOND AVERAGES, YIELDS (PERCENT), YEARLY, HIGH-LOW (yield ranges for current year and one year previous shown separately for Aa, A, Baa, and combined railroads). MOODY'S BOND SURVEY. Published weekly.

MOODY'S RAILROAD STOCK AVERAGE, DIVIDEND YIELD (PERCENT), MONTH-LY (yield for end of each of last 13 or 14 months). MOODY'S STOCK SURVEY. This data normally appears in second issue of each month.

MOODY'S RAILROAD STOCK AVERAGE, DIVIDEND YIELD (PERCENT), WEEK-LY (yield for end of each of last five weeks). MOODY'S STOCK SURVEY. Published weekly.

MOODY'S RAILROAD STOCK AVERAGE, DIVIDEND YIELD (PERCENT), YEAR-LY, HIGH-LOW (range of yield during current year and each of two previous years). MOODY'S STOCK SURVEY. Published weekly.

MOODY'S RAILROAD STOCK AVERAGE, DIVIDENDS, MONTHLY (dividend dollar average per share as of end of each of last 13 or 14 months). MOODY'S STOCK SURVEY. This data appears normally in second issue of each month.

MOODY'S RAILROAD STOCK AVERAGE, DIVIDENDS, WEEKLY (dividend dollar average per share for each of last five weeks). MOODY'S STOCK SUR-VEY. Published weekly.

MOODY'S RAILROAD STOCK AVERAGE, DIVIDENDS, YEARLY (dividend dollar average per share, as of end of two previous years). MOODY'S STOCK SUR-VEY. Published weekly.

MOODY'S RAILROAD STOCK AVERAGE, DIVIDENDS, YEARLY, CHART (dividend average per share is charted on annual rate basis for about 40 years). MOODY'S HANDBOOK OF COMMON STOCKS. Published quarterly.

MOODY'S RAILROAD STOCK AVERAGE, EARNINGS PER SHARE, QUARTERLY (for each of nine previous quarters). MOODY'S STOCK SURVEY. This data normally appears in second issue of each month.

MOODY'S RAILROAD STOCK AVERAGE, EARNINGS PER SHARE, QUARTERLY,

CHART (earnings average per share is charted quarterly on annual rate basis for about 40 years). MOODY'S HANDBOOK OF COMMON STOCKS. Published quarterly.

MOODY'S RAILROAD STOCK AVERAGE, EARNINGS PER SHARE, YEARLY (estimated figure for current year and actual figure for each of two previous years). MOODY'S STOCK SURVEY. This data normally appears in second issue of each month.

MOODY'S RAILROAD STOCK AVERAGE, NAMES OF STOCKS COMPRISING (24 stocks are listed). MOODY'S HANDBOOK OF COMMON STOCKS. Published quarterly.

MOODY'S RAILROAD STOCK AVERAGE, PRICE, MONTHLY, CLOSE (for end of each of last 13 or 14 months). MOODY'S STOCK SURVEY. This data normally appears in second issue of each month.

MOODY'S RAILROAD STOCK AVERAGE, PRICE, MONTHLY, CLOSE, CHART (end-of-month prices charted for about 40 years). MOODY'S HANDBOOK OF COMMON STOCKS. Published quarterly.

MOODY'S RAILROAD STOCK AVERAGE, PRICE, WEEKLY, CLOSE (for end of each of last five weeks). MOODY'S STOCK SURVEY. Published weekly.

MOODY'S RAILROAD STOCK AVERAGE, PRICE, YEARLY, HIGH-LOW (price range for current year and each of two previous years). MOODY'S STOCK SURVEY. Published weekly.

MOODY'S RAILROAD STOCK AVERAGE, PRICE-EARNINGS RATIO, MONTHLY (for end of each of last 13 or 14 months). MOODY'S STOCK SURVEY. This data normally appears in second issue of each month.

MOODY'S RAILROAD STOCK AVERAGE, PRICE-EARNINGS RATIO, WEEKLY (for end of each of last five weeks). MOODY'S STOCK SURVEY. Published weekly.

MOODY'S RAILROAD STOCK AVERAGE, PRICE-EARNINGS RATIO, YEARLY, HIGH-LOW (range of price-earnings ratio during each of two previous years. MOODY'S STOCK SURVEY. Published weekly. (Note: the same data for each of previous three years normally appears in second issue of each month).

Moody's state bond averages (ten-year).

    SEE: Moody's municipal bond averages. . .

Moody's stock group averages.

    SEE: Moody's industry group stock averages. . .

MOODY'S TREASURY BILL AVERAGES, YIELDS (PERCENT), MONTHLY (average yields for 91-day and 182-day bills for each of previous two months). MOODY'S BOND SURVEY. Published weekly.

MOODY'S TREASURY BILL AVERAGES, YIELDS (PERCENT), WEEKLY (average yields for 91-day and 182-day bills for each of previous four weeks). MOODY'S BOND SURVEY. Published weekly.

MOODY'S TREASURY BILL AVERAGES, YIELDS (PERCENT), YEAR TO DATE, HIGH-LOW (range of yields for 91-day and 182-day bills for current year). MOODY'S BOND SURVEY. Published weekly.

MOODY'S UTILITY BOND AVERAGE, COMBINED, PRICE, WEEKLY-MONTH-LY-YEARLY (daily average price for latest week, previous week, month ago, and same week one year ago). COMMERCIAL AND FINANCIAL CHRONICLE. Thursday edition.

MOODY'S UTILITY BOND AVERAGE, COMBINED, YIELD (PERCENT), WEEK-LY-MONTHLY-YEARLY (average yield for latest week, previous week, month ago, and same week one year ago). COMMERCIAL AND FINANCIAL CHRON-ICLE. Thursday edition.

MOODY'S UTILITY BOND AVERAGES, YIELDS (PERCENT), DAILY (yield averages based on closing prices for each of previous five days. Separate yields for Aaa, Aa, A, Baa, and combined utilities). MOODY'S BOND SURVEY. Published weekly.

MOODY'S UTILITY BOND AVERAGES, YIELDS (PERCENT), YEARLY, HIGH-LOW (yield ranges for current year and one year previous shown separately for Aaa, Aa, A, Baa, and combined utilities). MOODY'S BOND SURVEY. Published weekly.

Moody's utility preferred stock averages.

SEE: Moody's preferred stock averages. . .

MOODY'S UTILITY STOCK AVERAGE, DIVIDEND YIELD (PERCENT), MONTH-LY (yield at end of each of last 13 or 14 months). MOODY'S STOCK SURVEY. This data normally appears in second issue of each month.

MOODY'S UTILITY STOCK AVERAGE, DIVIDEND YIELD (PERCENT), WEEKLY (yield at end of each of last five weeks). MOODY'S STOCK SURVEY. Published weekly.

MOODY'S UTILITY STOCK AVERAGE, DIVIDEND YIELD (PERCENT), YEARLY, HIGH-LOW (range of yield during current year and each of previous two years). MOODY'S STOCK SURVEY. Published weekly.

MOODY'S UTILITY STOCK AVERAGE, DIVIDENDS, MONTHLY (dividend dollar average per share as of end of each of last 13 or 14 months). MOODY'S STOCK SURVEY. This data normally appears in second issue of each month.

MOODY'S UTILITY STOCK AVERAGE, DIVIDENDS, WEEKLY (dividend dollar average per share for each of last five weeks). MOODY'S STOCK SURVEY. Published weekly.

MOODY'S UTILITY STOCK AVERAGE, DIVIDENDS, YEARLY (dividend dollar

CHART (earnings average per share is charted quarterly on annual rate basis for about 40 years). MOODY'S HANDBOOK OF COMMON STOCKS. Published quarterly.

MOODY'S RAILROAD STOCK AVERAGE, EARNINGS PER SHARE, YEARLY (estimated figure for current year and actual figure for each of two previous years). MOODY'S STOCK SURVEY. This data normally appears in second issue of each month.

MOODY'S RAILROAD STOCK AVERAGE, NAMES OF STOCKS COMPRISING (24 stocks are listed). MOODY'S HANDBOOK OF COMMON STOCKS. Published quarterly.

MOODY'S RAILROAD STOCK AVERAGE, PRICE, MONTHLY, CLOSE (for end of each of last 13 or 14 months). MOODY'S STOCK SURVEY. This data normally appears in second issue of each month.

MOODY'S RAILROAD STOCK AVERAGE, PRICE, MONTHLY, CLOSE, CHART (end-of-month prices charted for about 40 years). MOODY'S HANDBOOK OF COMMON STOCKS. Published quarterly.

MOODY'S RAILROAD STOCK AVERAGE, PRICE, WEEKLY, CLOSE (for end of each of last five weeks). MOODY'S STOCK SURVEY. Published weekly.

MOODY'S RAILROAD STOCK AVERAGE, PRICE, YEARLY, HIGH-LOW (price range for current year and each of two previous years). MOODY'S STOCK SURVEY. Published weekly.

MOODY'S RAILROAD STOCK AVERAGE, PRICE-EARNINGS RATIO, MONTHLY (for end of each of last 13 or 14 months). MOODY'S STOCK SURVEY. This data normally appears in second issue of each month.

MOODY'S RAILROAD STOCK AVERAGE, PRICE-EARNINGS RATIO, WEEKLY (for end of each of last five weeks). MOODY'S STOCK SURVEY. Published weekly.

MOODY'S RAILROAD STOCK AVERAGE, PRICE-EARNINGS RATIO, YEARLY, HIGH-LOW (range of price-earnings ratio during each of two previous years. MOODY'S STOCK SURVEY. Published weekly. (Note: the same data for each of previous three years normally appears in second issue of each month).

Moody's state bond averages (ten-year).

    SEE: Moody's municipal bond averages. . .

Moody's stock group averages.

    SEE: Moody's industry group stock averages. . .

MOODY'S TREASURY BILL AVERAGES, YIELDS (PERCENT), MONTHLY (average yields for 91-day and 182-day bills for each of previous two months). MOODY'S BOND SURVEY. Published weekly.

MOODY'S TREASURY BILL AVERAGES, YIELDS (PERCENT), WEEKLY (average
yields for 91-day and 182-day bills for each of previous four weeks). MOODY'S
BOND SURVEY. Published weekly.

MOODY'S TREASURY BILL AVERAGES, YIELDS (PERCENT), YEAR TO DATE,
HIGH-LOW (range of yields for 91-day and 182-day bills for current year).
MOODY'S BOND SURVEY. Published weekly.

MOODY'S UTILITY BOND AVERAGE, COMBINED, PRICE, WEEKLY-MONTH-
LY-YEARLY (daily average price for latest week, previous week, month ago,
and same week one year ago). COMMERCIAL AND FINANCIAL CHRONICLE.
Thursday edition.

MOODY'S UTILITY BOND AVERAGE, COMBINED, YIELD (PERCENT), WEEK-
LY-MONTHLY-YEARLY (average yield for latest week, previous week, month
ago, and same week one year ago). COMMERCIAL AND FINANCIAL CHRON-
ICLE. Thursday edition.

MOODY'S UTILITY BOND AVERAGES, YIELDS (PERCENT), DAILY (yield averages based on closing prices for each of previous five days. Separate yields
for Aaa, Aa, A, Baa, and combined utilities). MOODY'S BOND SURVEY.
Published weekly.

MOODY'S UTILITY BOND AVERAGES, YIELDS (PERCENT), YEARLY, HIGH-
LOW (yield ranges for current year and one year previous shown separately for
Aaa, Aa, A, Baa, and combined utilities). MOODY'S BOND SURVEY. Pub-
lished weekly.

Moody's utility preferred stock averages.
    SEE: Moody's preferred stock averages. . .

MOODY'S UTILITY STOCK AVERAGE, DIVIDEND YIELD (PERCENT), MONTH-
LY (yield at end of each of last 13 or 14 months). MOODY'S STOCK SURVEY.
This data normally appears in second issue of each month.

MOODY'S UTILITY STOCK AVERAGE, DIVIDEND YIELD (PERCENT), WEEKLY
(yield at end of each of last five weeks). MOODY'S STOCK SURVEY. Published weekly.

MOODY'S UTILITY STOCK AVERAGE, DIVIDEND YIELD (PERCENT), YEARLY,
HIGH-LOW (range of yield during current year and each of previous two years).
MOODY'S STOCK SURVEY. Published weekly.

MOODY'S UTILITY STOCK AVERAGE, DIVIDENDS, MONTHLY (dividend dollar
average per share as of end of each of last 13 or 14 months). MOODY'S
STOCK SURVEY. This data normally appears in second issue of each month.

MOODY'S UTILITY STOCK AVERAGE, DIVIDENDS, WEEKLY (dividend dollar
average per share for each of last five weeks). MOODY'S STOCK SURVEY.
Published weekly.

MOODY'S UTILITY STOCK AVERAGE, DIVIDENDS, YEARLY (dividend dollar average per share as of end of each of two previous years). MOODY'S STOCK SURVEY. Published weekly.

MOODY'S UTILITY STOCK AVERAGE, DIVIDENDS, YEARLY, CHART (dividend average per share is charted on annual rate basis for about 40 years). MOODY'S HANDBOOK OF COMMON STOCKS. Published quarterly.

MOODY'S UTILITY STOCK AVERAGE, EARNINGS PER SHARE, QUARTERLY (for each of nine previous quarters). MOODY'S STOCK SURVEY. This data normally appears in second issue of each month.

MOODY'S UTILITY STOCK AVERAGE, EARNINGS PER SHARE, QUARTERLY, CHART (earnings average per share is charted quarterly on annual rate basis for about 40 years). MOODY'S HANDBOOK OF COMMON STOCKS. Published quarterly.

MOODY'S UTILITY STOCK AVERAGE, EARNINGS PER SHARE, YEARLY (esti-mated figure for current year and actual figure for each of two previous years). MOODY'S STOCK SURVEY. This data normally appears in second issue of each month.

MOODY'S UTILITY STOCK AVERAGE, NAMES OF STOCKS COMPRISING (24 stocks are listed). MOODY'S HANDBOOK OF COMMON STOCKS. Pub-lished quarterly.

MOODY'S UTILITY STOCK AVERAGE, PRICE, MONTHLY, CLOSE (for end of each of last 13 or 14 months). MOODY'S STOCK SURVEY. This data normal-ly appears in second issue of each month.

MOODY'S UTILITY STOCK AVERAGE, PRICE, MONTHLY, CLOSE, CHART (end-of-month price charted for about 40 years). MOODY'S HANDBOOK OF COMMON STOCKS. Published quarterly.

MOODY'S UTILITY STOCK AVERAGE, PRICE, WEEKLY, CLOSE (for end of each of last five weeks). MOODY'S STOCK SURVEY. Published weekly.

MOODY'S UTILITY STOCK AVERAGE, PRICE, YEARLY, HIGH-LOW (price range for current year and each of two previous years). MOODY'S STOCK SURVEY. Published weekly.

MOODY'S UTILITY STOCK AVERAGE, PRICE-EARNINGS RATIO, MONTHLY (for end of each of last 14 months). MOODY'S STOCK SURVEY. This data appears in second issue of each month.

MOODY'S UTILITY STOCK AVERAGE, PRICE-EARNINGS RATIO, WEEKLY (for end of each of last five weeks). MOODY'S STOCK SURVEY. Published weekly.

MOODY'S UTILITY STOCK AVERAGE, PRICE-EARNINGS RATIO, YEARLY, HIGH-LOW (range of price-earnings ratio during each of two previous years). MOODY'S STOCK SURVEY. Published weekly. (Note: the same information for each of previous three years appears in second issue of each month.)

Mortgage totals, real estate companies.

SEE: Real estate companies, mortgage and debt totals. . .

Mortgage totals, savings and loan companies.

SEE: Savings and loan companies, loan totals. . .

Most active ratio.

SEE: Most active stocks, New York Stock Exchange, ratio of volume (percentage) to total volume. . .

Most active stocks.

SEE ALSO: High volume stocks. . .

MOST ACTIVE STOCKS, AMERICAN STOCK EXCHANGE, LIST OF, DAILY (five most active stocks, with closing price and volume for each, for previous day). NEW YORK TIMES. Published weekdays.

MOST ACTIVE STOCKS, AMERICAN STOCK EXCHANGE, LIST OF, DAILY (ten most active stocks, with closing price and volume for each, for previous day). WALL STREET JOURNAL. Published business days.

MOST ACTIVE STOCKS, AMERICAN STOCK EXCHANGE, LIST OF, WEEKLY (ten most active stocks during week just past, with high-low-close prices and volume for each). BARRON'S. Published weekly.

MOST ACTIVE STOCKS, AMERICAN STOCK EXCHANGE, LIST OF, WEEKLY (five most active stocks during week just past, with closing price and volume for each). NEW YORK TIMES. Sunday edition.

Most active stocks, average price.

SEE: Most active stocks, New York Stock Exchange, average closing price. . .

MOST ACTIVE STOCKS, NEW YORK STOCK EXCHANGE, AVERAGE CLOS-ING PRICE, DAILY (average closing price of ten most active stocks, for each day of week just past). BARRON'S. Published weekly.

MOST ACTIVE STOCKS, NEW YORK STOCK EXCHANGE, AVERAGE CLOS-ING PRICE, DAILY (average closing price of ten most active stocks, for previous day). WALL STREET JOURNAL. Published business days.

MOST ACTIVE STOCKS, NEW YORK STOCK EXCHANGE, AVERAGE CLOS-ING PRICE, WEEKLY-YEARLY (average of closing prices of 20 stocks most active during week just past, week before that, and same week one year ago). BARRON'S. Published weekly.

MOST ACTIVE STOCKS, NEW YORK STOCK EXCHANGE, LIST OF, DAILY (15 most active stocks, with closing price and volume for each, for previous day). NEW YORK TIMES. Published weekdays.

MOST ACTIVE STOCKS, NEW YORK STOCK EXCHANGE, LIST OF, DAILY (ten most active stocks, with price range and volume for each, for previous day). WALL STREET JOURNAL. Published business days.

MOST ACTIVE STOCKS, NEW YORK STOCK EXCHANGE, LIST OF, WEEKLY (20 most active stocks during week just past, with high-low-close prices and volume for each). BARRON'S. Published weekly.

MOST ACTIVE STOCKS, NEW YORK STOCK EXCHANGE, LIST OF WEEKLY (15 most active stocks during week just past, with closing price and volume for each). NEW YORK TIMES. Sunday edition.

MOST ACTIVE STOCKS, NEW YORK STOCK EXCHANGE, RATIO OF VOLUME (PERCENT) TO TOTAL VOLUME, DAILY (for ten most active stocks combined, for each day of week just past). BARRON'S. Published weekly.

MOST ACTIVE STOCKS, NEW YORK STOCK EXCHANGE, RATIO OF VOLUME (PERCENT) TO TOTAL VOLUME, WEEKLY-YEARLY (for 20 most active stocks combined, for week just past, week before that, and same week one year ago). BARRON'S. Published weekly.

Moving average, stock prices.

> SEE: Stock prices, moving average. . .

Moving average ratio.

> SEE: Over 200-day moving average ratio. . .

Municipal bond average.

> SEE: Moody's municipal bond averages. . .
> Standard & Poor's municipal bond index. . .

Municipal bonds.

> SEE ALSO: Public authority bonds. . .
> Toll revenue bonds. . .

MUNICIPAL BONDS, CANADIAN, LIST OF (about 35 bonds are listed, with quality ratings). STANDARD & POOR'S EARNINGS AND RATINGS BOND GUIDE. Published monthly.

MUNICIPAL BONDS, "LARGER ISSUES SCHEDULED FOR SALE" (new, large issues of municipal bonds to be sold within next couple of weeks are listed by day and hour of offering. Issuing body, total amount, and years of maturity are given for each issue). COMMERCIAL AND FINANCIAL CHRONICLE. Thursday edition.

MUNICIPAL BONDS, LIST OF (about 7,000 municipal bonds are arranged geographically by state, with listings for each state arranged according to whether bonds are direct obligations, general obligations, or revenue bonds. Quality ratings are indicated, but not prices). STANDARD & POOR'S EARNINGS AND RATINGS BOND GUIDE. Published monthly.

Municipal bonds, new issues.

    SEE: New issues, municipal bonds. . .

MUNICIPAL BONDS, PRICES, MONTHLY, CLOSE (end-of-month, bid-asked prices for about 350 U.S. and Canadian "State and Municipal Bonds"). BANK AND QUOTATION RECORD. Published monthly.

Municipal bonds, ratings.

    SEE: Rating changes, municipal bonds. . .
             Ratings, municipal bonds. . .

MUNICIPAL BONDS, YIELD AVERAGE (PERCENT), MONTHLY, CHART (small chart shows "Monthly Average of Twenty 20-Year Bonds," over a period of about three years). WALL STREET JOURNAL. This chart normally appears in Monday edition.

MUNICIPAL BONDS, YIELD AVERAGE (PERCENT), WEEKLY, CHART (small chart shows weekly average of twenty 20-year bonds, over a period of about six months). WALL STREET JOURNAL. This chart normally appears in Monday edition.

MUTUAL FUND AVERAGES (percentage change for year to date and for week just past is shown for each of the following mutual fund price averages: all funds, growth funds, growth and income, balanced, income, and bank & insurance. Same percentage changes also shown for each of the following "Unmanaged Portfolios": Dow-Jones industrial stock average, Standard & Poor's industrial stock index, Standard & Poor's composite stock index, and American Stock Exchange price level index. Labeled "Mutual Fund Performance Index"). BARRON'S. Published weekly.

Mutual fund holdings.

    SEE: Institutional holdings. . .
             Investment company transactions. . .

MUTUAL FUND INDUSTRY TOTALS, QUARTERLY-YEARLY (quarterly and annual totals given over last five years for gross sales, redemptions, net sales, net assets, and percentage ratio of redemptions to net assets, for all mutual funds combined). COMMERCIAL AND FINANCIAL CHRONICLE. This data normally appears in Thursday edition around the 20th of February, May, August, and November.

Mutual fund redemptions.

    SEE: Mutual fund industry totals. . .

Mutual fund transactions.

    SEE: Investment company transactions. . .

Mutual funds.

    SEE ALSO: Exchange funds. . .

Investment companies. . .
Mutual fund averages. . .
Mutual fund industry totals. . .

MUTUAL FUNDS, ASSET TOTALS (NET), CURRENT (for each of about 300 funds, as of recent date). STANDARD & POOR'S SECURITY OWNER'S STOCK GUIDE. Published monthly.

MUTUAL FUNDS, ASSET TOTALS (NET), QUARTERLY-YEARLY (for each of about 200 funds, for end of latest quarter, and for end of corresponding quarter for each of last ten years). BARRON'S. This data normally appears around the beginning of February, May, August, and November.

MUTUAL FUNDS, ASSET TOTALS (NET), YEARLY (for end of each of past eleven years, for each of largest funds). MOODY'S HANDBOOK OF COM-MON STOCKS. Published quarterly.

Mutual funds, asset value per share (net).

SEE ALSO: Mutual funds, prices. . .

MUTUAL FUNDS, ASSET VALUE PER SHARE (NET), QUARTERLY (for end of current year's quarters and each of quarters for three previous years, for each of largest funds). MOODY'S HANDBOOK OF COMMON STOCKS. Publish-ed quarterly.

MUTUAL FUNDS, ASSET VALUE PER SHARE (NET), YEARLY (for end of each of past eleven years, for each of largest funds). MOODY'S HANDBOOK OF COMMON STOCKS. Published quarterly.

MUTUAL FUNDS, ASSET VALUE PER SHARE (NET), YEARLY, PERCENTAGE CHANGE (year end to year end percentage changes for each of about 300 funds, for each of last five years). STANDARD & POOR'S SECURITY OWN-ER'S STOCK GUIDE. Published monthly.

Mutual funds, averages.

SEE: Mutual fund averages. . .

MUTUAL FUNDS, BONDS AND PREFERRED STOCKS AS PERCENTAGE OF AS-SETS, QUARTERLY (for each of about 75 major funds, for end of latest and previous quarters. Total average percentages also given). COMMERCIAL AND FINANCIAL CHRONICLE. This data normally appears in Thursday edition around the 20th of February, May, August, and November.

MUTUAL FUNDS, CANADIAN (yearly net asset value and dividends from in-vestment income for each of about seven Canadian funds, for each of last ten years). BARRON'S. This data normally appears around the first of February, May, August, and November.

Mutual funds, capital gains distributions.

SEE: Mutual funds, dividends from capital gains. . .

MUTUAL FUNDS, CASH ASSET TOTALS (NET), CURRENT (for each of about 300 funds, as of recent date). STANDARD & POOR'S SECURITY OWNER'S STOCK GUIDE. Published monthly.

MUTUAL FUNDS, CASH ASSET TOTALS (NET), QUARTERLY (for each of about 75 major funds, for end of latest and previous quarters. Totals for combined funds also given). COMMERCIAL AND FINANCIAL CHRONICLE. This data normally appears in Thursday edition around the 20th of February, May, August, and November.

MUTUAL FUNDS, CASH ASSET TOTALS (NET), YEARLY (for each of past eleven years, for each of largest funds). MOODY'S HANDBOOK OF COMMON STOCKS. Published quarterly.

MUTUAL FUNDS, CASH ASSETS AS PERCENTAGE OF TOTAL ASSETS, QUARTERLY (for each of about 75 major funds, for end of latest and previous quarters. Total average percentages also given). COMMERCIAL AND FINANCIAL CHRONICLE. This data normally appears in Thursday edition around the 20th of February, May, August, and November.

MUTUAL FUNDS, CASH POSITION TOTAL (PERCENT), MONTHLY-YEARLY ("Month-end cash position as percent of total net assets." This is a total figure, not for individual funds. Labeled "Mutual Fund Liquidity", and quoted for latest month, previous month, and same month one year ago. BARRON'S. This data normally appears in first issue of each month.

Mutual funds, changes in holdings.

SEE: Investment company transactions. . .

Mutual funds, commission charge.

SEE: Mutual funds, sales charge. . .

MUTUAL FUNDS, COMMON STOCK TRANSACTIONS, DOLLAR VALUE, QUARTERLY (for each of about 75 major funds, for end of latest and previous quarters, totals are shown for purchases and sales. Grand totals for combined funds are also given). COMMERCIAL AND FINANCIAL CHRONICLE. This data normally appears in Thursday edition around the 20th of February, May, August, and November.

MUTUAL FUNDS, COMMON STOCKS AS PERCENTAGE OF ASSETS, QUARTERLY (for each of about 75 major funds, for end of latest and previous quarters. Total average percentages also given). COMMERCIAL AND FINANCIAL CHRONICLE. This data normally appears in Thursday edition around the 20th of February, May, August, and November.

Mutual funds, dates of founding.

SEE: Founding dates, mutual funds. . .

MUTUAL FUNDS, DIVIDEND YIELDS (PERCENT) FROM INVESTMENT INCOME,

MONTHLY (as of end of month prior to month of publication, for each of about 300 funds). STANDARD & POOR'S SECURITY OWNER'S STOCK GUIDE. Published monthly.

MUTUAL FUNDS, DIVIDENDS FROM CAPITAL GAINS, YEARLY (per share payment during latest 12 month period, for each of about 300 funds). STANDARD & POOR'S SECURITY OWNER'S STOCK GUIDE. Published monthly.

MUTUAL FUNDS, DIVIDENDS FROM CAPITAL GAINS, YEARLY (per share payment during latest 12 month period, for each of about 200 mutual funds. For each fund, for each of past ten years, per share payment is also shown for corresponding period). BARRON'S. This data normally appears around the beginning of February, May, August, and November.

MUTUAL FUNDS, DIVIDENDS FROM CAPITAL GAINS, YEARLY (per share payments for each of past eleven years, for each of largest funds). MOODY'S HANDBOOK OF COMMON STOCKS. Published quarterly.

MUTUAL FUNDS, DIVIDENDS FROM CAPITAL GAINS, YEARLY (per share payments for current year and one year previous, for each of about 300 funds). STANDARD & POOR'S SECURITY OWNER'S STOCK GUIDE. Published monthly.

MUTUAL FUNDS, DIVIDENDS FROM INVESTMENT INCOME, YEARLY (per share payment during latest 12 month period, for each of about 300 funds). BARRON'S. Published weekly.

MUTUAL FUNDS, DIVIDENDS FROM INVESTMENT INCOME, YEARLY (per share payment during latest 12 month period, for each of about 200 funds. Payment during corresponding period shown for each of past ten years, for each fund). BARRON'S. This data normally appears around the beginning of February, May, August, and November.

MUTUAL FUNDS, DIVIDENDS FROM INVESTMENT INCOME, YEARLY (per share payments for each of past eleven years, for each of largest funds). MOODY'S HANDBOOK OF COMMON STOCKS. Published quarterly.

MUTUAL FUNDS, DIVIDENDS FROM INVESTMENT INCOME, YEARLY (per share payments for current year and one year previous, for each of about 300 funds). STANDARD & POOR'S SECURITY OWNER'S STOCK GUIDE. Published monthly.

Mutual funds, foreign.

SEE: Foreign mutual funds. . .

Mutual funds, founding dates.

SEE: Founding dates, mutual funds. . .

Mutual funds, holdings.

SEE: Institutional holdings. . .
Investment company transactions. . .

Mutual funds, indexes.

    SEE: Mutual fund averages. . .

Mutual funds, initial purchase requirements.

    SEE: Mutual funds, minimum initial purchase. . .

Mutual funds, investment income per share (net).

    SEE ALSO: Mutual funds, dividends from investment income. . .

MUTUAL FUNDS, INVESTMENT INCOME PER SHARE (NET), YEARLY (for each of past eleven years, for each of largest funds). MOODY'S HANDBOOK OF COMMON STOCKS. Published quarterly.

MUTUAL FUNDS, INVESTMENT INCOME TOTAL (NET), YEARLY (for each of past eleven years, for each of largest funds). MOODY'S HANDBOOK OF COMMON STOCKS. Published quarterly.

MUTUAL FUNDS, INVESTMENTS OTHER THAN GOVERNMENT SECURITIES, VALUE OF, YEARLY (for each of past eleven years, for each of largest funds). MOODY'S HANDBOOK OF COMMON STOCKS. Published quarterly.

Mutual funds, liquidity.

    SEE: Mutual funds, cash asset totals. . .
          Mutual funds, cash position total (percent). . .

MUTUAL FUNDS, MINIMUM INITIAL PURCHASE (smallest initial purchase allowed for each of about 300 funds. Labeled "Min. Unit"). STANDARD & POOR'S SECURITY OWNER'S STOCK GUIDE. Published monthly.

Mutual funds, net asset value.

    SEE: Mutual funds, asset value per share (net). . .

Mutual funds, net total assets.

    SEE: Mutual funds, asset totals (net). . .

Mutual funds, percentage change in asset value.

    SEE: Mutual funds, asset value per share (net), yearly, percentage change. . .

Mutual funds, performance index.

    SEE: Mutual fund averages. . .

Mutual funds, portfolios.

    SEE: Institutional holdings. . .
          Investment company transactions. . .
          Mutual funds, bonds and preferred stocks. . .

Mutual funds, cash. . .
Mutual funds, common stocks. . .

Mutual funds, prices.

SEE ALSO: Mutual funds, asset value per share (net). . .

MUTUAL FUNDS, PRICES, DAILY (bid and asked prices for previous day for each of about 300 funds, with former bid). NEW YORK TIMES. Published weekdays.

MUTUAL FUNDS, PRICES, DAILY (bid and asked prices for previous day for each of about 300 funds, with net change in bid). WALL STREET JOURNAL. Published business days.

MUTUAL FUNDS, PRICES, MONTHLY, CLOSE (tabulation of over-the-counter "Investing Companies Stocks and Bonds" includes mutual funds. Bid and asked prices quoted for end of month prior to month of publication). BANK AND QUOTATION RECORD. Published monthly.

MUTUAL FUNDS, PRICES, MONTHLY, CLOSE (net asset value per share and asked price per share for each of about 300 funds, for a day near end of month prior to month of publication). STANDARD & POOR'S SECURITY OWNER'S STOCK GUIDE. Published monthly.

MUTUAL FUNDS, PRICES, WEEKLY, CLOSE (bid and asked prices for end of week just past for each of about 300 mutual funds. Latest 12 month payments from income and capital gain also shown). BARRON'S. Published weekly.

MUTUAL FUNDS, PRICES, WEEKLY, CLOSE (bid and asked prices for end of week just past are given for each of about 300 mutual funds). COMMERCIAL AND FINANCIAL CHRONICLE. Monday edition.

MUTUAL FUNDS, PRICES, WEEKLY, HIGH-LOW-CLOSE (bid prices for each of about 300 funds, for week just past). NEW YORK TIMES. Sunday edition.

MUTUAL FUNDS, PRICES, YEAR TO DATE, HIGH-LOW (range of bid prices for current year for each of about 300 mutual funds. Same as net asset value per share--labeled "Price Record NAV Per Sh"). STANDARD & POOR'S SE-CURITY OWNER'S STOCK GUIDE. Published monthly.

MUTUAL FUNDS, PRICES, YEARLY (FIVE YEAR PERIOD), HIGH-LOW (range of bid prices over total five year period, for each of about 300 funds. Same as net asset value per share--labeled "Price Record NAV Per Sh"). STANDARD & POOR'S SECURITY OWNER'S STOCK GUIDE. Published monthly.

Mutual funds, purchase requirements, initial.

SEE: Mutual funds, minimum initial purchase. . .

Mutual funds, redemptions.

SEE: Mutual fund industry totals. . .

MUTUAL FUNDS, SALES CHARGE (maximum percentage sales charge for each of about 300 mutual funds). STANDARD & POOR'S SECURITY OWNER'S STOCK GUIDE. Published monthly.

Mutual funds, sales totals.

SEE: Mutual fund industry totals. . .

Mutual funds, total assets.

SEE: Mutual funds, asset totals. . .

Mutual funds, transactions.

SEE: Investment company transactions. . .

Mutual funds, year of formation.

SEE: Founding dates, mutual funds. . .

Mutual funds, yields.

SEE: Mutual funds, dividend yields (percent) from
investment income. . .

NAME CHANGES, STOCKS (both old and new names are shown for listed and unlisted companies recently having name changes). BARRON'S. Published weekly.

NAME CHANGES, STOCKS (recent name changes are included with price information for roughly 26,000 corporations). NATIONAL MONTHLY STOCK SUMMARY. Published monthly.

NAME CHANGES, STOCKS (both old and new names are shown for listed and unlisted companies recently having name changes). STANDARD & POOR'S SECURITY OWNER'S STOCK GUIDE. Published monthly.

NAME CHANGES, STOCKS, NEW YORK STOCK EXCHANGE (all name changes for "big board" companies are included with price information extending over a 24 year period). COMMERCIAL AND FINANCIAL CHRONICLE. This information is included in special "Stock and Bond Outlook Supplement," normally published on an annual basis as part of Thursday edition, in the latter part of each year.

Names of stocks making up various averages.

See names of the averages, such as "Dow-Jones industrial stock average, names of stocks comprising. . ." or "Standard & Poor's industrial 425 stock index, names of stocks comprising. . ."

NATIONAL QUOTATION BUREAU OVER-THE-COUNTER INDUSTRIAL STOCK AVERAGE, PRICE, DAILY, CLOSE (for each day of week just past). BARRON'S. Published weekly.

NATIONAL QUOTATION BUREAU OVER-THE-COUNTER INDUSTRIAL STOCK AVERAGE, PRICE, DAILY, CLOSE (for each day of week just past). COMMERCIAL AND FINANCIAL CHRONICLE. Monday edition.

NATIONAL QUOTATION BUREAU OVER-THE-COUNTER INDUSTRIAL STOCK AVERAGE, PRICE, DAILY-YEARLY, CLOSE (closing price for previous day and same day one year ago). WALL STREET JOURNAL. Published business days.

NATIONAL QUOTATION BUREAU OVER-THE-COUNTER INSURANCE STOCK AVERAGE, PRICE, DAILY, CLOSE (for each day of week just past). BARRON'S. Published weekly.

NATIONAL QUOTATION BUREAU OVER-THE-COUNTER INSURANCE STOCK AVERAGE, PRICE, DAILY, CLOSE (for each day of week just past). COMMERCIAL AND FINANCIAL CHRONICLE. Monday edition.

National Stock Exchange.
> SEE: Stock prices on National Stock Exchange. . .
> Volume of trading in stocks, individual stocks on
> National Stock Exchange. . .
> Volume of trading in stocks, total for National
> Stock Exchange. . .

Net asset value per share.
> SEE: Closed-end investment companies, asset value per
> share. . .
> Mutual funds, asset value per share. . .

NET INCOME, DAILY LIST (short summaries each day for individual companies having new earnings reports. Includes sales--corporate revenue--and net income for latest period and same period one year ago. Labeled "Other Company Reports"). NEW YORK TIMES. Published weekdays.

NET INCOME, DAILY LIST (short summaries each day for individual companies having new earnings reports. Includes sales--corporate revenue--and net income for latest period and same period one year ago. Labeled "Digest of Earnings Reports"). WALL STREET JOURNAL. Published business days.

NET INCOME, YEARLY (for each of past eleven years, for each of over 1,000 companies having actively traded common stock). MOODY'S HANDBOOK OF COMMON STOCKS. Published quarterly.

NET PLANT, YEARLY (amounts for each of past 18 or so years, for each of about 1,400 leading companies. Net plant is net value of plant and equipment). VALUE LINE INVESTMENT SURVEY. Part three: published weekly, a few industries each week.

Net sales.
> SEE: Sales (corporate revenue). . .

Netherlands stocks.
> SEE: Foreign stock price indexes. . .
> Stock prices on Amsterdam Stock Exchange. . .

New exchange listings.

SEE: New listings. . .

New highs, stock groups.

SEE: Barron's group stock averages, prices, new highs. . .

New highs and new lows.

SEE ALSO: Stock prices, dates of highs and lows. . .

NEW HIGHS AND NEW LOWS, BOND PRICES ON AMERICAN STOCK EX-CHANGES, NUMBER OF, DAILY (number of issues reaching new highs for current year and number reaching new lows, on each of last four trading days). WALL STREET JOURNAL. Published business days.

NEW HIGHS AND NEW LOWS, BOND PRICES ON NEW YORK STOCK EX-CHANGE, NUMBER OF, DAILY (total number of issues reaching new highs for current year and number reaching new lows, on each of last three trading days). NEW YORK TIMES. Published weekdays.

NEW HIGHS AND NEW LOWS, BOND PRICES ON NEW YORK STOCK EX-CHANGE, NUMBER OF, DAILY (number of issues reaching new highs for current year and number reaching new lows, on each of last two trading days, in each of three following categories: foreign, domestic, all issues). WALL STREET JOURNAL. Published business days.

NEW HIGHS AND NEW LOWS, STOCK PRICES ON AMERICAN STOCK EX-CHANGE, LIST OF, WEEKLY (list of stocks reaching new highs for the year during past week and list of stocks reaching new lows). BARRON'S. Published weekly.

NEW HIGHS AND NEW LOWS, STOCK PRICES ON AMERICAN STOCK EX-CHANGE, NUMBER OF, DAILY (number of issues reaching new highs for current year and number reaching new lows, on each day of week just past). BARRON'S. Published weekly.

NEW HIGHS AND NEW LOWS, STOCK PRICES ON AMERICAN STOCK EX-CHANGE, NUMBER OF, DAILY (number of issues reaching new highs for current year and number reaching new lows, on each of last two trading days. Labeled "The Summary"). NEW YORK TIMES. Published weekdays.

NEW HIGHS AND NEW LOWS, STOCK PRICES ON AMERICAN STOCK EX-CHANGE, NUMBER OF, DAILY (number of issues reaching new highs for current year and number reaching new lows, on each of last six trading days). WALL STREET JOURNAL. Published business days.

NEW HIGHS AND NEW LOWS, STOCK PRICES ON AMERICAN STOCK EX-CHANGE, NUMBER OF, WEEKLY (number of issues reaching new highs for the year during past week and number of issues reaching new lows). BARRON'S. Published weekly.

NEW HIGHS AND NEW LOWS, STOCK PRICES ON AMERICAN STOCK EX-CHANGE, NUMBER OF, WEEKLY (number of issues reaching new highs for the year during each of the past two weeks and number of issues reaching new lows. Labeled "Market Breadth"). NEW YORK TIMES. Sunday edition.

NEW HIGHS AND NEW LOWS, STOCK PRICES ON NEW YORK STOCK EX-CHANGE, LIST OF, DAILY (list of stocks reaching new highs for current year and list of those reaching new lows, for previous trading day). NEW YORK TIMES. Published weekdays.

NEW HIGHS AND NEW LOWS, STOCK PRICES ON NEW YORK STOCK EX-CHANGE, LIST OF, DAILY (list of stocks reaching new highs for current year and list of those reaching new lows, for previous trading day). WALL STREET JOURNAL. Published business days.

NEW HIGHS AND NEW LOWS, STOCK PRICES ON NEW YORK STOCK EX-CHANGE, LIST OF, WEEKLY (list of stocks reaching new highs for the year during past week and list of stocks reaching new lows). BARRON'S. Published weekly.

NEW HIGHS AND NEW LOWS, STOCK PRICES ON NEW YORK STOCK EX-CHANGE, MOVING AVERAGES, CHART (ten day moving averages of number of new highs and new lows are charted on daily basis for about six months. Labeled "High-Low Index"). TRENDLINE DAILY BASIS STOCK CHARTS. Published weekly.

NEW HIGHS AND NEW LOWS, STOCK PRICES ON NEW YORK STOCK EX-CHANGE, MOVING AVERAGES, CHART (ten week moving average of number of new highs and new lows are charted on weekly basis for about six years. Labeled "High-Low Index"). TRENDLINE'S CURRENT MARKET PERSPECTIVES. Published monthly.

NEW HIGHS AND NEW LOWS, STOCK PRICES ON NEW YORK STOCK EX-CHANGE, NUMBER OF, DAILY (number of issues reaching new highs for current year and number reaching new lows, on each day of week just past). BARRON'S. Published weekly.

NEW HIGHS AND NEW LOWS, STOCK PRICES ON NEW YORK STOCK EX-CHANGE, NUMBER OF, DAILY (number of issues reaching new highs for current year and number reaching new lows, on each of last two trading days. Labeled "Market Summary"). NEW YORK TIMES. Published weekdays.

NEW HIGHS AND NEW LOWS, STOCK PRICES ON NEW YORK STOCK EX-CHANGE, NUMBER OF, DAILY (number of issues reaching new highs for current year and number reaching new lows, on each of last six trading days. Labeled "Market Diary"). WALL STREET JOURNAL. Published business days.

NEW HIGHS AND NEW LOWS, STOCK PRICES ON NEW YORK STOCK EX-CHANGE, NUMBER OF, WEEKLY (number of issues reaching new highs for current year and number reaching new lows, during past week). BARRON'S. Published weekly.

NEW HIGHS AND NEW LOWS, STOCK PRICES ON NEW YORK STOCK EX-CHANGE, NUMBER OF, WEEKLY (number of issues reaching new highs for current year and number reaching new lows, during each of last two weeks. Labeled "Market Breadth"). NEW YORK TIMES. Sunday edition.

"New Issue Calendar."

    SEE: New issues, corporate offerings, probable. . .

New issues, bonds.

    SEE ALSO: New issues, convertible bonds. . .
               New issues, municipal bonds. . .

NEW ISSUES, BONDS, LIST OF, MONTHLY ("New Issues Registered with SEC," including amounts, preliminary Standard & Poor's quality ratings, and dates of filing). STANDARD & POOR'S EARNINGS AND RATINGS BOND GUIDE. Published monthly.

NEW ISSUES, BONDS, LIST OF, WEEKLY ("Recent Taxable-Bond Offerings," including offering date, amount, call price, offering price, yield on offering price, recent price, yield on recent price, and Moody's rating, for individual issues). MOODY'S BOND SURVEY. Published weekly.

NEW ISSUES, BONDS, LIST OF PROSPECTIVE OFFERINGS, WEEKLY (new bonds are listed according to offering date, up to a couple of months or so in advance. Amount is given in each case, and quality rating where available. Labeled "New Issues Calendar"). BOND OUTLOOK. Published weekly.

NEW ISSUES, BONDS, LIST OF PROSPECTIVE OFFERINGS, WEEKLY (new bonds are listed according to offering date, up to a couple of months or so in advance. Amount and type of underwriting given in each case, with quality rating where available. Labeled "Prospective Taxable-Bond Offerings"). MOODY'S BOND SURVEY. Published weekly.

New issues, bonds, municipal.

    SEE: New issues, municipal bonds. . .

NEW ISSUES, BONDS, PRICES, DAILY (current asked price, original offering price, and yield for each of "Recent Issues". Divided into "Straight Debt" and "Convertibles"). NEW YORK TIMES. Published weekdays.

NEW ISSUES, BONDS, PRICES, DAILY (current bid-asked and original offering price for each of "recent issues of senior securities that are not listed on a principal exchange." Divided into "Straight Debt" and "Convertibles" under heading "Prices of Recent Issues"). WALL STREET JOURNAL. Published business days.

NEW ISSUES, BONDS, PRICES, WEEKLY, CLOSE (bid and asked prices are shown for end of week just past for each of "Recent Security Bond Issues"). COMMERCIAL AND FINANCIAL CHRONICLE. Monday edition.

New issues, bonds, tax-exempt.

    SEE: New issues, municipal bonds. . .

NEW ISSUES, BONDS, TOTAL VALUE OF, WEEKLY-YEARLY (total dollar value of new bond offerings for latest week, previous week, and same week one year ago). BARRON'S. Published weekly.

NEW ISSUES, BONDS, YIELDS (PERCENT), DAILY (yield for each of "recent issues of senior securities that are not listed on a principal exchange." Labeled

"Prices of Recent Issues"). WALL STREET JOURNAL. Published business days.

NEW ISSUES, BONDS, YIELDS (PERCENT), MONTHLY (yield average for latest month for each of newly issued industrial and utility bond groups, by Aaa, Aa, A, and Baa ratings. Yields on bonds formerly distributed given for comparison. Labeled "Yields on Corporate Bonds, Newly Issued versus Distributed" or "Yields on Public Utility Bonds, Newly Issued versus Distributed"). MOODY'S BOND SURVEY. This data normally appears in first or second issue of each month.

NEW ISSUES, CONVERTIBLE BONDS, MONTHLY LIST ("New Convertible Issues Registered with SEC," including amounts, preliminary Standard & Poor's quality ratings, and dates of filing). STANDARD & POOR'S EARNINGS AND RATINGS BOND GUIDE. Published monthly. This information also appears in monthly supplement to BOND OUTLOOK, second week of each month.

NEW ISSUES, CONVERTIBLE BONDS, PRICES, DAILY (current bid and asked prices for individual "Convertibles" under 'Recent Issues" label). NEW YORK TIMES. Published weekdays.

NEW ISSUES, CONVERTIBLE BONDS, PRICES, DAILY (current bid-asked and original offering prices for each of "recent issues of senior securities that are not listed on a principal exchange." Divided into "Straight Debt" and "Convertibles" under label "Prices of Recent Issues"). WALL STREET JOURNAL. Published business days.

NEW ISSUES, CONVERTIBLE BONDS, LIST OF, WEEKLY (list of "New Convertible Offerings," with amount, interest rate, and conversion price per share in each case). BARRON'S. Published weekly.

New issues, corporate offerings, probable.

    SEE ALSO: New issues, bonds, list of prospective offerings. . .

NEW ISSUES, CORPORATE OFFERINGS, PROBABLE ("Week's Probable Corporate Offerings" are individually listed, with number of shares or dollar amount, probable day of offering, and principal underwriter). BARRON'S. Published weekly.

NEW ISSUES, CORPORATE OFFERINGS, PROBABLE (new issues are listed by date of expected offering, up to six months or so in advance. Number of shares or dollar amount given in each case, plus name of underwriter. Labeled "New Issue Calendar"). COMMERCIAL AND FINANCIAL CHRONICLE. Thursday edition.

New issues, dates of expected offerings.

    SEE: New issues, corporate offerings, probable. . .

New issues, filings.

    SEE: New issues, SEC registrations. . .

NEW ISSUES, MUNICIPAL BONDS, LIST OF, DAILY (individual, new, tax-exempt bond issues are listed, with amounts and dates. Details of recent large

"Sales" of new tax-exempt issues also given. Labeled "Tax-Exempts"). WALL STREET JOURNAL. Published business days.

NEW ISSUES, MUNICIPAL BONDS, LIST OF, WEEKLY ("This Week's Municipal Offerings," including amount, rating where available, maturities, call provisions, interest cost, syndicate, and range of offering yields, for each issue). BOND OUTLOOK. Published weekly.

NEW ISSUES, MUNICIPAL BONDS, LIST OF, WEEKLY ("New Tax-Exempt Issues Offered," including date, amount, rating where available, and yields by selected maturities, for each issue). MOODY'S BOND SURVEY. Published weekly.

NEW ISSUES, MUNICIPAL BONDS, LIST OF PROSPECTIVE OFFERINGS, WEEK-LY ("New Tax-Exempt Issues Scheduled," including date, amount, rating, population, estimated true value, and various debt figures for individual "General Obligations;" and date, amount, rating, debt, source of payment, debt service, gross revenues, and coverage for individual "Revenue Bonds"). BOND OUT-LOOK. Published weekly.

NEW ISSUES, MUNICIPAL BONDS, LIST OF PROSPECTIVE OFFERINGS, WEEK-LY (details of "Proposals and Negotiations" listed in "State and City Department"). COMMERCIAL AND FINANCIAL CHRONICLE. Monday edition.

NEW ISSUES, MUNICIPAL BONDS, LIST OF PROSPECTIVE OFFERINGS, WEEK-LY ("Prospective Tax-Exempt Bond Offerings," including scheduled date and hour, amount, Moody's rating or provisional rating, purpose, assessed valuation, and over-all debt for individual "General and Limited Liability Obligations;" and scheduled sale date and hour, amount, Moody's rating or provisional rating, purpose, security basis, revenues, and times charges earned for individual "Revenue Obligations"). MOODY'S BOND SURVEY. Published weekly.

New issues, number of.

SEE ALSO: New issues, total value of. . .

NEW ISSUES, NUMBER OF, WEEKLY-YEARLY ("Total Supply of New Issues to be Publicly Offered." Number and total dollar value for new taxable bonds, municipal bonds, and corporate stocks, for latest week, previous week, and same week one year ago). COMMERCIAL AND FINANCIAL CHRONICLE. Monday edition.

New issues, offering dates, expected.

SEE: New issues, corporate offerings, probable. . .
New issues, municipal bonds, list of prospective offerings. . .

NEW ISSUES, SEC REGISTRATIONS, COMPREHENSIVE LIST ("Securities Now in Registration" with SEC. Following information usually given: date of filing, amount, expected offering price, nature of business, expected use of proceeds, address of company, and name of underwriter). COMMERCIAL AND FINAN-CIAL CHRONICLE. Thursday edition.

NEW ISSUES, SEC REGISTRATIONS, DAILY (dollar amount or number of shares and name of underwriter for proposed major offering filed with the Securities and Exchange Commission. Labeled "SEC Registrations"). WALL STREET JOURNAL. Published business days.

NEW ISSUES, SEC REGISTRATIONS, WEEKLY ("New Offerings Filed" with Securities and Exchange Commission are individually listed, with number of shares or dollar amount). BARRON'S. Published weekly.

NEW ISSUES, SEC REGISTRATIONS, WEEKLY ("SEC Registrations" individually listed, with information as to date, price, kind of business, etc.). COMMERCIAL AND FINANCIAL CHRONICLE. Monday edition.

NEW ISSUES, SEC REGISTRATIONS, WEEKLY ("Issues Filed With SEC This Week" are individually listed, with information regarding date, price, nature of business, etc.). COMMERCIAL AND FINANCIAL CHRONICLE. Thursday edition.

NEW ISSUES, SEC REGISTRATIONS, WEEKLY (selected new issues filed with Securities and Exchange Commission during past week are listed in paragraph form, with number of shares in each case). NEW YORK TIMES. This information appears in Saturday edition.

NEW ISSUES, SEC REGISTRATIONS (EFFECTIVE), WEEKLY (list of companies whose registration statements were "declared effective this week by the SEC." Amount, date, price, and underwriter are given in each case. COMMERCIAL AND FINANCIAL CHRONICLE. Thursday edition.

NEW ISSUES, STOCKS, ORIGINAL OFFERINGS (dates and amounts of new issues since 1933 are given for many of roughly 26,000 unlisted and listed corporations. Offerings may have been "New," "Additional," "Block Issue," or "Secondary"). NATIONAL MONTHLY STOCK SUMMARY. This data appears in semiannual cumulative volumes, dated April 1 and October 1.

NEW ISSUES, STOCKS, PRICES, WEEKLY (offering price and recent bid price given for stock of individual companies going public within past eight months or so. Date of offering also indicated in each case). COMMERCIAL AND FINANCIAL CHRONICLE. Thursday edition.

NEW ISSUES, STOCKS, PRICES, WEEKLY (offering price and end of week bid and asked prices for each of selected, initial public offerings made during past week). NEW YORK TIMES. This information appears in Saturday edition.

New issues, stocks, probable offering dates.

SEE: New issues, corporate offerings, probable. . .

NEW ISSUES, STOCKS, TOTAL VALUE OF, WEEKLY-YEARLY (total dollar value of new stock offerings for latest week, previous week, and same week one year ago). BARRON'S. Published weekly.

New issues, tax-exempt.

SEE: New issues, municipal bonds. . .

NEW ISSUES, TOTAL VALUE OF, WEEKLY-YEARLY ("Total Supply of New Issues to be Publicly Offered." Number and total dollar value for new taxable bonds, municipal bonds, and corporate stocks, for latest week, previous week, and same week one year ago). COMMERCIAL AND FINANCIAL CHRONICLE. Monday edition.

New issues, value of, total.
SEE: New issues, stocks, total value of. . .
New issues, total value of. . .

NEW LISTINGS, BONDS, WEEKLY (names of bonds newly listed on American and New York Stock Exchange. Weekly and yearly price ranges and weekly volume are given in each case). COMMERCIAL AND FINANCIAL CHRONICLE. Monday edition.

NEW LISTINGS, STOCKS, MONTHLY (names of stocks newly listed on American, New York, and other exchanges). STANDARD & POOR'S SECURITY OWNER'S STOCK GUIDE. Published monthly.

NEW LISTINGS, STOCKS, WEEKLY (names of stocks newly listed on American and New York Stock Exchanges). BARRON'S. Published weekly.

NEW LISTINGS, STOCKS, WEEKLY (names of stocks newly listed on American and New York Stock Exchanges. Current year's price range, weekly price range for week just past, and week's volume are given in each case). COMMERCIAL AND FINANCIAL CHRONICLE. Monday edition.

NEW LISTINGS, STOCKS (PENDING), MONTHLY (names of stocks for which listings on major exchanges are pending). STANDARD & POOR'S SECURITY OWNER'S STOCK GUIDE. Published monthly.

NEW LISTINGS, STOCKS (PENDING), WEEKLY (names of stocks for which listings on American and New York Stock Exchanges are pending. Labeled "Applied for Listing"). BARRON'S. Published weekly.

New lows.
SEE: New highs and new lows. . .

New names, stocks.
SEE: Name changes, stocks. . .

New ratings.
SEE: Rating changes. . .

New York bank stock average, Moody's.
SEE: Moody's New York bank stock average. . .

New York bank stock average, Standard & Poor's.

SEE: Standard & Poor's stock group indexes. . .

NEW YORK CITY BONDS, LISTED, PRICES AND VOLUME (price range for current year, daily prices, and daily sales volume). NEW YORK TIMES. Published weekdays.

NEW YORK CITY BONDS, LISTED, PRICES AND VOLUME (price range for current year, weekly prices, and weekly sales volume). NEW YORK TIMES. Sunday edition.

NEW YORK CITY BONDS, LISTED, PRICES AND VOLUME (price range for current year, daily prices, and daily sales volume). WALL STREET JOURNAL. Published business days.

NEW YORK CITY BONDS, OVER-THE-COUNTER, PRICES, DAILY (bid and asked prices for previous day, with former bid). NEW YORK TIMES. Published weekdays.

NEW YORK CITY BONDS, OVER-THE-COUNTER, PRICES, WEEKLY, HIGH-LOW-CLOSE (range and closing of bid prices, for week just past). NEW YORK TIMES. Sunday edition.

New York Stock Exchange.

SEE: Advances and declines, bond prices on New York
        Stock Exchange. . .
     Advances and declines, stock prices on New York
        Stock Exchange. . .
     Bond prices on New York Stock Exchange. . .
     Call loan rates (percent), New York Stock
        Exchange. . .
     Commission rates, major stock exchanges. . .
     Dividends, amount, current, New York Stock
        Exchange. . .
     Dividends, amount, indicated annual rate, New
        York Stock Exchange. . .
     Earnings per share, interim, New York Stock
        Exchange. . .
     Exchange seats on New York Stock Exchange,
        price. . .
     Floor trader's volume, New York Stock
        Exchange. . .
     Issues traded, bonds on New York Stock
        Exchange. . .
     Issues traded, stocks on New York Stock
        Exchange. . .
     Large block transactions. . .
     Market value total of all shares listed. . .
     Market value total of share sales on New York
        Stock Exchange. . .
     Member trading, New York Stock Exchange. . .
     Most active stocks, New York Stock Exchange. . .
     Name changes, stocks, New York Stock
        Exchange. . .

New highs and new lows, bond prices on New York
Stock Exchange. . .
New highs and new lows, stock prices on New York
Stock Exchange. . .
New listings, stocks. . .
New York Stock Exchange composite stock
index. . .
New York Stock Exchange financial stock
index. . .
New York Stock Exchange industrial stock
index. . .
New York Stock Exchange transportation stock
index. . .
New York Stock Exchange utility stock index. . .
Odd-lot short sales, total for New York Stock
Exchange. . .
Odd-lot volume of trading in stocks, total for
New York Stock Exchange. . .
Short interest, individual stocks on New York Stock
Exchange. . .
Short interest, total for New York Stock
Exchange. . .
Short sales, total for New York Stock Exchange. . .
Specialists' trading, New York Stock Exchange. . .
Stock prices on New York Stock Exchange. . .
Stock splits, New York Stock Exchange. . .
Ticker symbols. . .
Upside-downside volume, New York Stock
Exchange. . .
Volume of trading in bonds, individual bonds on
New York Stock Exchange. . .
Volume of trading in bonds, total for New York
Stock Exchange. . .
Volume of trading in stocks, individual stocks on
New York Stock Exchange. . .
Volume of trading in stocks, total for New York
Stock Exchange. . .

New York Stock Exchange composite stock index, percentage change.

SEE: New York Stock Exchange composite stock index,
price, weekly, percentage change. . .
New York Stock Exchange composite stock index,
price, year to date, percentage change. . .

NEW YORK STOCK EXCHANGE COMPOSITE STOCK INDEX, PRICE, DAILY,
CLOSE (closing price for each day of month prior to month of publication).
BANK AND QUOTATION RECORD. Published monthly.

NEW YORK STOCK EXCHANGE COMPOSITE STOCK INDEX, PRICE, DAILY, CLOSE (closing price for each day of week just past). BARRON'S. Published weekly.

NEW YORK STOCK EXCHANGE COMPOSITE STOCK INDEX, PRICE, DAILY, HIGH-LOW-CLOSE (for each day of week just past). COMMERCIAL AND FINANCIAL CHRONICLE. Monday edition.

NEW YORK STOCK EXCHANGE COMPOSITE STOCK INDEX, PRICE, DAILY, HIGH-LOW-CLOSE (for previous trading day). NEW YORK TIMES. Published weekdays.

NEW YORK STOCK EXCHANGE COMPOSITE STOCK INDEX, PRICE, DAILY-YEARLY, CLOSE (closing price for previous day and same day one year ago). WALL STREET JOURNAL. Published business days.

NEW YORK STOCK EXCHANGE COMPOSITE STOCK INDEX, PRICE, MONTH-LY, HIGH-LOW (price range for month prior to month of publication). BANK AND QUOTATION RECORD. Published monthly.

NEW YORK STOCK EXCHANGE COMPOSITE STOCK INDEX, PRICE, MONTH-LY, HIGH-LOW, CHART (monthly price range charted for about 30 years). MOODY'S HANDBOOK OF COMMON STOCKS. Published quarterly.

NEW YORK STOCK EXCHANGE COMPOSITE STOCK INDEX, PRICE, MONTH-LY AVERAGE (average of daily closing prices for month prior to month of publication). BANK AND QUOTATION RECORD. Published monthly.

NEW YORK STOCK EXCHANGE COMPOSITE STOCK INDEX, PRICE, WEEK-LY, HIGH-LOW, CHART (weekly price range charted for about two years). MOODY'S HANDBOOK OF COMMON STOCKS. Published quarterly.

NEW YORK STOCK EXCHANGE COMPOSITE STOCK INDEX, PRICE, WEEKLY, HIGH-LOW-CLOSE (for week just past, with dates of high and low for week). NEW YORK TIMES. Sunday edition.

NEW YORK STOCK EXCHANGE COMPOSITE STOCK INDEX, PRICE, WEEKLY, PERCENTAGE CHANGE (for end of week just past. Included with data labeled "Mutual Fund Investment Performance Index"). BARRON'S. Published weekly.

NEW YORK STOCK EXCHANGE COMPOSITE STOCK INDEX, PRICE, WEEKLY AVERAGE, CHART (weekly average of daily closing prices charted for about two years). TRENDLINE DAILY BASIS STOCK CHARTS. Published weekly.

NEW YORK STOCK EXCHANGE COMPOSITE STOCK INDEX, PRICE, YEAR TO DATE, PERCENTAGE CHANGE (up to end of week just past. Included with data labeled "Mutual Fund Investment Performance Index"). BARRON'S. Published weekly.

NEW YORK STOCK EXCHANGE FINANCIAL STOCK INDEX, PRICE, DAILY, CLOSE (closing price is given for each day of month prior to month of publication). BANK AND QUOTATION RECORD. Published monthly.

NEW YORK STOCK EXCHANGE FINANCIAL STOCK INDEX, PRICE, DAILY, CLOSE (for each day of week just past). BARRON'S. Published weekly.

NEW YORK STOCK EXCHANGE FINANCIAL STOCK INDEX, PRICE, DAILY, HIGH-LOW-CLOSE (for each day of week just past). COMMERCIAL AND FINANCIAL CHRONICLE. Monday edition.

NEW YORK STOCK EXCHANGE FINANCIAL STOCK INDEX, PRICE, DAILY, HIGH-LOW-CLOSE (for previous trading day). NEW YORK TIMES. Published weekdays.

NEW YORK STOCK EXCHANGE FINANCIAL STOCK INDEX, PRICE, DAILY-YEARLY, CLOSE (closing price for previous day and same day one year ago). WALL STREET JOURNAL. Published business days.

NEW YORK STOCK EXCHANGE FINANCIAL STOCK INDEX, PRICE, MONTH-LY, HIGH-LOW (price range for month prior to month of publication). BANK AND QUOTATION RECORD. Published monthly.

NEW YORK STOCK EXCHANGE FINANCIAL STOCK INDEX, PRICE, MONTH-LY AVERAGE (average of daily closing prices for month prior to month of pub-lication). BANK AND QUOTATION RECORD. Published monthly.

NEW YORK STOCK EXCHANGE FINANCIAL STOCK INDEX, PRICE, WEEKLY, HIGH-LOW-CLOSE (for week just past, with dates of high and low for week). NEW YORK TIMES. Sunday edition.

NEW YORK STOCK EXCHANGE INDUSTRIAL STOCK INDEX, PRICE, DAILY, CLOSE (closing price for each day of month prior to month of publication). BANK AND QUOTATION RECORD. Published monthly.

NEW YORK STOCK EXCHANGE INDUSTRIAL STOCK INDEX, PRICE, DAILY, CLOSE (closing price for each day of week just past). BARRON'S. Published weekly.

NEW YORK STOCK EXCHANGE INDUSTRIAL STOCK INDEX, PRICE, DAILY, HIGH-LOW-CLOSE (for each day of week just past). COMMERCIAL AND FI-NANCIAL CHRONICLE. Monday edition.

NEW YORK STOCK EXCHANGE INDUSTRIAL STOCK INDEX, PRICE, DAILY, HIGH-LOW-CLOSE (for previous trading day). NEW YORK TIMES. Published weekdays.

NEW YORK STOCK EXCHANGE INDUSTRIAL STOCK INDEX, PRICE, DAILY-YEARLY, CLOSE (closing price for previous trading day and same day one year ago). WALL STREET JOURNAL. Published business days.

NEW YORK STOCK EXCHANGE INDUSTRIAL STOCK INDEX, PRICE, MONTH-LY, HIGH-LOW (price range for month prior to month of publication). BANK AND QUOTATION RECORD. Published monthly.

NEW YORK STOCK EXCHANGE INDUSTRIAL STOCK INDEX, PRICE, MONTH-LY AVERAGE (average of daily closing prices for month prior to month of publication). BANK AND QUOTATION RECORD. Published monthly.

NEW YORK STOCK EXCHANGE INDUSTRIAL STOCK INDEX, PRICE, WEEK-LY, HIGH-LOW-CLOSE (for week just past, with dates of high and low for week). NEW YORK TIMES. Sunday edition.

New York Stock Exchange public utility index.

    SEE: New York Stock Exchange utility stock index. . .

NEW YORK STOCK EXCHANGE TRANSPORTATION STOCK INDEX, PRICE, DAILY, CLOSE (closing price for each day of month prior to month of publication). BANK AND QUOTATION RECORD. Published monthly.

NEW YORK STOCK EXCHANGE TRANSPORTATION STOCK INDEX, PRICE, DAILY, CLOSE (closing price for each day of week just past). BARRON'S. Published weekly.

NEW YORK STOCK EXCHANGE TRANSPORTATION STOCK INDEX, PRICE, DAILY, HIGH-LOW-CLOSE (for each day of week just past). COMMERCIAL AND FINANCIAL CHRONICLE. Monday edition.

NEW YORK STOCK EXCHANGE TRANSPORTATION STOCK INDEX, PRICE, DAILY, HIGH-LOW-CLOSE (for previous trading day). NEW YORK TIMES. Published weekdays.

NEW YORK STOCK EXCHANGE TRANSPORTATION STOCK INDEX, PRICE, DAILY-YEARLY, CLOSE (closing price for previous day and same day one year ago). WALL STREET JOURNAL. Published business days.

NEW YORK STOCK EXCHANGE TRANSPORTATION STOCK INDEX, PRICE, MONTHLY, HIGH-LOW (price range for month prior to month of publication). BANK AND QUOTATION RECORD. Published monthly.

NEW YORK STOCK EXCHANGE TRANSPORTATION STOCK INDEX, PRICE, MONTHLY AVERAGE (average of daily closing prices for month prior to month of publication). BANK AND QUOTATION RECORD. Published monthly.

NEW YORK STOCK EXCHANGE TRANSPORTATION STOCK INDEX, PRICE, WEEKLY, HIGH-LOW-CLOSE (for week just past, with dates of high and low for week). NEW YORK TIMES. Sunday edition.

NEW YORK STOCK EXCHANGE UTILITY STOCK INDEX, PRICE, DAILY, CLOSE (for each day of month prior to month of publication). BANK AND QUOTATION RECORD. Published monthly.

NEW YORK STOCK EXCHANGE UTILITY STOCK INDEX, PRICE, DAILY, CLOSE (for each day of week just past). BARRON'S. Published weekly.

NEW YORK STOCK EXCHANGE UTILITY STOCK INDEX, PRICE, DAILY, HIGH-LOW-CLOSE (for each day of week just past). COMMERCIAL AND FINANCIAL CHRONICLE. Monday edition.

NEW YORK STOCK EXCHANGE UTILITY STOCK INDEX, PRICE, DAILY, HIGH-LOW-CLOSE (for previous trading day). NEW YORK TIMES. Published weekdays.

NEW YORK STOCK EXCHANGE UTILITY STOCK INDEX, PRICE, DAILY-YEARLY, CLOSE (closing price for previous trading day and same day one year ago). WALL STREET JOURNAL. Published business days.

NEW YORK STOCK EXCHANGE UTILITY STOCK INDEX, PRICE, MONTHLY, HIGH-LOW (price range for month prior to month of publication). BANK AND QUOTATION RECORD. Published monthly.

NEW YORK STOCK EXCHANGE UTILITY STOCK INDEX, PRICE, MONTHLY AVERAGE (average of daily closing prices for month prior to month of publication). BANK AND QUOTATION RECORD. Published monthly.

NEW YORK STOCK EXCHANGE UTILITY STOCK INDEX, PRICE, WEEKLY, HIGH-LOW-CLOSE (for week just past, with dates of high and low for week). NEW YORK STOCK EXCHANGE. Sunday edition.

New York Times combined bond average.

    SEE: New York Times composite bond average. . .

New York Times combined stock average.

    SEE: New York Times composite stock average. . .

NEW YORK TIMES COMPOSITE BOND AVERAGE, PRICE, DAILY, CLOSE (for each of seven previous trading days. Labeled "Domestic Bonds" and "Daily Range of Domestic Bonds"). NEW YORK TIMES. Published weekdays.

NEW YORK TIMES COMPOSITE BOND AVERAGE, PRICE, YEAR TO DATE, HIGH-LOW (labeled "Yearly Range of Domestic Bonds." Includes date of yearly high so far and date of low). NEW YORK TIMES. Published weekdays.

NEW YORK TIMES COMPOSITE STOCK AVERAGE, PRICE, DAILY, HIGH-LOW-CLOSE (for each of seven previous trading days. Labeled "50 stocks"). NEW YORK TIMES. Published weekdays.

NEW YORK TIMES COMPOSITE STOCK AVERAGE, PRICE, DAILY, HIGH-LOW-CLOSE, CHART (daily prices charted for about three months). NEW YORK TIMES. Published weekdays.

NEW YORK TIMES COMPOSITE STOCK AVERAGE, PRICE, MONTHLY, HIGH-LOW-CLOSE (for current month, as well as each of previous twelve months). NEW YORK TIMES. Published weekdays.

NEW YORK TIMES COMPOSITE STOCK AVERAGE, PRICE, WEEKLY, CLOSE, CHART (weekly closing prices charted for about twelve months. Labeled "12 Month Trend"). NEW YORK TIMES. Published weekdays.

NEW YORK TIMES COMPOSITE STOCK AVERAGE, PRICE, WEEKLY, HIGH-LOW-CLOSE (for week just past, with dates of high and low for week). NEW YORK TIMES. Sunday edition.

NEW YORK TIMES COMPOSITE STOCK AVERAGE, PRICE, WEEKLY, HIGH-LOW-CLOSE, CHART (weekly prices charted for about two years). NEW YORK TIMES. Sunday edition.

New York Times domestic bond average.

SEE: New York Times composite bond average. . .

New York Times 50 stock average.

SEE: New York Times composite stock average. . .

NEW YORK TIMES INDUSTRIAL BOND AVERAGE, PRICE, DAILY, CLOSE (for previous trading day). NEW YORK TIMES. Published weekdays.

NEW YORK TIMES INDUSTRIAL STOCK AVERAGE, PRICE, DAILY, HIGH-LOW-CLOSE (for each of five previous trading days). NEW YORK TIMES. Published weekdays.

NEW YORK INDUSTRIAL STOCK AVERAGE, PRICE, WEEKLY, HIGH-LOW-CLOSE (for week just past, with dates of high and low for week). NEW YORK TIMES. Sunday edition.

NEW YORK TIMES RAILROAD BOND AVERAGE, PRICE, DAILY, CLOSE (for previous trading day). NEW YORK TIMES. Published weekdays.

NEW YORK TIMES RAILROAD STOCK AVERAGE, PRICE, DAILY, HIGH-LOW-CLOSE (for each of five previous trading days). NEW YORK TIMES. Published weekdays.

NEW YORK TIMES RAILROAD STOCK AVERAGE, PRICE, WEEKLY, HIGH-LOW-CLOSE (for week just past, with dates of high and low for week). NEW YORK TIMES. Sunday edition.

NEW YORK TIMES UTILITY BOND AVERAGE, PRICE, DAILY, CLOSE (for previous trading day). NEW YORK TIMES. Published weekdays.

Notes, treasury.

SEE: Treasury notes. . .

Odd-lot activity.

SEE ALSO: Odd-lot volume of trading. . .

ODD-LOT ACTIVITY, WEEKLY, <u>CHART</u> (Trendline's seasonally adjusted "Odd-Lot Index" is charted weekly for about two years. "Normal Buying Line" equals 100). TRENDLINE DAILY BASIS STOCK CHARTS. Published weekly.

ODD-LOT ACTIVITY, WEEKLY, <u>CHART</u> (Trendline's seasonally adjusted "Odd-Lot Index" is charted weekly for about six years. "Normal Buying Line" equals 100). TRENDLINE'S CURRENT MARKET PERSPECTIVES. Published monthly.

Odd-lot commission rates.

 SEE: Commission rates, major stock exchanges. . .

Odd-lot customers' purchases and sales of individual stocks.

 SEE: Odd-lot volume of trading in stocks, individual
     stocks. . .

ODD-LOT DIFFERENTIAL CHARGES, STOCKS (explanation and amounts). STANDARD & POOR'S SECURITY OWNER'S STOCK GUIDE. Published monthly.

ODD-LOT DOLLAR VALUE OF VOLUME, TOTAL FOR NEW YORK STOCK EX-CHANGE, WEEKLY-MONTHLY-YEARLY (dollar value of odd-lot trading volume --sales and purchases separately--for latest week, previous week, month ago, and same week one year ago). COMMERCIAL AND FINANCIAL CHRONICLE. Thursday edition.

Odd-lot index.

 SEE: Odd-lot activity. . .

Odd-Lot sales.

 SEE: Odd-lot volume of trading. . .

ODD-LOT SHORT INTEREST, TOTAL FOR NEW YORK STOCK EXCHANGE, MONTHLY (number of shares short in odd-lot dealers' accounts, for middle of latest month and previous month). BARRON'S. This data appears in introduction to special short interest report, normally published about the 20th of each month.

ODD-LOT SHORT SALES, MOVING AVERAGE, <u>CHART</u> (ten-day moving average of volume of odd-lot short sales on New York Stock Exchange is charted daily for about six months). TRENDLINE DAILY BASIS STOCK CHARTS. Published weekly.

ODD-LOT SHORT SALES, MOVING AVERAGE, <u>CHART</u> (five-week moving average of volume of odd-lot short sales on New York Stock Exchange is charted weekly for about six years). TRENDLINE'S CURRENT MARKET PERSPECTIVES. Published monthly.

ODD-LOT SHORT SALES, TOTAL FOR NEW YORK STOCK EXCHANGE, DAILY (number of shares for each day of week just past). BARRON'S. Published weekly.

ODD-LOT SHORT SALES, TOTAL FOR NEW YORK STOCK EXCHANGE, DAILY (number of shares for latest available trading day). NEW YORK TIMES. Published weekdays.

ODD-LOT SHORT SALES, TOTAL FOR NEW YORK STOCK EXCHANGE, DAILY (number of shares for latest available trading day). WALL STREET JOURNAL. Published business days.

ODD-LOT SHORT SALES, TOTAL FOR NEW YORK STOCK EXCHANGE, WEEKLY-MONTHLY-YEARLY (totals in both dollars and number of shares, for latest week, previous week, month ago, and same week one year ago). COMMERCIAL AND FINANCIAL CHRONICLE. Thursday edition.

ODD-LOT SHORT SALES, TOTAL FOR NEW YORK STOCK EXCHANGE, WEEKLY-YEARLY (number of shares for latest week, previous week, and same week one year ago). BARRON'S. Published weekly.

Odd-lot volume of trading in stocks.

> SEE ALSO: Odd-lot activity. . .

Odd-lot volume of trading in stocks, dollar value.

> SEE: Odd-lot dollar value of volume. . .

ODD-LOT VOLUME OF TRADING IN STOCKS, INDIVIDUAL STOCKS ON NEW YORK STOCK EXCHANGE, WEEKLY ("Odd-Lot Customers' Purchases and Sales in 100 Selected Common Stocks," for recent week. Purchase and sales figures given separately for each stock). BARRON'S. Published weekly.

ODD-LOT VOLUME OF TRADING IN STOCKS, TOTAL FOR NEW YORK STOCK EXCHANGE, DAILY (number of shares, purchases and sales separately, for each day of week just past. Odd-lot short sales also given). BARRON'S. Published weekly.

ODD-LOT VOLUME OF TRADING IN STOCKS, TOTAL FOR NEW YORK STOCK EXCHANGE, DAILY (number of shares separately for customer purchases, short sales, other sales, and total sales, for latest available trading day). NEW YORK TIMES. Published weekdays.

ODD-LOT VOLUME OF TRADING IN STOCKS, TOTAL FOR NEW YORK STOCK EXCHANGE, DAILY (number of shares separately for customer purchases, short sales, other sales, and total sales, for latest available trading day). WALL STREET JOURNAL. Published business days.

ODD-LOT VOLUME OF TRADING IN STOCKS, TOTAL FOR NEW YORK STOCK EXCHANGE, WEEKLY-MONTHLY-YEARLY (totals in both dollars and number of shares for sales and purchases separately, for latest week, previous week, month ago, and same week one year ago. Odd-lot short sales also given). COMMERCIAL AND FINANCIAL CHRONICLE. Thursday edition.

ODD-LOT VOLUME OF TRADING IN STOCKS, TOTAL FOR NEW YORK STOCK EXCHANGE, WEEKLY-YEARLY (totals in both dollars and number of shares for sales and purchases separately, for latest week, previous week, and same week one year ago. Odd-lot short sale totals are also quoted). BARRON'S. Published weekly.

Odd-lot volume of trading in stocks, value of.

>   SEE: Odd-lot dollar value of volume. . .

Offering prices.

>   SEE: Bond prices, offering. . .
>   Foreign bonds, prices, offering. . .
>   New issues, stocks, original offerings. . .
>   New issues, stocks, prices. . .

Officer-director transactions.

>   SEE: Insider transactions. . .

OFFICERS, CORPORATE (Chairman, President, Secretary, and Treasurer are named for each of over 1,000 companies with actively traded common stock). MOODY'S HANDBOOK OF COMMON STOCKS. Published quarterly.

OFFICERS, CORPORATE (Chairman and President are named for each of about 1,400 leading corporations). VALUE LINE INVESTMENT SURVEY. Part three: published weekly, a few industries each week.

Oil companies.

>   SEE: Petroleum companies. . .

Omitted dividends.

>   SEE: Dividend omissions. . .

100% margin stocks.

>   SEE: Margin 100%. . .

Open-end investment companies.

>   SEE: Mutual funds. . .

Open market rate, federal funds.

>   SEE: Federal funds open market rate. . .

Operating profit margin.

>   SEE: Profit margin, operating. . .

Operating revenues, gross.

>   SEE: Sales (corporate revenue). . .

Options.

>   SEE: Puts and calls. . .

Original offerings (stocks).

>   SEE: New issues, stocks, original offerings. . .

Outstanding shares.

>   SEE: Shares outstanding. . .

Over-the-counter issues.

>   SEE: Bond prices, over-the-counter. . .
>   Dividends, amount, indicated annual rate,
>   over-the-counter. . .
>   Earnings per share, interim, over-the-counter. . .
>   National Quotation Bureau over-the-counter
>   industrial stock average. . .
>   National Quotation Bureau over-the-counter insurance
>   stock average. . .
>   Stock prices, over-the-counter. . .

OVER 200-DAY MOVING AVERAGE RATIO ("Daily Basis Stocks--Five Week Moving Average" charted for about two years). TRENDLINE DAILY BASIS STOCK CHARTS. Published weekly.

P-E ratio.

>   SEE: Price-earnings ratio. . .

Pacific Coast Stock Exchange.

>   SEE: Dividends, amount, indicated annual rate, Pacific
>   Coast Stock Exchange. . .
>   Earnings per share, interim, Pacific Coast Stock
>   Exchange. . .
>   Stock prices on Pacific Coast Stock Exchange. . .
>   Volume of trading in stocks, individual stocks on
>   Pacific Coast Stock Exchange. . .
>   Volume of trading in stocks, total for Pacific
>   Coast Stock Exchange. . .

Paid-in capital.

>   SEE: Capitalization stated as dollar amounts. . .

PAR VALUES, STOCK (for each of about 9,000 listed and unlisted issues). BANK AND QUOTATION RECORD. Published monthly.

PAR VALUES, STOCK (shown for each of stocks listed on New York, American, Cincinnati, Philadelphia-Baltimore-Washington, and National Stock Exchanges). COMMERCIAL AND FINANCIAL CHRONICLE. Monday edition.

PAR VALUES, STOCK (for each of about 30,000 listed and unlisted issues).
NATIONAL MONTHLY STOCK SUMMARY. Published monthly.

PAR VALUES, STOCK (for each of about 5,000 listed and unlisted issues).
STANDARD & POOR'S SECURITY OWNER'S STOCK GUIDE. Published monthly.

Paris Stock Exchange prices.

> SEE: Foreign stock price indexes. . .
> Stock prices on Paris Stock Exchange (Bourse). . .

Parity (conversion).

> SEE: Convertible bonds, conversion parity. . .

Passenger load factor (airlines).

> SEE: Airlines, passenger load factor. . .

Payment dates.

> SEE: Bond interest payment dates. . .
> Dividends, dates of payment. . .

Payout (dividends).

> SEE: Dividend payout. . .

Pending listings.

> SEE: New listings, stocks (pending). . .

PENNSYLVANIA TAX STATUS, STOCKS ("Tax Free in Penna." included where
appropriate for each of over 1,000 actively traded common stocks). MOODY'S
HANDBOOK OF COMMON STOCKS. Published quarterly.

Performance index (mutual funds).

> SEE: Mutual fund averages. . .

Personnel (corporate).

> SEE: Officers, corporate. . .

PETROLEUM COMPANIES, DRILLING AND EXPLORATION COSTS PER SHARE,
YEARLY (for each of about 50 leading petroleum companies, gives amount per
common share that is "written off in full against current earnings," for each of
about past 18 years). VALUE LINE INVESTMENT SURVEY. Part three: published weekly, a few industries each week.

Philadelphia-Baltimore-Washington Stock Exchange.

> SEE: Dividends, amount, indicated annual rate, Phila-
> delphia-Baltimore-Washington Stock
> Exchange. . .

    Earnings per share, interim, Philadelphia–
        Baltimore–Washington Stock Exchange. . .
    Stock prices on Philadelphia–Baltimore–Washington
        Stock Exchange. . .
    Volume of trading in stocks, individual stocks on
        Philadelphia–Baltimore–Washington Stock
        Exchange. . .
    Volume of trading in stocks, total for Philadelphia–
        Baltimore–Washington Stock Exchange. . .

Pittsburgh Stock Exchange.

    SEE: Dividends, amount, indicated annual rate, Pitts-
        burgh Stock Exchange. . .
        Earnings per share, interim, Pittsburgh Stock
        Exchange. . .
        Stock prices on Pittsburgh Stock Exchange. . .
        Volume of trading in stocks, individual stocks on
        Pittsburgh Stock Exchange. . .
        Volume of trading in stocks, total for Pittsburgh
        Stock Exchange. . .

Place of incorporation.

    SEE: State of incorporation. . .

Plant and equipment, net value of.

    SEE: Net Plant, yearly. . .

Plant and equipment, spending for.

    SEE: Capital spending per share. . .

Portfolio changes.

    SEE: Investment company transactions. . .

Potential purchasing power, margin.

    SEE: Margin purchasing power. . .

PREFERRED STOCK, TERMS OF (brief descriptions and recent prices of individual issues are included in main list of stocks). STANDARD & POOR'S SECURITY OWNER'S STOCK GUIDE. Published monthly.

PREFERRED STOCK, TOTAL CORPORATE DOLLAR AMOUNT OF DIVIDENDS PAYABLE ANNUALLY (for each of about 1,400 leading corporations, where applicable). VALUE LINE INVESTMENT SURVEY. Part three: published weekly, a few industries each week.

Preferred stock average, Moody's.

    SEE: Moody's preferred stock averages. . .

Preferred stock average, Standard & Poor's.

SEE: Standard & Poor's preferred stock index. . .

Preferred stock call prices.

SEE: Call prices, preferred stocks.

PREFERRED STOCK EQUITY (for each of about 1,000 corporations with actively traded common stock, shows dollar amount of total capital currently represented by preferred ·stock, if any). MOODY'S HANDBOOK OF COMMON STOCKS. Published quarterly.

PREFERRED STOCK EQUITY (for each of about 1,400 leading corporations, shows dollar amount of total capital currently represented by preferred stock, if any. Short description of each preferred stock is given). VALUE LINE INVESTMENT SURVEY. Part three: published weekly, a few industries each week.

Preferred stock prices.

SEE: Preferred stock, terms of. . .
Stock prices. . .

Preferred stock shares outstanding.

SEE: Shares outstanding, preferred stock. . .

Premium over net asset value, closed-end investment companies.

SEE: Closed-end investment companies, discount or premium relative to net asset value. . .

Premiums, insurance.

SEE: Insurance companies, premiums written. . .
Insurance companies, unearned premium totals. . .

Price, conversion.

SEE: Convertible bonds, conversion price. . .

Price-earnings ratio, Barron's 50-stock average.

SEE: Barron's 50-stock average, price-earnings ratio. . .

Price-earnings ratio, Dow-Jones stock averages.

SEE: Dow-Jones industrial stock average, price-earnings ratio. . .
Dow-Jones railroad stock average, price-earnings ratio. . .
Dow-Jones utility stock average, price-earnings ratio. . .

PRICE-EARNINGS RATIO, INDIVIDUAL STOCKS, ARBITRARY, QUARTERLY, CHARTS (arbitrary high and low price-earnings ratio lines are drawn above and below actual, weekly price ranges for most of about 960 individual stocks. Time covered is about four years). TRENDLINE'S CURRENT MARKET PER-SPECTIVES. Published monthly.

PRICE-EARNINGS RATIO, INDIVIDUAL STOCKS, CURRENT (P-E ratio shown for most of about 4,300 listed and unlisted common stocks). STANDARD & POOR'S SECURITY OWNER'S STOCK GUIDE. Published monthly.

PRICE-EARNINGS RATIO, INDIVIDUAL STOCKS, CURRENT (for each of about 1,400 leading common stocks). VALUE LINE INVESTMENT SURVEY. Part three: published weekly, a few industries each week.

PRICE-EARNINGS RATIO, INDIVIDUAL STOCKS, YEARLY AVERAGE (annual average for each of past eleven years for each of over 1,000 actively traded common stocks, and for most recent year only for over 1,200 less actively traded common stocks). MOODY'S HANDBOOK OF COMMON STOCKS. Published quarterly.

PRICE-EARNINGS RATIO, INDIVIDUAL STOCKS, YEARLY AVERAGE (annual average for each of past 18 or so years for each of about 1,400 leading common stocks. Labeled "Average Annual P/E Ratio"). VALUE LINE INVEST-MENT SURVEY. Part three: published weekly, a few industries each week.

PRICE-EARNINGS RATIO, INDIVIDUAL STOCKS, YEARLY AVERAGE--15 YEAR AVERAGE (a 15 year median price-earnings ratio is shown for each of about 1,400 leading common stocks). VALUE LINE INVESTMENT SURVEY. Part three: published weekly, a few industries each week.

Price-earnings ratio, long range average.

    SEE: Barron's 50-stock average, price-earnings ratio based on five-year average earnings. . .

Price-earnings ratio, Moody's stock averages.

    SEE: Moody's composite stock average, price-earnings ratio. . .
          Moody's industrial stock average, price-earnings ratio. . .
          Moody's New York bank stock average, price-earnings ratio. . .
          Moody's railroad stock average, price-earnings ratio. . .
          Moody's utility stock average, price-earnings ratio. . .

Price-earnings ratio, Standard & Poor's stock indexes.

    SEE: Standard & Poor's composite 500 stock index, price-earnings ratio. . .
          Standard & Poor's industrial 425 stock index, price-earnings ratio. . .
          Standard & Poor's railroad stock index, price-earnings ratio. . .
          Standard & Poor's utility stock index, price-earnings ratio. . .

Prices.

    SEE: Bond prices. . .
              Call prices. . .
              Convertible bonds, prices. . .
              Foreign bonds, prices. . .
              Government bonds, prices. . .
              Municipal bonds, prices. . .
              Mutual funds, prices. . .
              Stock prices. . .
              Stock prices, over-the-counter. . .

PRIME RATE (current percentage rate, with date that it became effective. Labeled "Money"). NEW YORK TIMES. Published weekdays.

Principal office address.

    SEE: Address of principal office. . .

Privileges expiring or changing (convertibles).

    SEE: Convertible bonds, conversion privileges, recent
                  expirations or changes. . .

Profit margin.

    SEE ALSO: Earnings rate. . .

PROFIT MARGIN, OPERATING (PERCENT), YEARLY (shown for each of past four years, for each of about 960 listed companies). TRENDLINE'S CURRENT MARKET PERSPECTIVES. Published monthly.

PROFIT MARGIN, OPERATING (PERCENT), YEARLY (for each of past eleven years, for each of about 1,000 companies having actively traded common stock). MOODY'S HANDBOOK OF COMMON STOCKS. Published quarterly.

PROFIT MARGIN, OPERATING (PERCENT), YEARLY (for each of past 18 or so years, for each of about 1,200 leading corporations). VALUE LINE INVESTMENT SURVEY. Part three: published weekly, a few industries each week.

Profits.

    SEE: Earnings. . .
              Net income. . .
              Profit margin, operating. . .

Pro-forma earnings per share.

    SEE: Diluted earnings per share. . .

Property, net.

    SEE: Funded debt to net property ratio. . .
              Net plant, yearly. . .

Prospective offerings.

> SEE: New issues. . .

Public authority bonds.

> SEE ALSO: Toll revenue bonds. . .

PUBLIC AUTHORITY BONDS, PRICES, DAILY (bid-asked prices for each of about 50 issues, for previous trading day, with former bid). NEW YORK TIMES. Published weekdays.

PUBLIC AUTHORITY BONDS, PRICES, WEEKLY, HIGH-LOW-CLOSE (range and closing of bid prices for each of about 50 issues, for week just past). NEW YORK TIMES. Sunday edition.

Public offerings.

> SEE: New issues. . .

Public utilities.

> SEE: Utilities. . .
> Utility. . .

Public utility bonds (unlisted).

> SEE: Utility bonds (unlisted). . .

Public utility preferred stock averages, Moody's.

> SEE: Moody's preferred stock averages. . .

Purchase warrants.

> SEE: Warrants. . .

Purchasing power, margin.

> SEE: Margin purchasing power. . .

PUTS AND CALLS (OPTIONS), PRICES (advertisements of put and call dealers quote prices and dates for "special" options). NEW YORK TIMES. Published weekdays. Also in Sunday edition.

PUTS AND CALLS (OPTIONS), PRICES (advertisements of put and call dealers quote prices and dates for "special" options). WALL STREET JOURNAL. Published business days.

Quality ratings.

> SEE: Ratings, bonds. . .
> Ratings, stocks. . .

Quarterly dividends.

>   SEE: Dividends, amount, quarterly. . .

Quarterly earnings.

>   SEE: Earnings per share, interim. . .

Railroad bond averages.

>   SEE: Dow-Jones railroad bond average (higher grade). . .
>   Dow-Jones railroad bond average (income bonds). . .
>   Dow-Jones railroad bond average (second grade). . .
>   Moody's railroad bond average. . .
>   New York Times railroad bond average. . .
>   Standard & Poor's railroad bond indexes. . .

Railroad bonds.

>   SEE ALSO: Railroad equipment trust certificates. . .

RAILROAD BONDS (UNLISTED), PRICES, MONTHLY, CLOSE (price for end of month prior to month of publication, for each of about 65 over-the-counter railroad bonds). BANK AND QUOTATION RECORD. Published monthly.

RAILROAD EQUIPMENT TRUST CERTIFICATES (a listing, with quality ratings). STANDARD & POOR'S EARNINGS AND RATINGS BOND GUIDE. Published monthly.

RAILROAD EQUIPMENT TRUST CERTIFICATES, PRICES (approximate bid prices are indicated for each of about 600 issues). BANK AND QUOTATION RECORD. Published monthly.

Railroad income bond average, Dow-Jones.

>   SEE: Dow-Jones railroad bond average (income bonds). . .

Railroad stock averages.

>   SEE: Dow-Jones railroad stock average. . .
>   Moody's railroad stock average. . .
>   New York Times railroad stock average. . .
>   Standard & Poor's railroad stock index. . .
>   Value Line railroad stock index. . .

RAILROAD STOCKS (UNLISTED), PRICES, MONTHLY, CLOSE (bid and asked prices for end of month prior to month of publication are given for each of about 100 over-the-counter railroad stocks, many quaranteed). BANK AND QUOTATION RECORD. Published monthly.

RAILROADS, COMMON STOCK EQUITY (PERCENT), YEARLY (for each of past 18 or so years, for each of about 30 large railroads. Refers to common stock as percentage of total capitalization. Labeled "Common Equity Ratio"). VALUE LINE INVESTMENT SURVEY. Part three: published weekly, a few industries each week.

RAILROADS, DEBT DUE IN ONE YEAR (for about 30 leading railroads, as of latest balance sheet or report). VALUE LINE INVESTMENT SURVEY. Part three: published weekly, a few industries each week.

RAILROADS, MAINTENANCE RATIO (PERCENT), YEARLY (for each of past eleven years for each of large railroads with actively traded common stock. Maintenance ratio refers to the portion of gross revenues allotted to maintenance expenses). MOODY'S HANDBOOK OF COMMON STOCKS. Published quarterly.

RAILROADS, MAINTENANCE RATIO (PERCENT), YEARLY (for each of past 18 or so years for each of about 30 large railroads). VALUE LINE INVESTMENT SURVEY. Part three: published weekly, a few industries each week.

RAILROADS, OPERATING RATIO (PERCENT), YEARLY (for each of past eleven years for each of large railroads with actively traded common stock. Operating ratio refers to the portion of gross revenues allotted to total, direct, operating expenditures). MODDY'S HANDBOOK OF COMMON STOCKS. Published quarterly.

RAILROADS, OPERATING RATIO (PERCENT), YEARLY (for each of past four years for each of about 14 major railroads). TRENDLINE'S CURRENT MARKET PERSPECTIVES. Published monthly.

RAILROADS, OPERATING RATIO (PERCENT), YEARLY (for each of past 18 or so years for each of about 30 large railroads). VALUE LINE INVESTMENT SURVEY. Part three: published weekly, a few industries each week.

RAILROADS, TRANSPORTATION RATIO (PERCENT), YEARLY (for each of past eleven years for each of large railroads with actively traded common stock. Transportation ratio refers to the portion of gross revenues spent for the actual movement of trains). MOODY'S HANDBOOK OF COMMON STOCKS. Published quarterly.

RAILROADS, TRANSPORTATION RATIO (PERCENT), YEARLY (for each of past 18 or so years for each of about 30 large railroads). VALUE LINE INVESTMENT SURVEY. Part three: published weekly, a few industries each week.

Railway equipment trust certificates.

    SEE: Railroad equipment trust certificates. . .

Rallies and declines.

    SEE: Trading swings. . .

Rankings, bond and stock.

    SEE: Ratings. . .

Rates of interest, bonds.

    SEE: Bonds, interest rates. . .

RATING CHANGES, BONDS, MONTHLY ("Changes in Bond Quality Ratings."
Old and new ratings are given for municipal and corporate issues). STANDARD
& POOR'S EARNINGS AND RATINGS BOND GUIDE. Published monthly.

RATING CHANGES, BONDS, WEEKLY ("New and Revised Ratings" for tax-
exempt as well as taxable bonds). MOODY'S BOND SURVEY. Published weekly.

RATING CHANGES, MUNICIPAL BONDS, WEEKLY ("New Municipal Ratings"
and "Municipal Rating Changes"). BOND OUTLOOK. Published weekly.

RATING CHANGES, STOCKS, MONTHLY (both "old ranking" and "new ranking" are shown). STANDARD & POOR'S SECURITY OWNER'S STOCK GUIDE.
Published monthly.

RATINGS, BONDS, STANDARD & POOR'S (letter ratings of individual corporate, municipal, and convertible bonds, based upon safety of principal and interest. About 2,600 corporate, 7,000 municipal, and 500 convertible issues are
rated). STANDARD & POOR'S EARNINGS AND RATINGS BOND GUIDE.
Published monthly.

RATINGS, CONVERTIBLE BONDS, MOODY'S (letter ratings for each of about
350 convertible issues). MOODY'S BOND SURVEY. This data appears in
special section, third week of each month.

RATINGS, MUNICIPAL BONDS, STANDARD & POOR'S (about 7,000 municipal
bonds are arranged geographically by state, with listings for each state arranged
alphabetically by city, and according to whether bonds are direct obligations,
general obligations, or revenue bonds. Quality ratings are indicated, but not
prices). STANDARD & POOR'S EARNINGS AND RATINGS BOND GUIDE.
Published monthly.

RATINGS, STOCKS, STANDARD & POOR'S (letter ratings of individual common
and preferred stock issues, based on past earnings and dividends. Roughly half
of 5,000 stocks are rated). STANDARD & POOR'S SECURITY OWNER'S STOCK
GUIDE. Published monthly.

RATINGS, STOCKS, STANDARD & POOR'S, UTILITIES (special list of "Quality
Ratings of Utility Preferred Stocks"). STANDARD & POOR'S SECURITY OWN-
ER'S STOCK GUIDE. Published monthly.

RATINGS, STOCKS, VALUE LINE (letter ratings of each of about 1,400 leading common stocks. Quality is defined as "dependability over the very long
term"). VALUE LINE INVESTMENT SURVEY. Part one, published weekly.
Also in part three: published weekly, a few industries each week.

Ratios.

    See specific subjects, such as "Price-earnings ratio. . ."
        or "Short interest ratio. . ."

REAL ESTATE COMPANIES, MORTGAGE AND DEBT TOTALS, YEARLY (for each of past 18 or so years, for each of about five leading real estate companies). VALUE LINE INVESTMENT SURVEY. Part three: published weekly, a few industries each week.

Receivables, finance companies.

SEE: Finance companies, receivables. . .

Recent issues.

SEE: New issues. . .

Record dates (dividends).

SEE: Dividends, dates of record. . .

Redemption ratio (mutual funds).

SEE: Mutual fund industry totals. . .

Redemption totals (mutual funds).

SEE: Mutual fund industry totals. . .

REDEMPTIONS, WEEKLY ("Bonds Called for Payment" -- major issues, with amount called, price, call date, and paying agent for each issue). BOND OUTLOOK. Published weekly.

REDEMPTIONS, WEEKLY (list of "Redemption Calls & Sinking Fund Notices" for corporate bonds and preferred stocks). COMMERCIAL AND FINANCIAL CHRONICLE. Monday edition.

REDEMPTIONS, WEEKLY ("Bonds Called for Redemption" -- major issues, with amount called, price, announcement date, and call date for each issue). NEW YORK TIMES. This information normally appears in Monday edition.

REDEMPTIONS (OVER-THE-COUNTER), MONTHLY ("Securities Called for Redemption" -- includes not only over-the-counter issues "being called for redemption, but also the details of any contemplated mergers, purchase or exchange offers, special interest payments or dissolutions of. . . over-the-counter issues"). BANK AND QUOTATION RECORD. Published monthly.

Reduced dividends.

SEE: Dividend decreases. . .

Refunding of bonds.

SEE: Bonds, refunding. . .
Foreign bonds, refunding. . .

Registered and exempt collateral (margin accounts).

SEE: Collateral, registered and exempt, total. . .

Registered bond form.

    SEE: Bonds, form of. . .

Registered exchanges, market value of trading.

    SEE: Market value total of share sales on all
           registered exchanges. . .

Registrars.

    SEE ALSO: Transfer agents. . .

REGISTRARS (name and city of bank serving as registrar for each of over 1,000
companies having actively traded common stock). MOODY'S HANDBOOK OF
COMMON STOCKS. Published quarterly.

Registration, securities in.

    SEE: New issues, SEC registrations. . .

Regulation of bank investments.

    SEE: Bonds, eligibility for bank investment. . .
           Comptroller of the Currency regulations. . .

Relative price performance of industries.

    SEE: Industries, price performance. . .

RETAILERS, INVENTORY TURNOVER, YEARLY (times inventory has turned over
per year (for each of about 50 leading retailers, for each of past 18 or so years).
VALUE LINE INVESTMENT SURVEY. Part three: published weekly, a few industries each week.

RETAILERS, NUMBER OF STORES, YEARLY (number of stores for each of about
50 leading retailers is shown yearly for each of about 18 or so years). VALUE
LINE INVESTMENT SURVEY. Part three: published weekly, a few industries
each week.

Revenue, gross.

    SEE: Sales (corporate revenue). . .

Revenue bonds.

    SEE: Municipal bonds. . .
           Public authority bonds. . .
           Toll revenue bonds. . .

Revenue per share.

    SEE: Sales (corporate revenue) per share. . .

Round lot commission rates.

    SEE: Commission rates, major stock exchanges. . .

SBIC's.

> SEE: Small business investment companies. . .

SEC.

> SEE: New issues, SEC registrations. . .
> Securities and Exchange Commission fee. . .

SALES (CORPORATE REVENUE), DAILY LIST (short summaries each day for in-dividual companies having new earnings reports. Includes sales or corporate revenue and total net income for latest period and same period one year ago. Labeled "Other Company Reports"). NEW YORK TIMES. Published weekdays.

SALES (CORPORATE REVENUE), DAILY LIST (short summaries each day for individual companies having new earnings reports. Includes sales or corporate revenue and total net income for latest period and same period one year ago. Labeled "Digest of Earnings Reports"). WALL STREET JOURNAL. Published business days.

SALES (CORPORATE REVENUE), QUARTERLY (sales for each quarter for about seven years, for each of about 1,400 leading corporations). VALUE LINE IN-VESTMENT SURVEY. Part three: published weekly, a few industries each week.

SALES (CORPORATE REVENUE), YEARLY (annual sales for each of past eleven years, for each of over 1,000 companies having actively traded com-mon stock, and for most recent year only for over 1,200 companies with less actively traded common stock). MOODY'S HANDBOOK OF COMMON STOCKS. Published quarterly.

SALES (CORPORATE REVENUE), YEARLY (annual sales for each of past four years, for each of about 960 listed companies). TRENDLINE'S CURRENT MARKET PERSPECTIVES. Published monthly.

SALES (CORPORATE REVENUE), YEARLY (annual sales for each of past 18 or so years, for each of about 1,400 leading companies). VALUE LINE INVEST-MENT SURVEY. Part three: published weekly, a few industries each week.

SALES (CORPORATE REVENUE) PER SHARE, YEARLY (sales per share for each of past 18 or so years, for each of over 1,200 leading industrial common stocks). VALUE LINE INVESTMENT SURVEY. Part three: published weekly, a few in-dustries each week.

Sales volume of securities.

> SEE: Volume of trading in bonds. . .
> Volume of trading in stocks. . .

Salt Lake City Stock Exchange.

> SEE: Stock prices on Salt Lake City Stock Exchange. . .

Volume of trading in stocks, individual stocks on Salt Lake City Stock Exchange. . .
Volume of trading in stocks, total for Salt Lake City Stock Exchange. . .

SAVINGS AND LOAN COMPANIES, ASSET TOTALS, YEARLY (for each of past 15 or so years, for each of about eleven leading companies). VALUE LINE INVESTMENT SURVEY. Part three: published weekly, a few industries each week.

SAVINGS AND LOAN COMPANIES, BOOK VALUE PER SHARE, YEARLY (for each of past eleven years, for each of large companies with actively traded common stock). MOODY'S HANDBOOK OF COMMON STOCKS. Published quarterly.

SAVINGS AND LOAN COMPANIES, CAPITAL FUNDS AS PERCENTAGE OF DEPOSITS, YEARLY (for each of past 15 or so years, for each of about eleven leading companies. "Capital Funds" refers to total capital from various sources). VALUE LINE INVESTMENT SURVEY. Part three: published weekly, a few industries each week.

SAVINGS AND LOAN COMPANIES, CAPITAL FUNDS AS PERCENTAGE OF MORTGAGE LOANS, YEARLY (for each of past 15 or so years, for each of about eleven leading companies). VALUE LINE INVESTMENT SURVEY. Part three: published weekly, a few industries each week.

SAVINGS AND LOAN COMPANIES, CAPITAL FUNDS TOTALS, YEARLY (for each of past 15 or so years, for each of about eleven leading companies). VALUE LINE INVESTMENT SURVEY. Part three: published weekly, a few industries each week.

Savings and loan companies, deposit totals.
SEE: Savings and loan companies, savings totals. . .

SAVINGS AND LOAN COMPANIES, EXPENSES AS PERCENTAGE OF ASSETS, YEARLY (for each of past 15 or so years, for each of about eleven leading companies). VALUE LINE INVESTMENT SURVEY. Part three: published weekly, a few industries each week.

SAVINGS AND LOAN COMPANIES, GROSS INCOME, YEARLY (for each of past eleven years, for each of large companies with actively traded common stock). MOODY'S HANDBOOK OF COMMON STOCKS. Published quarterly.

SAVINGS AND LOAN COMPANIES, GROSS INCOME, YEARLY (for each of past 15 or so years, for each of about eleven leading companies). VALUE LINE INVESTMENT SURVEY. Part three: published weekly, a few industries each week.

SAVINGS AND LOAN COMPANIES, INTEREST EXPENSE AS PERCENTAGE OF GROSS INCOME, YEARLY (For each of past 15 or so years, for each of about eleven leading companies). VALUE LINE INVESTMENT SURVEY. Part three:

published weekly, a few industries each week.

SAVINGS AND LOAN COMPANIES, LOAN TOTALS, YEARLY (for each of past eleven years, for each of large companies with actively traded common stock). MOODY'S HANDBOOK OF COMMON STOCKS. Published quarterly.

SAVINGS AND LOAN COMPANIES, LOAN TOTALS, YEARLY (for each of past 15 or so years, for each of about eleven leading companies. Labeled "Mortgage Loans"). VALUE LINE INVESTMENT SURVEY. Part three: published weekly, a few industries each week.

Savings and loan companies, mortgage totals.

SEE: Savings and loan companies, loan totals. . .

SAVINGS AND LOAN COMPANIES, OPERATING EARNINGS TOTALS, YEARLY (for each of past eleven years, for each of large companies with actively traded common stock). MOODY'S HANDBOOK OF COMMON STOCKS. Published quarterly.

SAVINGS AND LOAN COMPANIES, SAVINGS TOTALS, YEARLY (for each of past eleven years, for each of large companies with actively traded common stock). MOODY'S HANDBOOK OF COMMON STOCK. Published quarterly.

SAVINGS AND LOAN COMPANIES, SAVINGS TOTALS, YEARLY (for each of past 15 or so years, for each of about eleven leading companies). VALUE LINE INVESTMENT SURVEY. Part three: published weekly, a few industries each week.

SAVINGS AND LOAN COMPANIES, SCHEDULED ASSETS AS PERCENTAGE OF MORTGAGE LOANS, YEARLY (for each of past 15 or so years, for each of about eleven leading companies). VALUE LINE INVESTMENT SURVEY. Part three: published weekly, a few industries each week.

School bonds.

SEE: Municipal bonds. . .

Seats on stock exchanges.

SEE: Exchange seats. . .

SECONDARY DISTRIBUTIONS (list of recent secondary distributions, with name of stock, number of shares involved, price per share, and approximate total value for each distribution). BARRON'S. Published weekly.

Securities, market value total of trading on all registered exchanges. . .

SEE: Market value total of share sales on all registered exchanges. . .

Securities, prices.

SEE: Bond prices. . .
Stock prices. . .

SECURITIES AND EXCHANGE COMMISSION FEE (amount of fee for transactions on any registered exchange). STANDARD & POOR'S SECURITY OWNER'S STOCK GUIDE. Published monthly.

Securities and Exchange Commission registrations.

    SEE: New issues, SEC registrations. . .

Security dealers.

    SEE: Brokers. . .
          Underwriters. . .

Senior capital.

    SEE ALSO: Funded debt. . .
                Long term debt. . .

SENIOR CAPITAL, YEARLY (dollar amount for each of past eleven years, for each of over 1,000 companies having actively traded common stock, and for most recent year only for over 1,200 companies with less actively traded stock. Senior capital generally represents bonds and preferred stock). MOODY'S HANDBOOK OF COMMON STOCKS. Published quarterly.

SENIOR CAPITAL, YEARLY (dollar amount for each of past 18 or so years, for each of over 1,200 leading industrial companies. Labeled "Bonds and Pfd."). VALUE LINE INVESTMENT SURVEY. Part three: published weekly, a few industries each week.

Share earnings.

    SEE: Earnings per share. . .

Shareholders.

    SEE: Stockholders. . .

Shares held by institutions.

    SEE: Institutional holdings. . .

SHARES OUTSTANDING, COMMON STOCK, CURRENT (for each of roughly 26,000 unlisted and listed corporations). NATIONAL MONTHLY STOCK SUMMARY. This data appears in semiannual cumulative volumes, April 1 and October 1.

SHARES OUTSTANDING, COMMON STOCK, CURRENT (for each of about 4,300 listed and unlisted companies). STANDARD & POOR'S SECURITY OWNER'S STOCK GUIDE. Published monthly.

SHARES OUTSTANDING, COMMON STOCK, CURRENT (for each of about 700 active, listed corporations). TRENDLINE DAILY BASIS STOCK CHARTS. Published weekly.

SHARES OUTSTANDING, COMMON STOCK, CURRENT (for each of about 960 listed companies). TRENDLINE'S CURRENT MARKET PERSPECTIVES. Published monthly.

SHARES OUTSTANDING, COMMON STOCK, CURRENT (for each of about 1,400 leading corporations). VALUE LINE INVESTMENT SURVEY. Part three: published weekly, a few industries each week.

SHARES OUTSTANDING, COMMON STOCK, YEARLY (for current year and each of past eleven years for each of over 1,000 companies with actively traded stock, and for current year only for each of over 1,200 companies with less actively traded stock). MOODY'S HANDBOOK OF COMMON STOCKS. Published quarterly.

Shares outstanding, preferred stock.

> NOTE: publications mentioned under "Shares outstanding, common stock, current" also indicate number of preferred shares outstanding, where appropriate.

Shares per convertible bond.

> SEE: Convertible bonds, shares per bond. . .

Short interest.

> SEE ALSO: Short sales. . .

SHORT INTEREST, INDIVIDUAL STOCKS ON AMERICAN STOCK EXCHANGE, MONTHLY (for each stock in which a short position of at least 20,000 shares existed, or in which there was a monthly change in short interest of 10,000 shares or more, number of shares short is shown for middle of latest available month and previous month). This data published around the 20th of each month in both BARRON'S and the WALL STREET JOURNAL.

SHORT INTEREST, INDIVIDUAL STOCKS ON AMERICAN STOCK EXCHANGE, MONTHLY (for each of about 25 stocks "which have relatively high short interest," shows number of shares short for latest available month, one month ago, and two months ago). TRENDLINE DAILY BASIS STOCK CHARTS. Published weekly.

SHORT INTEREST, INDIVIDUAL STOCKS ON NEW YORK STOCK EXCHANGE, MONTHLY (for each stock in which a short position of at least 20,000 shares existed, or in which there was a monthly change in short interest of 10,000 shares or more, number of shares short is shown for middle of latest available month and previous month. "Shares Listed" also shown). This data published about the 20th of each month in both BARRON'S and the WALL STREET JOURNAL. The same data is also published in the weekday edition of the NEW YORK TIMES around the 20th of each month, but without the "Shares Listed" feature.

SHORT INTEREST, INDIVIDUAL STOCKS ON NEW YORK STOCK EXCHANGE,

MONTHLY (for each of about 135 stocks "which have relatively high short interest," shows number of shares short for latest available month, previous month, and two months ago). TRENDLINE DAILY BASIS STOCK CHARTS. Published weekly.

SHORT INTEREST, NUMBER OF ISSUES WITH SHORT POSITION, AMERICAN STOCK EXCHANGE, MONTHLY (number of individual stock issues in which short position was reported, for middle of latest available month). BARRON'S. This data appears in special short interest report, around the 20th of each month.

SHORT INTEREST, NUMBER OF ISSUES WITH SHORT POSITION, NEW YORK STOCK EXCHANGE, MONTHLY (number of stock issues in which short position was reported, for middle of latest month available and previous month). BARRON'S. This data appears in special short interest report, about the 20th of each month.

Short interest, odd lot.

SEE: Odd-lot short interest. . .

SHORT INTEREST, TOTAL FOR AMERICAN STOCK EXCHANGE, MONTHLY (number of shares short for entire Exchange, for middle of latest available month and previous month). This data published around the 20th of each month in both BARRON'S and the WALL STREET JOURNAL.

SHORT INTEREST, TOTAL FOR NEW YORK STOCK EXCHANGE, MONTHLY (number of shares short for entire Exchange, for middle of latest available month and previous month). This data published around the 20th of each month in BARRON'S, the WALL STREET JOURNAL, and the NEW YORK TIMES -- weekday edition.

SHORT INTEREST, TOTAL FOR NEW YORK STOCK EXCHANGE, MONTHLY-YEARLY (number of shares short for entire Exchange, for middle of latest available month, previous month, and same month one year ago. Labeled "Short Int th shs" -- short interest in thousands of shares). BARRON'S. Published weekly.

SHORT INTEREST RATIO, NEW YORK STOCK EXCHANGE, MONTHLY, CHART (charted on monthly basis for about two years. Represents total short interest as a percentage of average volume). TRENDLINE DAILY BASIS STOCK CHARTS. Published weekly.

SHORT INTEREST RATIO, NEW YORK STOCK EXCHANGE, MONTHLY, CHART (charted on monthly basis for about six years. Represents total short interest as a percentage of average volume). TRENDLINE'S CURRENT MARKET PERSPECTIVES. Published monthly.

SHORT INTEREST RATIO, NEW YORK STOCK EXCHANGE, MONTHLY-YEARLY (for latest available month, previous month, and same period one year ago. Represents total short interest as a percentage of average volume. Labeled "Ratio to d'ly vol" under "N.Y. Exchange Monthly Figures"). BARRON'S Published weekly.

Short sales, odd-lot.

>   SEE: Odd-lot short sales. . .

Short sales, total for New York Stock Exchange.

>   SEE ALSO: Member trading, New York Stock Exchange. . .

SHORT SALES, TOTAL FOR NEW YORK STOCK EXCHANGE, WEEKLY-MONTH-LY-YEARLY (short sale share volume for latest available week, previous week, month ago, and same week one year ago). COMMERCIAL AND FINANCIAL CHRONICLE. Thursday edition.

Sinking fund call prices, bonds.

>   SEE: Call prices, bonds, sinking fund. . .

Sinking fund notices.

>   SEE: Redemptions. . .

65 stocks average.

>   SEE: Dow-Jones composite stock average. . .

Skipped dividends.

>   SEE: Dividend omissions. . .

SMALL BUSINESS INVESTMENT COMPANIES (price range, dividends, net as-set value, and other information for leading SBIC's included in main list of stocks). STANDARD & POOR'S SECURITY OWNER'S STOCK GUIDE. Publish-ed monthly.

South African stocks.

>   SEE: Stock prices on Johannesburg Stock Exchange. . .

SPECIALISTS' TRADING, NEW YORK STOCK EXCHANGE, WEEKLY-MONTH-LY-YEARLY (total round-lot purchases, sales, and short sales by "specialists in stocks in which registered," in number of shares, for latest week, previous week, month ago, and same week one year ago). COMMERCIAL AND FINANCIAL CHRONICLE. Thursday edition.

Splits, stock.

>   SEE: Stock splits. . .

Spread, yield.

>   SEE: Yield spread. . .

Standard & Poor's bank stock indexes.

>   SEE: Standard & Poor's stock group indexes. . .

Standard & Poor's bill average.

>   SEE: Standard & Poor's treasury bill index. . .

Standard & Poor's bond ratings.

SEE: Ratings, bonds, Standard & Poor's. . .

STANDARD & POOR'S CAPITAL GOODS STOCK INDEX, PRICE, WEEKLY, CLOSE (closing price at middle of each of last two weeks, with percentage change). THE OUTLOOK. Published weekly.

STANDARD & POOR'S CAPITAL GOODS STOCK INDEX, PRICE, WEEKLY, CLOSE (closing figures for last four weeks, plus high-low for current year). STANDARD & POOR'S SECURITY OWNER'S STOCK GUIDE. Published monthly.

STANDARD & POOR'S CAPITAL GOODS STOCK INDEX, PRICE, YEAR TO DATE, HIGH-LOW (range for year so far). THE OUTLOOK. Published weekly. Also published monthly in STANDARD & POOR'S SECURITY OWNER'S STOCK GUIDE.

STANDARD & POOR'S CLOSED-END INVESTMENT COMPANIES STOCK INDEX, PRICE, WEEKLY (closing price for last four weeks, plus high-low for current year). STANDARD & POOR'S SECURITY OWNER'S STOCK GUIDE. Published monthly. Also published weekly with stock group indexes in THE OUTLOOK.

Standard & Poor's combined stock index.

SEE: Standard & Poor's composite 500 stock index. . .

Standard & Poor's composite bond index.

SEE: Standard & Poor's corporate (composite) AAA
bond index. . .
Standard & Poor's corporate (composite) bond
indexes. . .

STANDARD & POOR'S COMPOSITE 500 STOCK INDEX, DIVIDEND YIELD (PERCENT), WEEKLY (for middle of each of two weeks just past). THE OUTLOOK. Published weekly.

STANDARD & POOR'S COMPOSITE 500 STOCK INDEX, DIVIDEND YIELD (PERCENT), YEARLY, HIGH-LOW (yield range for current year and one year previous). THE OUTLOOK. Published weekly.

STANDARD & POOR'S COMPOSITE 500 STOCK INDEX, NAMES OF STOCKS COMPRISING, ALPHABETICAL LIST (500 stocks listed alphabetically. Labeled "alphabetical Listing of Stocks in S.&P. Indexes," with a "Key to Industry Groups"). THE OUTLOOK. This listing appears on the back of every other blue "Cumulative Index." Alternates with group list.

STANDARD & POOR'S COMPOSITE 500 STOCK INDEX, NAMES OF STOCKS COMPRISING, GROUP LIST (425 industrials listed by groups, plus 20 railroads and 55 public utilities, for a total of 500 stocks). THE OUTLOOK. This grouping appears on the back of every other blue "Cumulative Index." Alternates with alphabetical list.

Standard & Poor's composite 500 stock index, percentage change.

> SEE: Standard & Poor's composite 500 stock index,
> price, weekly, percentage change. . .
> Standard & Poor's composite 500 stock index, price,
> year to date, percentage change. . .

STANDARD & POOR"S COMPOSITE 500 STOCK INDEX, PRICE, DAILY, CLOSE (for each day of week just past). BARRON'S. Published weekly.

STANDARD & POOR'S COMPOSITE 500 STOCK INDEX, PRICE, DAILY, HIGH-LOW-CLOSE (for previous trading day--labeled "500 Stocks"). NEW YORK TIMES. Published weekdays.

STANDARD & POOR'S COMPOSITE 500 STOCK INDEX, PRICE, DAILY, HIGH-LOW-CLOSE (for each day of week just past). THE OUTLOOK. Published weekly.

STANDARD & POOR'S COMPOSITE 500 STOCK INDEX, PRICE, DAILY, HIGH-LOW-CLOSE, CHART (about four years are charted on daily basis). TREND-LINE DAILY BASIS STOCK CHARTS. Published weekly.

STANDARD & POOR'S COMPOSITE 500 STOCK INDEX, PRICE, MOVING AVERAGE, CHART (200-day moving average is shown on daily chart covering about four years). TRENDLINE DAILY BASIS STOCK CHARTS. Published weekly.

STANDARD & POOR'S COMPOSITE 500 STOCK INDEX, PRICE, MOVING AVERAGE, CHART (200-day moving average is charted weekly for about five years). TRENDLINE'S CURRENT MARKET PERSPECTIVES. Published monthly.

STANDARD & POOR'S COMPOSITE 500 STOCK INDEX, PRICE, WEEKLY, CLOSE (closing price at middle of each of last two weeks, with percentage change from week to week). THE OUTLOOK. Published weekly.

STANDARD AND POOR'S COMPOSITE 500 STOCK INDEX, PRICE, WEEKLY, CLOSE (closing figures for last four weeks, plus high-low for current year). STANDARD & POOR'S SECURITY OWNER'S STOCK GUIDE. Published monthly.

STANDARD & POOR'S COMPOSITE 500 STOCK INDEX, PRICE, WEEKLY, HIGH-LOW-CLOSE (for week just past, with dates of high and low for week-- labeled "500 Stocks"). NEW YORK TIMES. Sunday edition.

STANDARD & POOR'S COMPOSITE 500 STOCK INDEX, PRICE, WEEKLY, HIGH-LOW-CLOSE, CHART (about five years are charted on weekly basis). TRENDLINE'S CURRENT MARKET PERSPECTIVES. Published monthly.

STANDARD & POOR'S COMPOSITE 500 STOCK INDEX, PRICE, WEEKLY, PERCENTAGE CHANGE (for end of week just past--week to week percentage change. Included with data labeled "Mutual Fund Investment Performance Index"). BARRON'S. Published weekly.

STANDARD & POOR'S COMPOSITE 500 STOCK INDEX, PRICE, WEEKLY, PERCENTAGE CHANGE (price at middle of each of last two weeks, with percentage change from week to week). THE OUTLOOK. Published weekly.

STANDARD & POOR'S COMPOSITE 500 STOCK INDEX, PRICE, YEAR TO DATE, HIGH-LOW (range for year so far). STANDARD & POOR'S SECURITY OWNER'S STOCK GUIDE. Published monthly.

STANDARD & POOR'S COMPOSITE 500 STOCK INDEX, PRICE, YEAR TO DATE, PERCENTAGE CHANGE (change in percent from beginning of year to end of week just past. Included with data labeled "Mutual Fund Investment Performance Index"). BARRON'S. Published weekly.

STANDARD & POOR'S COMPOSITE 500 STOCK INDEX, PRICE, YEARLY, HIGH-LOW (range for current year and one year previous). THE OUTLOOK. Published weekly.

STANDARD & POOR'S COMPOSITE 500 STOCK INDEX, PRICE, YEARLY, HIGH-LOW, CHART (annual price ranges charted for about twelve years). TRENDLINE DAILY BASIS STOCK CHARTS. Published weekly.

STANDARD & POOR'S COMPOSITE 500 STOCK INDEX, PRICE-EARNINGS RATIO, WEEKLY (for middle of each of two weeks just past). THE OUTLOOK. Published weekly.

STANDARD & POOR'S COMPOSITE 500 STOCK INDEX, PRICE-EARNINGS RATIO, YEARLY, HIGH-LOW (range of price-earnings ratio for current year and previous year). THE OUTLOOK. Published weekly.

Standard & Poor's composite 500 stock index, yield.

      SEE: Standard & Poor's composite 500 stock index,
               dividend yield. . .

STANDARD & POOR'S CONSUMER GOODS STOCK INDEX, PRICE, WEEKLY, CLOSE (closing price at middle of each of last two weeks, with percentage change). THE OUTLOOK. Published weekly.

STANDARD & POOR'S CONSUMER GOODS STOCK INDEX, PRICE, WEEKLY, CLOSE (closing figures for last four weeks, plus high-low for current year). STANDARD & POOR'S SECURITY OWNER'S STOCK GUIDE. Published monthly.

STANDARD & POOR'S CONSUMER GOODS STOCK INDEX, PRICE, YEAR TO DATE, HIGH-LOW (price range for year so far). THE OUTLOOK. Published weekly.

STANDARD & POOR'S CONSUMER GOODS STOCK INDEX, PRICE, YEAR TO DATE, HIGH-LOW (price range for year so far). STANDARD & POOR'S SECURITY OWNER'S STOCK GUIDE. Published monthly.

STANDARD & POOR'S CORPORATE (COMPOSITE) AAA BOND INDEX, PRICE, WEEKLY (for middle of each of two weeks just past). THE OUTLOOK. Published weekly. Also published weekly in the BOND OUTLOOK.

STANDARD & POOR'S CORPORATE (COMPOSITE) AAA BOND INDEX, PRICE, YEAR TO DATE, HIGH-LOW (price range for year so far). THE OUTLOOK. Published weekly. Also published weekly in the BOND OUTLOOK.

STANDARD & POOR'S CORPORATE (COMPOSITE) AAA BOND INDEX, YIELD (PERCENT), MONTHLY, CHART (covers about 28 years). STANDARD & POOR'S EARNINGS AND RATINGS BOND GUIDE. Published monthly.

STANDARD & POOR'S CORPORATE (COMPOSITE) AAA BOND INDEX, YIELD (PERCENT), QUARTERLY, CHART (covers about 50 years). TRENDLINE'S CURRENT MARKET PERSPECTIVES. Published monthly.

STANDARD & POOR'S CORPORATE (COMPOSITE) BOND INDEXES, YIELDS (PERCENT), MONTHLY (average yield for each of twelve recent months, for each of AAA, AA, A, and BBB ratings). STANDARD & POOR'S EARNINGS AND RATINGS BOND GUIDE. Published monthly.

STANDARD & POOR'S CORPORATE (COMPOSITE) BOND INDEXES, YIELDS (PERCENT), WEEKLY (for the middle of each of two weeks just past, for each of AAA, AA, A, and BBB ratings). THE OUTLOOK. Published weekly. Also published weekly in the BOND OUTLOOK.

STANDARD & POOR'S CORPORATE (COMPOSITE) BOND INDEXES, YIELDS (PERCENT), WEEKLY (average yield for each of five recent weeks, for each of AAA, AA, A, and BBB ratings). STANDARD & POOR'S EARNINGS AND RATINGS BOND GUIDE. Published monthly.

STANDARD & POOR'S CORPORATE (COMPOSITE) BOND INDEXES, YIELDS (PERCENT), YEARLY, HIGH-LOW (yield range for current year and one previous year, for each of AAA, AA, A, and BBB ratings). THE OUTLOOK. Published weekly. Yield range for current year also published weekly in the BOND OUTLOOK.

STANDARD & POOR'S CORPORATE (COMPOSITE) BOND INDEXES, YIELDS (PERCENT), YEARLY, HIGH-LOW (annual range of weekly average yields for each of nine recent years, for each of AAA, AA, A, and BBB ratings). STANDARD & POOR'S EARNINGS AND RATINGS BOND GUIDE. Published monthly.

Standard & Poor's 500 stock index.

    SEE: Standard & Poor's composite 500 stock index. . .

Standard & Poor's 425 stock index.

    SEE: Standard & Poor's industrial 425 stock index. . .

STANDARD & POOR'S GOVERNMENT BOND INDEX, YIELD (PERCENT), MONTHLY, CHART (covers about 28 years). STANDARD & POOR'S EARNINGS AND RATINGS BOND GUIDE. Published monthly.

STANDARD & POOR'S GOVERNMENT BOND INDEXES, PRICES, WEEKLY (for middle of each of two weeks just past, for each of long term, intermediate, and short term indexes). THE OUTLOOK. Published weekly. Also published weekly in the BOND OUTLOOK.

STANDARD & POOR'S GOVERNMENT BOND INDEXES, PRICES, YEAR TO DATE, HIGH–LOW (price range for year so far, for each of long term, intermediate, and short term indexes). THE OUTLOOK. Published weekly. Also published weekly in the BOND OUTLOOK.

STANDARD & POOR'S GOVERNMENT BOND INDEXES, YIELDS (PERCENT), WEEKLY (for middle of each of two weeks just past, for each of long term, intermediate, and short term indexes). THE OUTLOOK. Published weekly. Also published weekly in the BOND OUTLOOK.

STANDARD & POOR'S GOVERNMENT BOND INDEXES, YIELDS (PERCENT), YEAR TO DATE, HIGH–LOW (yield range for current year so far, for each of long term, intermediate, and short term indexes). THE OUTLOOK. Published weekly. Also published weekly in the BOND OUTLOOK.

Standard & Poor's group indexes.

SEE: Standard & Poor's stock group indexes. . .

STANDARD & POOR'S HIGH–GRADE COMMON STOCK INDEX, NAMES OF STOCKS COMPRISING (25 stocks are listed). THE OUTLOOK. This list appears on the back of every other blue "Cumulative Index".

STANDARD & POOR'S HIGH–GRADE COMMON STOCK INDEX, PRICE, MONTHLY AVERAGE, CHART (small chart of monthly averages over four year period). STANDARD & POOR'S SECURITY OWNER'S STOCK GUIDE. Published monthly.

STANDARD & POOR'S HIGH–GRADE COMMON STOCK INDEX, PRICE, WEEKLY, CLOSE (closing price at middle of each of last two weeks, with percentage change). THE OUTLOOK. Published weekly.

STANDARD & POOR'S HIGH–GRADE COMMON STOCK INDEX, PRICE, WEEKLY, CLOSE (closing figures for last four weeks, plus high–low for current year). STANDARD & POOR'S SECURITY OWNER'S STOCK GUIDE. Published monthly.

STANDARD & POOR'S HIGH–GRADE COMMON STOCK INDEX, PRICE, YEAR TO DATE, HIGH–LOW (price range for year so far). THE OUTLOOK. Published weekly. Also published monthly in STANDARD & POOR'S SECURITY OWNER'S STOCK GUIDE.

STANDARD & POOR'S INDUSTRIAL BOND INDEXES, YIELDS (PERCENT), MONTHLY (average yield for each of twelve recent months for each of AAA, AA, A, and BBB ratings). STANDARD & POOR'S EARNINGS AND RATINGS BOND GUIDE. Published monthly.

STANDARD & POOR'S INDUSTRIAL BOND INDEXES, YIELDS (PERCENT), WEEKLY (for middle of each of two weeks just past, for each of AAA, AA, A, and BBB ratings). THE OUTLOOK. Published weekly. Also published weekly in the BOND OUTLOOK.

STANDARD & POOR'S INDUSTRIAL BOND INDEXES, YIELDS (PERCENT), WEEKLY (average yield for each of five recent weeks, for each of AAA, AA, A, and BBB ratings). STANDARD & POOR'S EARNINGS AND RATINGS BOND GUIDE. Published monthly.

STANDARD & POOR'S INDUSTRIAL BOND INDEXES, YIELDS (PERCENT), YEARLY, HIGH-LOW (yield range for current year and one previous year for each of AAA, AA, A, and BBB ratings). THE OUTLOOK. Published weekly. Yield range for current year also published weekly in the BOND OUTLOOK.

STANDARD & POOR'S INDUSTRIAL BOND INDEXES, YIELDS (PERCENT), YEARLY, HIGH-LOW (yearly range of average weekly yields for each of nine recent years, for each of AAA, AA, A, and BBB ratings). STANDARD & POOR'S EARNINGS AND RATINGS BOND GUIDE. Published monthly.

STANDARD & POOR'S INDUSTRIAL 425 STOCK INDEX, DIVIDEND YIELD (PERCENT), QUARTERLY, CHART (average yield charted on quarterly basis back to 1926). TRENDLINE'S CURRENT MARKET PERSPECTIVES. Published monthly.

STANDARD & POOR'S INDUSTRIAL 425 STOCK INDEX, DIVIDEND YIELD (PERCENT), WEEKLY (for middle of each of two weeks just past). THE OUTLOOK. Published weekly.

STANDARD & POOR'S INDUSTRIAL 425 STOCK INDEX, DIVIDEND YIELD (PERCENT), YEARLY, HIGH-LOW (yield range for current year and one previous year). THE OUTLOOK. Published weekly.

STANDARD & POOR'S INDUSTRIAL 425 STOCK INDEX, NAMES OF STOCKS COMPRISING (425 individual stocks are listed, divided into about 80 industry groups). THE OUTLOOK. This listing appears on the back of every other blue "Cumulative Index."

Standard & Poor's industrial 425 stock index, percentage change.

    SEE: Standard & Poor's industrial 425 stock index, price,
          weekly, percentage change. . .
        Standard & Poor's industrial 425 stock index, price,
          year to date, percentage change. . .

STANDARD & POOR'S INDUSTRIAL 425 STOCK INDEX, PRICE, DAILY, CLOSE (for each day of week just past). BARRON'S. Published weekly.

STANDARD & POOR'S INDUSTRIAL 425 STOCK INDEX, PRICE, DAILY, HIGH-LOW, CHART (price range charted on daily basis for about twelve months). THE OUTLOOK. Published weekly.

STANDARD & POOR'S INDUSTRIAL 425 STOCK INDEX, PRICE, DAILY, HIGH-LOW, CHART (price range charted on daily basis for about twelve months). STANDARD & POOR'S SECURITY OWNER'S STOCK GUIDE. Published monthly.

STANDARD & POOR'S INDUSTRIAL 425 STOCK INDEX, PRICE, DAILY, HIGH-LOW-CLOSE (for each day of week just past). THE OUTLOOK. Published weekly.

STANDARD & POOR'S INDUSTRIAL 425 STOCK INDEX, PRICE, DAILY, HIGH-LOW-CLOSE (for previous trading day). NEW YORK TIMES. Published week-days.

STANDARD & POOR'S INDUSTRIAL 425 STOCK INDEX, PRICE, DAILY-YEAR-LY, CLOSE (closing price for previous trading day and same day one year ago). WALL STREET JOURNAL. Published business days.

STANDARD & POOR'S INDUSTRIAL 425 STOCK INDEX, PRICE, MONTHLY, HIGH-LOW, CHART (price range charted on monthly basis for about 24 years). THE OUTLOOK. This chart normally appears in the first issue of each month.

Standard & Poor's industrial 425 stock index, price, rallies and declines.

SEE: Trading swings, Standard & Poor's stock indexes. . .

STANDARD & POOR'S INDUSTRIAL 425 STOCK INDEX, PRICE, WEEKLY, CLOSE (closing price at middle of each of last two weeks, with percentage change). THE OUTLOOK. Published weekly.

STANDARD & POOR'S INDUSTRIAL 425 STOCK INDEX, PRICE, WEEKLY, CLOSE (closing figures for each of last four weeks, plus high-low for current year). STANDARD & POOR'S SECURITY OWNER'S STOCK GUIDE. Published monthly.

STANDARD & POOR'S INDUSTRIAL 425 STOCK INDEX, PRICE, WEEKLY, HIGH-LOW-CLOSE (for week just past, with dates of high and low for week). NEW YORK TIMES. Sunday edition.

STANDARD & POOR'S INDUSTRIAL 425 STOCK INDEX, PRICE, WEEKLY, PERCENTAGE CHANGE (for end of week just past--percentage change week to week. Included with data under "Mutual Fund Investment Performance Index"). BARRON'S. Published weekly.

STANDARD & POOR'S INDUSTRIAL 425 STOCK INDEX, PRICE, WEEKLY, PERCENTAGE CHANGE (closing price at middle of each of last two weeks, with percentage change from week to week). THE OUTLOOK. Published weekly.

STANDARD & POOR'S INDUSTRIAL 425 STOCK INDEX, PRICE, YEAR TO DATE, HIGH-LOW (price range for current year). STANDARD & POOR'S SECURITY OWNER'S STOCK GUIDE. Published monthly.

STANDARD & POOR'S INDUSTRIAL 425 STOCK INDEX, PRICE, YEAR TO

DATE, PERCENTAGE CHANGE (from beginning of current year to end of week just past. Included with data under "Mutual Fund Investment Performance Index"). BARRON'S. Published weekly.

STANDARD & POOR'S INDUSTRIAL 425 STOCK INDEX, PRICE, YEARLY, HIGH-LOW (price range for current year and one previous year). THE OUTLOOK. Published weekly.

STANDARD & POOR'S INDUSTRIAL 425 STOCK INDEX, PRICE-EARNINGS RATIO, WEEKLY (for middle of each of two weeks just past). THE OUTLOOK. Published weekly.

STANDARD & POOR'S INDUSTRIAL 425 STOCK INDEX, PRICE-EARNINGS RATIO, YEARLY, HIGH-LOW (range of price-earnings ratio for current year and one previous year). THE OUTLOOK. Published weekly.

Standard & Poor's industrial 425 stock index, rallies and declines.

SEE: Trading swings, Standard & Poor's stock indexes. . .

Standard & Poor's industrial 425 stock index, yield.

SEE: Standard & Poor's industrial 425 stock index,
dividend yield. . .

Standard & Poor's industry group stock indexes.

SEE: Standard & Poor's stock group indexes. . .

Standard & Poor's insurance stock indexes (life and property).

SEE: Standard & Poor's stock group indexes. . .

STANDARD & POOR'S LOW-PRICED COMMON STOCK INDEX, NAMES OF STOCKS COMPRISING (20 stocks are listed). THE OUTLOOK. This list appears on the back of every other blue "Cumulative Index".

STANDARD & POOR'S LOW-PRICED COMMON STOCK INDEX, PRICE, MONTHLY AVERAGE, CHART (small chart of monthly averages over four year period). STANDARD & POOR'S SECURITY OWNER'S STOCK GUIDE. Published monthly.

STANDARD & POOR'S LOW-PRICED COMMON STOCK INDEX, PRICE, MONTHLY AVERAGE, CHART (monthly averages are charted for about 18 years). TRENDLINE'S CURRENT MARKET PERSPECTIVES. Published monthly.

STANDARD & POOR'S LOW-PRICED COMMON STOCK INDEX, PRICE, WEEKLY, CLOSE (closing price at middle of each of last two weeks, with percentage change). THE OUTLOOK. Published weekly.

STANDARD & POOR'S LOW-PRICED COMMON STOCK INDEX, PRICE, WEEKLY, CLOSE (closing figures for each of last four weeks, plus high-low for current year). STANDARD & POOR'S SECURITY OWNER'S STOCK GUIDE. Published monthly.

STANDARD & POOR'S LOW-PRICED COMMON STOCK INDEX, PRICE, YEAR TO DATE, HIGH-LOW (current year's price range). THE OUTLOOK. Published weekly. Also published monthly in STANDARD & POOR'S SECURITY OWNER'S STOCK GUIDE.

STANDARD & POOR'S MUNICIPAL BOND INDEX, PRICE, WEEKLY (for middle of each of two weeks just past). THE OUTLOOK. Published weekly. Also published weekly in the BOND OUTLOOK.

STANDARD & POOR'S MUNICIPAL BOND INDEX, PRICE, YEAR TO DATE, HIGH-LOW (price range for current year). THE OUTLOOK. Published weekly. Also published weekly in the BOND OUTLOOK.

STANDARD & POOR'S MUNICIPAL BOND INDEX, YIELD (PERCENT), MONTHLY (average yield for each of twelve recent months). STANDARD & POOR'S EARNINGS AND RATINGS BOND GUIDE. Published monthly.

STANDARD & POOR'S MUNICIPAL BOND INDEX, YIELD (PERCENT), MONTHLY, CHART (yield charted on monthly basis for about 28 years). STANDARD & POOR'S EARNINGS AND RATINGS BOND GUIDE. Published monthly.

STANDARD & POOR'S MUNICIPAL BOND INDEX, YIELD (PERCENT), WEEKLY (for middle of each of two weeks just past). THE OUTLOOK. Published weekly. Also published weekly in the BOND OUTLOOK.

STANDARD & POOR'S MUNICIPAL BOND INDEX, YIELD (PERCENT), WEEKLY (average yield for each of five recent weeks). STANDARD & POOR'S EARNINGS AND RATINGS BOND GUIDE. Published monthly.

STANDARD & POOR'S MUNICIPAL BOND INDEX, YIELD (PERCENT), YEAR TO DATE, HIGH-LOW (range of yields for current year). THE OUTLOOK. Published weekly. Also published weekly in the BOND OUTLOOK.

STANDARD & POOR'S MUNICIPAL BOND INDEX, YIELD (PERCENT), YEARLY, HIGH-LOW (range of average weekly yields for each of eight recent years). STANDARD & POOR'S EARNINGS AND RATINGS BOND GUIDE. Published monthly.

STANDARD & POOR'S PREFERRED STOCK INDEX, DIVIDEND YIELD (PERCENT), WEEKLY (for middle of each of two weeks just past). THE OUTLOOK. Published weekly.

STANDARD & POOR'S PREFERRED STOCK INDEX, DIVIDEND YIELD (PERCENT), YEARLY, HIGH-LOW (range of yields for current year and one previous year). THE OUTLOOK. Published weekly.

STANDARD & POOR'S PREFERRED STOCK INDEX, PRICE, WEEKLY, CLOSE (closing price at middle of each of two weeks just past). THE OUTLOOK. Published weekly.

STANDARD & POOR'S PREFERRED STOCK INDEX, PRICE, YEARLY, HIGH-LOW (range for current year and one previous year). THE OUTLOOK. Published weekly.

Standard & Poor's public utility indexes.

> SEE: Standard & Poor's utility bond indexes. . .
>   Standard & Poor's utility stock index. . .

STANDARD & POOR'S RAILROAD BOND INDEXES, YIELDS (PERCENT), MONTHLY (average yields for each of twelve recent months for each of AAA, AA, A, and BBB ratings). STANDARD & POOR'S EARNINGS AND RATINGS BOND GUIDE. Published monthly.

STANDARD & POOR'S RAILROAD BOND INDEXES, YIELDS (PERCENT), WEEKLY (for the middle of each of two weeks just past, for each of AAA, AA, A, and BBB ratings). THE OUTLOOK. Published weekly. Also published weekly in the BOND OUTLOOK.

STANDARD & POOR'S RAILROAD BOND INDEXES, YIELDS (PERCENT), WEEKLY (average yields for each of five recent weeks, for each of AAA, AA, A, and BBB ratings). STANDARD & POOR'S EARNINGS AND RATINGS BOND GUIDE. Published monthly.

STANDARD & POOR'S RAILROAD BOND INDEXES, YIELDS (PERCENT), YEARLY, HIGH-LOW (yield ranges for current year and one previous year, for each of AAA, AA, A, and BBB ratings). THE OUTLOOK. Published weekly. Also published weekly in the BOND OUTLOOK.

STANDARD & POOR'S RAILROAD BOND INDEXES, YIELDS (PERCENT), YEARLY, HIGH-LOW (yearly ranges of weekly averages for each of nine recent years, for each of AAA, AA, A, and BBB ratings). STANDARD & POOR'S EARNINGS AND RATINGS BOND GUIDE. Published monthly.

STANDARD & POOR'S RAILROAD STOCK INDEX, DIVIDEND YIELD (PERCENT), WEEKLY (for middle of each of two weeks just past). THE OUTLOOK. Published weekly.

STANDARD & POOR'S RAILROAD STOCK INDEX, DIVIDEND YIELD (PERCENT), YEARLY, HIGH-LOW (yield range for current year and one previous year). THE OUTLOOK. Published weekly.

STANDARD & POOR'S RAILROAD STOCK INDEX, NAMES OF STOCKS COMPRISING (20 railroad stocks are listed). THE OUTLOOK. This list appears on the back of every other blue "Cumulative Index".

STANDARD & POOR'S RAILROAD STOCK INDEX, PRICE, DAILY, HIGH-LOW, CHART (daily price range charted for about twelve months). THE OUTLOOK. Published weekly.

STANDARD & POOR'S RAILROAD STOCK INDEX, PRICE, DAILY, HIGH-LOW, CHART (daily price range charted for about twelve months). STANDARD & POOR'S SECURITY OWNER'S STOCK GUIDE. Published monthly.

STANDARD & POOR'S RAILROAD STOCK INDEX, PRICE, DAILY, HIGH-LOW-CLOSE (for previous trading day). NEW YORK TIMES. Published weekdays.

STANDARD & POOR'S RAILROAD STOCK INDEX, PRICE, DAILY, HIGH-LOW-CLOSE (for each day of week just past). THE OUTLOOK. Published weekly.

STANDARD & POOR'S RAILROAD STOCK INDEX, PRICE, MONTHLY, HIGH-LOW, CHART (monthly price range charted for about 24 years). THE OUTLOOK. This chart normally appears in first issue of each month.

STANDARD & POOR'S RAILROAD STOCK INDEX, PRICE, WEEKLY, CLOSE (closing price at middle of each of last two weeks, with percentage change). THE OUTLOOK. Published weekly.

STANDARD & POOR'S RAILROAD STOCK INDEX, PRICE, WEEKLY, CLOSE (for each of last four weeks, with high-low for current year). STANDARD & POOR'S SECURITY OWNER'S STOCK GUIDE. Published monthly.

STANDARD & POOR'S RAILROAD STOCK INDEX, PRICE, WEEKLY, HIGH-LOW-CLOSE (for week just past, with dates of high and low for week). NEW YORK TIMES. Sunday edition.

STANDARD & POOR'S RAILROAD STOCK INDEX, PRICE, WEEKLY, PERCENTAGE CHANGE (closing price at middle of each of last two weeks, with percentage change week to week). THE OUTLOOK. Published weekly.

STANDARD & POOR'S RAILROAD STOCK INDEX, PRICE, YEARLY, HIGH-LOW (price range for current year and one previous year). THE OUTLOOK. Published weekly.

STANDARD & POOR'S RAILROAD STOCK INDEX, PRICE, YEARLY, HIGH-LOW (price range for current year). STANDARD & POOR'S SECURITY OWNER'S STOCK GUIDE. Published monthly.

STANDARD & POOR'S RAILROAD STOCK INDEX, PRICE-EARNINGS RATIO, WEEKLY (for middle of each of last two weeks). THE OUTLOOK. Published weekly.

STANDARD & POOR'S RAILROAD STOCK INDEX, PRICE-EARNINGS RATIO, YEARLY, HIGH-LOW (range for current year and one previous year). THE OUTLOOK. Published weekly.

Standard & Poor's railroad stock index, yield.

SEE: Standard & Poor's railroad stock index, dividend
      yield. . .

Standard & Poor's ratings.

SEE: Ratings, bonds, Standard & Poor's. . .
      Ratings, stocks, Standard & Poor's. . .

STANDARD & POOR'S STOCK GROUP INDEXES, NAMES OF STOCKS COMPRISING (individual stocks are listed for each of about 80 industrial groups, four public utility groups, and eight supplementary groups). THE OUTLOOK.

This list appears on the back of every other blue "Cumulative Index".

STANDARD & POOR'S STOCK GROUP INDEXES, PRICES, MONTHLY AVER-AGES, CHARTS (about 51 industry groups are charted on monthly basis for about four years). STANDARD & POOR'S SECURITY OWNER'S STOCK GUIDE. Published monthly.

STANDARD & POOR'S STOCK GROUP INDEXES, PRICES, WEEKLY, CLOSE (closing price at middle of each of last two weeks, for each of about 100 groups, including industrials, transportation, utilities, retailing, banks, insurance companies, closed-end investment companies, etc., with percentage change week to week for each group). THE OUTLOOK. Published weekly. Also published monthly in STANDARD & POOR'S SECURITY OWNER'S STOCK GUIDE.

STANDARD & POOR'S STOCK GROUP INDEXES, PRICES, WEEKLY, PERCENT-AGE CHANGES (week to week changes, for middle of each of last two weeks, for about 100 groups). THE OUTLOOK. Published weekly.

STANDARD & POOR'S STOCK GROUP INDEXES, PRICES, WEEKLY AVERAGES, CHARTS (each of about 36 industry groups is charted on weekly basis for about four years). TRENDLINE'S CURRENT MARKET PERSPECTIVES. Published monthly.

STANDARD & POOR'S STOCK GROUP INDEXES, PRICES, YEAR TO DATE, HIGH-LOW (price range for current year for each of about 100 groups, with percentage changes). THE OUTLOOK. Published weekly.

STANDARD & POOR'S STOCK GROUP INDEXES, PRICES, YEAR TO DATE, HIGH-LOW (price range for current year for each of about 100 groups). STANDARD & POOR'S SECURITY OWNER'S STOCK GUIDE. Published monthly.

STANDARD & POOR'S STOCK GROUP INDEXES, PRICES, YEAR TO DATE, PERCENTAGE CHANGES (change in percent since beginning of current year, for each of about 100 groups). THE OUTLOOK. Published weekly.

Standard & Poor's stock ratings.

　　SEE: Ratings, stocks, Standard & Poor's. . .

Standard & Poor's trading swings.

　　SEE: Trading swings, Standard & Poor's. . .

STANDARD & POOR'S TREASURY BILL INDEX, YIELD (PERCENT), WEEKLY (for middle of each of two weeks just past). BOND OUTLOOK. Published weekly.

STANDARD & POOR'S TREASURY BILL INDEX, YIELD (PERCENT), YEAR TO DATE, HIGH-LOW (yield range for current year). BOND OUTLOOK. Published weekly.

STANDARD & POOR'S UTILITY BOND INDEXES, YIELD (PERCENT), MONTH-

LY (average yields for each of twelve last months, for each of AAA, AA, A, and BBB ratings). STANDARD & POOR'S EARNINGS AND RATINGS BOND GUIDE. Published monthly.

STANDARD & POOR'S UTILITY BOND INDEXES, YIELDS (PERCENT), WEEKLY (for the middle of each of two weeks just past, for each of AAA, AA, A, and BBB ratings). THE OUTLOOK. Published weekly. Also published weekly in the BOND OUTLOOK.

STANDARD & POOR'S UTILITY BOND INDEXES, YIELDS (PERCENT), WEEKLY (average yields for each of five last weeks, for each of AAA, AA, A, and BBB ratings). STANDARD & POOR'S EARNINGS AND RATINGS BOND GUIDE. Published monthly.

STANDARD & POOR'S UTILITY BOND INDEXES, YIELDS (PERCENT), YEARLY, HIGHLOW (yield range for current year and one previous year, for each of AAA, AA, A, and BBB ratings). THE OUTLOOK. Published weekly. Yield range for current year also published weekly in the BOND OUTLOOK.

STANDARD & POOR'S UTILITY BOND INDEXES, YIELDS (PERCENT), YEARLY, HIGHLOW (yearly range for each of nine recent years, for each of AAA, AA, A, and BBB ratings). STANDARD & POOR'S EARNINGS AND RATINGS BOND GUIDE. Published monthly.

STANDARD & POOR'S UTILITY STOCK INDEX, DIVIDEND YIELD (PERCENT), WEEKLY (for middle of each of two weeks just past). THE OUTLOOK. Published weekly.

STANDARD & POOR'S UTILITY STOCK INDEX, DIVIDEND YIELD (PERCENT), YEARLY, HIGHLOW (yield range for current year and one previous year). THE OUTLOOK. Published weekly.

STANDARD & POOR'S UTILITY STOCK INDEX, NAMES OF STOCKS COMPRISING (55 public utility stocks are listed). THE OUTLOOK. This list appears on the back of every other blue "Cumulative Index".

STANDARD & POOR'S UTILITY STOCK INDEX, PRICE, DAILY, HIGHLOW, CHART (daily price range charted for about twelve months). THE OUTLOOK. Published weekly.

STANDARD & POOR'S UTILITY STOCK INDEX, PRICE, DAILY, HIGHLOW, CHART (daily range charted for about twelve months). STANDARD & POOR'S SECURITY OWNER'S STOCK GUIDE. Published monthly.

STANDARD & POOR'S UTILITY STOCK INDEX, PRICE, DAILY, HIGHLOWCLOSE (for each day of week just past). THE OUTLOOK. Published weekly.

STANDARD & POOR'S UTILITY STOCK INDEX, PRICE, DAILY, HIGHLOWCLOSE (for previous trading day). NEW YORK TIMES. Published daily.

STANDARD & POOR'S UTILITY STOCK INDEX, PRICE, MONTHLY AVERAGE, CHART (monthly average based on closing prices is charted for about 24 years). THE OUTLOOK. This chart normally appears in the first issue of each month.

STANDARD & POOR'S UTILITY STOCK INDEX, PRICE, WEEKLY, CLOSE (closing figure for each of last four weeks, with high-low for current year). STANDARD & POOR'S SECURITY OWNER'S STOCK GUIDE. Published monthly.

STANDARD & POOR'S UTILITY STOCK INDEX, PRICE, WEEKLY, CLOSE (closing price at middle of each of last two weeks, with week to week percentage change). THE OUTLOOK. Published weekly.

STANDARD & POOR'S UTILITY STOCK INDEX, PRICE, WEEKLY, HIGH-LOW-CLOSE (for week just past, with dates of high and low for week). NEW YORK TIMES. Sunday edition.

STANDARD & POOR'S UTILITY STOCK INDEX, PRICE, WEEKLY, PERCENTAGE CHANGE (closing price at middle of each of last two weeks, with week to week percentage change). THE OUTLOOK. Published weekly.

STANDARD & POOR'S UTILITY STOCK INDEX, PRICE, YEARLY, HIGH-LOW (price range for current year and one previous year). THE OUTLOOK. Published weekly.

STANDARD & POOR'S UTILITY STOCK INDEX, PRICE, YEARLY, HIGH-LOW (price range for current year). STANDARD & POOR'S SECURITY OWNER'S STOCK GUIDE. Published monthly.

STANDARD & POOR'S UTILITY STOCK INDEX, PRICE-EARNINGS RATIO, WEEKLY (for middle of each of two weeks just past). THE OUTLOOK. Published weekly.

STANDARD & POOR'S UTILITY STOCK INDEX, PRICE-EARNINGS RATIO, YEARLY, HIGH-LOW (range for current year and one previous year). THE OUTLOOK. Published weekly.

Standard & Poor's utility stock index, yield.

    SEE: Standard & Poor's utility stock index, dividend
             yield. . .

State bond averages (ten year), Moody's.

    SEE: Moody's municipal bond averages. . .

State bonds.

    SEE: Municipal bonds. . .
          Public authority bonds. . .
          Toll revenue bonds. . .

STATE OF INCORPORATION (state and date of incorporation for each of over 1,000 companies with actively traded common stock). MOODY'S HANDBOOK OF COMMON STOCKS. Published quarterly.

STATE OF INCORPORATION (state of incorporation for each of roughly 26,000 unlisted and listed corporations). NATIONAL MONTHLY STOCK SUMMARY. Published monthly.

Stock advances and declines.

    SEE: Advances and declines. . .

Stock-bond yield spread.

    SEE: Yield spread. . .

Stock classification by industry.

    SEE: Industry classification, stocks. . .

Stock dividends.

    SEE ALSO: Dividends, amount, current, daily list. . .
             Stock splits. . .

STOCK DIVIDENDS, CURRENT (leading corporations with currently announced dividends to be paid in stock instead of in cash are listed, with amount and date of payment). VALUE LINE INVESTMENT SURVEY. Part three: published weekly, a few industries each week.

STOCK DIVIDENDS, CURRENT, DAILY LIST ("Dividends Announced" includes separate "Stock" category). NEW YORK TIMES. Published weekdays.

STOCK DIVIDENDS, CURRENT, PREVIOUSLY ANNOUNCED (all cash and stock dividends previously announced and to be paid in near future are listed alphabetically by company. Dates of record and payment dates are included). COMMERCIAL AND FINANCIAL CHRONICLE. Monday edition.

STOCK DIVIDENDS, CURRENT, WEEKLY LIST OF (includes all cash and stock dividends announced during current week. Alphabetical listing, with dates of record and payment dates). COMMERCIAL AND FINANCIAL CHRONICLE. Monday edition.

STOCK DIVIDENDS, YEARLY (month, year, and amount of dividends paid in stock instead of cash are included on price chart for each of over 1,000 actively traded common stocks. A period of about 20 years is covered, in most cases). MOODY'S HANDBOOK OF COMMON STOCKS. Published quarterly.

STOCK DIVIDENDS, YEARLY (footnotes indicate amount of dividends paid in stock instead of cash and year of payment for each of about 4,300 corporations over past five years). STANDARD & POOR'S SECURITY OWNER'S STOCK GUIDE. Published monthly.

STOCK DIVIDENDS, YEARLY (week, year, and amount of dividends paid in stock instead of cash indicated on price chart for each of about 960 listed stocks. A period of about four years is covered, in each case). TRENDLINE'S CURRENT MARKET PERSPECTIVES. Published monthly.

Stock exchange seats.

    SEE: Exchange seats. . .

Stock exchanges.

    See names of individual exchanges.

Stock exchanges, total volume for U.S.

    SEE: Market value total of share sales on all
           registered exchanges. . .

Stock group averages.

    SEE: Barron's group stock averages. . .
           Moody's industry group stock averages. . .
           Standard & Poor's stock group indexes. . .
           Value Line industry group stock indexes. . .

Stock group classification.

    SEE: Industry classification, stocks. . .

Stock holdings, institutional.

    SEE: Institutional holdings. . .

Stock markets.

    SEE: Markets where stocks are traded. . .

Stock offerings.

    SEE: New issues, stocks. . .

Stock options.

    SEE: Puts and calls. . .

Stock outstanding.

    SEE: Shares outstanding. . .

Stock par values.

    SEE: Par values, stock. . .

Stock price advances and declines.

    SEE: Advances and declines. . .

Stock price averages.

    See names of individual averages or indexes, such as "Dow-Jones Industrial

Stock Average" or "Standard & Poor's Industrial 425 Stock Index." Averages and indexes will be found listed as cross references under individual subjects, such as "Industrial Stock Averages," "Railroad Stock Averages," "Utility Stock Averages," and so forth.

Stock price averages, foreign.

    SEE: Foreign stock price indexes. . .

Stock price fluctuations.

    SEE: Trading swings. . .

Stock price highs and lows.

    SEE: New highs and new lows. . .
          Stock prices, dates of highs and lows. . .

Stock prices.

    SEE ALSO: Bank stocks, prices. . .
                 Closed-end investment companies, prices. . .
                 Foreign stocks, prices. . .
                 Insurance stocks (unlisted), prices. . .
                 Mutual funds, prices. . .
                 Railroad stocks (unlisted), prices. . .
                 Utility stocks (unlisted), prices. . .

STOCK PRICES, DAILY, HIGH-LOW-CLOSE, CHARTS (prices of each of about 700 active, listed stocks are charted on a daily basis for about nine months). TRENDLINE DAILY BASIS STOCK CHARTS. Published weekly.

STOCK PRICES, DATES OF HIGHS AND LOWS, MONTHLY (for month prior to month of publication, dates of high and low during month are given for each stock traded on New York, American, Pacific Coast, and five other stock exchanges). BANK AND QUOTATION RECORD. Published monthly.

STOCK PRICES, DATES OF HIGHS AND LOWS, YEAR TO DATE (for current year up to and including month prior to month of publication, dates of high and low are given for each stock traded on New York, American, Pacific Coast, and five other stock exchanges). BANK AND QUOTATION RECORD. Published monthly.

STOCK PRICES, DATES OF HIGHS AND LOWS, YEAR TO DATE, AMERICAN STOCK EXCHANGE (month of low and month of high given for each listed stock for year to date). COMMERCIAL AND FINANCIAL CHRONICLE. Monday edition.

STOCK PRICES, DATES OF HIGHS AND LOWS, YEARLY, NEW YORK STOCK EXCHANGE (month and day of high, and month and day of low given for each listed stock for current year and previous year). COMMERCIAL AND FINAN-CIAL CHRONICLE. Monday edition.

Stock prices, foreign.

SEE: Foreign stock price indexes. . .
Foreign stock prices. . .
(Also see stock prices on various foreign stock ex-
changes, such as "Stock prices on London Stock
Exchange. . .")

STOCK PRICES, MONTHLY, HIGH–LOW, CHARTS (monthly price ranges are charted for about 20 years for each of over 1,000 activity traded common stocks). MOODY'S HANDBOOK OF COMMON STOCKS. Published quarterly.

STOCK PRICES, MONTHLY, HIGH–LOW, CHARTS (monthly price ranges are charted for about 18 years for each of about 1,400 leading common stocks). VALUE LINE INVESTMENT SURVEY. Part three: published weekly, a few industries each week.

STOCK PRICES, MONTHLY, HIGH–LOW–CLOSE (for each of about 5,000 common and preferred, listed and unlisted issues for month previous to month of publication). STANDARD & POOR'S SECURITY OWNER'S STOCK GUIDE. Published monthly.

Stock prices, moving average.

SEE ALSO: Over 200–day moving average ratio. . .

STOCK PRICES, MOVING AVERAGE, CHARTS (200–day moving average line is superimposed on daily price chart covering about nine months, for each of about 700 active, listed stocks). TRENDLINE DAILY BASIS STOCK CHARTS. Published weekly.

Stock prices, new highs and lows.

SEE: New highs and new lows, stock prices. . .

Stock prices, New York Stock Exchange.

SEE: Stock prices on New York Stock Exchange. . .

Stock prices, over-the-counter.

SEE ALSO: Bank stocks, prices. . .
Insurance stocks (unlisted), prices. . .
Railroad stocks (unlisted), prices. . .
Utility stocks (unlisted), prices. . .

STOCK PRICES, OVER-THE-COUNTER, DAILY (previous day's bid and asked prices at twelve noon for each of over 1,200 unlisted industrial, utility, and miscellaneous stocks, with former bid). NEW YORK TIMES. Weekday edition.

STOCK PRICES, OVER-THE-COUNTER, DAILY (previous day's bid and asked prices at one p.m. for each of over 1,000 unlisted industrial, utility, and miscellaneous stocks, with net change in bid). WALL STREET JOURNAL. Published business days.

STOCK PRICES, OVER-THE-COUNTER, MONTHLY (bid and asked prices-- labeled "Wants" and "Offerings"-- for each of about 27,000 unlisted stocks,

both common and preferred. Names of brokers "making a market" in each
stock are shown, with various dates and prices, including end-of-the-month in
most cases. Prices of very inactive issues may appear only in cumulative volumes
issued twice a year in April and October. Monthly closing prices are also shown
for U.S. and Canadian listed stocks, making a total of about 30,000 listed and
unlisted issues). NATIONAL MONTHLY STOCK SUMMARY. Published monthly.

STOCK PRICES, OVER-THE-COUNTER, MONTHLY, CLOSE (bid and asked
prices for end of month prior to month of publication are given for each of over
3,200 unlisted "Industrial and Miscellaneous Stocks"). BANK AND QUOTA-
TION RECORD. Published monthly.

STOCK PRICES, OVER-THE-COUNTER, WEEKLY, CLOSE (bid and asked prices
for end of week just past, and bid price for end of previous week, are quoted
for each of over 1,500 unlisted industrial, utility, and miscellaneous stocks.
Less-active stocks are labeled "Weekly List"). BARRON'S. Published weekly.

STOCK PRICES, OVER-THE-COUNTER, WEEKLY, CLOSE (bid and asked prices
for end of week just past are given for each of over 1,200 unlisted "Industrials
and Utilities"). COMMERCIAL AND FINANCIAL CHRONICLE. Monday edition.

STOCK PRICES, OVER-THE-COUNTER, WEEKLY, CLOSE (bid and asked prices
for each of over 350, less widely held, unlisted stocks, for end of week just
past). NEW YORK TIMES. These prices appear in Monday edition.

STOCK PRICES, OVER-THE-COUNTER, WEEKLY, CLOSE (bid and asked prices
for each of over 600, less widely held, unlisted stocks, for end of week just
past). WALL STREET JOURNAL. These prices appear in Monday edition.

STOCK PRICES, OVER-THE-COUNTER, WEEKLY, HIGH-LOW-CLOSE (range
and close of bid prices for each of over 1,200 unlisted industrial, utility, and
miscellaneous stocks, for week just past). NEW YORK TIMES. Sunday edition.

STOCK PRICES, OVER-THE-COUNTER, YEAR TO DATE, HIGH-LOW (range
of bid prices for current year given for each of over 1,500 unlisted industrial,
utility, and miscellaneous stocks). BARRON'S. Published weekly.

Stock prices, unlisted.

   SEE: Stock prices, over-the-counter. . .

STOCK PRICES, WEEKLY, HIGH-LOW-CLOSE, CHARTS (weekly prices are
charted for about four years for each of about 960 listed stocks). TRENDLINE'S
CURRENT MARKET PERSPECTIVES. Published monthly.

STOCK PRICES, YEARLY, HIGH-LOW (price range for current year and each
of past eleven years for each of over 1,000 actively traded common stocks,
and for current year only for each of over 1,200 less active common stocks).
MOODY'S HANDBOOK OF COMMON STOCKS. Published quarterly.

STOCK PRICES, YEARLY, HIGH-LOW (price range, where available, for each of past couple of years, for each of about 30,000 unlisted and listed, common and preferred stocks). NATIONAL MONTHLY STOCK SUMMARY. Published monthly.

STOCK PRICES, YEARLY, HIGH-LOW (price ranges for current year and one previous year for each of about 5,000 common and preferred, listed and unlisted stocks). STANDARD & POOR'S SECURITY OWNER'S STOCK GUIDE. Published monthly.

STOCK PRICES, YEARLY, HIGH-LOW, CHARTS (small charts show yearly price rabge for each of past twelve or so years, for each of about 700 active, listed stocks). TRENDLINE DAILY BASIS STOCK CHARTS. Published weekly.

STOCK PRICES, YEARLY, HIGH-LOW, CHARTS (small charts show yearly price range for each of past ten or so years, for each of about 960 listed stocks). TRENDLINE'S CURRENT MARKET PERSPECTIVES. Published monthly.

STOCK PRICES, YEARLY (30-YEAR PERIOD), HIGH-LOW (highest and lowest prices reached by each of about 5,000 common and preferred, listed and unlisted stocks during recent 30-year period). STANDARD & POOR'S SECURITY OWNER'S STOCK GUIDE. Published monthly.

STOCK PRICES, YEARLY (12-YEAR PERIOD), HIGH-LOW (highest and lowest prices reached by each of over 1,200 less actively traded common stocks during recent 12-year period). MOODY'S HANDBOOK OF COMMON STOCKS. Published quarterly.

STOCK PRICES ON AMERICAN STOCK EXCHANGE, DAILY, OPEN-HIGH-LOW-CLOSE (for each stock traded on previous day). NEW YORK TIMES. Published weekdays.

STOCK PRICES ON AMERICAN STOCK EXCHANGE, DAILY, OPEN-HIGH-LOW-CLOSE (for each stock traded on previous day). WALL STREET JOURNAL. Published business days.

STOCK PRICES ON AMERICAN STOCK EXCHANGE, MONTHLY, OPEN-HIGH-LOW-CLOSE (for each stock traded, for month prior to month of publication). BANK AND QUOTATION RECORD. Published monthly.

STOCK PRICES ON AMERICAN STOCK EXCHANGE, WEEKLY, HIGH-LOW-CLOSE (price range and last sale price for week just past, for each listed stock). BARRON'S. Published weekly. Also published weekly in Monday edition of COMMERCIAL AND FINANCIAL CHRONICLE and Sunday edition of NEW YORK TIMES.

STOCK PRICES ON AMERICAN STOCK EXCHANGE, YEAR TO DATE, HIGH-LOW (current year's price range for each listed stock). BARRON'S. Published weekly. Also published weekly in Monday edition of COMMERCIAL AND FINANCIAL CHRONICLE and Sunday edition of NEW YORK TIMES. Published daily in NEW YORK TIMES and WALL STREET JOURNAL.

STOCK PRICES ON AMERICAN STOCK EXCHANGE, YEAR TO DATE, OPEN-HIGH-LOW (opening price and price range for current year given for each listed stock). BANK AND QUOTATION RECORD. Published monthly.

STOCK PRICES ON AMSTERDAM STOCK EXCHANGE, DAILY, CLOSE (for each of about 15 selected stocks, in Netherlands guilders, for previous trading day). NEW YORK TIMES. Published weekdays.

STOCK PRICES ON BOSTON STOCK EXCHANGE, DAILY, HIGH-LOW-CLOSE (for each exclusively listed stock traded on previous day). WALL STREET JOURNAL. Published business days.

STOCK PRICES ON BOSTON STOCK EXCHANGE, MONTHLY, OPEN-HIGH-LOW-CLOSE (individual monthly prices given for all stocks traded on Boston Stock Exchange for month prior to month of publication). BANK AND QUOTATION RECORD. Published monthly.

STOCK PRICES ON BOSTON STOCK EXCHANGE, WEEKLY, CLOSE (for each exclusively listed stock, closing price is given for week just past and week previous to that). BARRON'S. Published weekly.

STOCK PRICES ON BOSTON STOCK EXCHANGE, YEAR TO DATE, HIGH-LOW (current year's price range for each exclusively listed stock). BARRON'S. Published weekly.

STOCK PRICES ON BOSTON STOCK EXCHANGE, YEAR TO DATE, OPEN-HIGH-LOW (opening price and price range for current year given for each stock listed). BANK AND QUOTATION RECORD. Published monthly.

STOCK PRICES ON BRUSSELS STOCK EXCHANGE, DAILY, CLOSE (for each of about ten selected stocks, in Belgian francs, for previous trading day). NEW YORK TIMES. Published weekdays.

STOCK PRICES ON BUENOS AIRES STOCK EXCHANGE, DAILY, CLOSE (for each of about ten selected stocks, in Argentine pesos, for previous trading day). NEW YORK TIMES. Published weekdays.

STOCK PRICES ON CINCINNATI STOCK EXCHANGE, DAILY, HIGH-LOW-CLOSE (for each exclusively listed stock traded on previous day), WALL STREET JOURNAL. Published business days.

STOCK PRICES ON CINCINNATI STOCK EXCHANGE, WEEKLY, CLOSE (for each exclusively listed stock, closing price is given for week just past and for week previous to that). BARRON'S. Published weekly.

STOCK PRICES ON CINCINNATI STOCK EXCHANGE, WEEKLY, HIGH-LOW-CLOSE (for each stock for week just past). COMMERCIAL AND FINANCIAL CHRONICLE. Monday edition.

STOCK PRICES ON CINCINNATI STOCK EXCHANGE, YEAR TO DATE, HIGH-LOW (current year's price range for each exclusively listed stock). BARRON'S. Published weekly.

STOCK PRICES ON DETROIT STOCK EXCHANGE, DAILY, HIGH-LOW-CLOSE (for each exclusively listed stock traded on previous day). WALL STREET JOUR-NAL. Published business days.

STOCK PRICES ON DETROIT STOCK EXCHANGE, MONTHLY, OPEN-HIGH-LOW-CLOSE (for each stock traded, for month prior to month of publication). BANK AND QUOTATION RECORD. Published monthly.

STOCK PRICES ON DETROIT STOCK EXCHANGE, WEEKLY, CLOSE (for each exclusively listed stock, closing price is given for week just past and for week previous to that). BARRON'S. Published weekly.

STOCK PRICES ON DETROIT STOCK EXCHANGE, YEAR TO DATE, HIGH-LOW (current year's price range for each exclusively listed stocks). BARRON'S. Published weekly.

STOCK PRICES ON DETROIT STOCK EXCHANGE, YEAR TO DATE, OPEN-HIGH-LOW (opening price and range for current year for each listed stock). BANK AND QUOTATION RECORD. Published monthly.

STOCK PRICES ON FRANKFURT STOCK EXCHANGE, DAILY, CLOSE (for each of about 20 selected stocks, in German marks, for previous trading day). NEW YORK TIMES. Published weekdays.

STOCK PRICES ON HONOLULU STOCK EXCHANGE, DAILY, HIGH-LOW-CLOSE (for each stock traded two days ago). WALL STREET JOURNAL. Published business days.

STOCK PRICES ON JOHANNESBURG STOCK EXCHANGE, DAILY, CLOSE (for each of about ten selected stocks, in South African rands, for previous trading day). NEW YORK TIMES. Published weekdays.

STOCK PRICES ON LONDON STOCK EXCHANGE, DAILY, CLOSE (for each of about 50 selected stocks, in shillings and pence, for previous trading day). NEW YORK TIMES. Published weekdays.

STOCK PRICES ON MEXICO CITY STOCK EXCHANGE, DAILY, CLOSE (for each of about 20 selected stocks, in Mexican pesos, for previous trading day). NEW YORK TIMES. Published weekdays.

STOCK PRICES ON MIDWEST STOCK EXCHANGE, DAILY, CLOSE (for each stock traded on previous day). NEW YORK TIMES. Published weekdays.

STOCK PRICES ON MIDWEST STOCK EXCHANGE, DAILY, HIGH-LOW-CLOSE (for each exclusively listed stock traded on previous day). WALL STREET JOUR-NAL. Published business days.

STOCK PRICES ON MIDWEST STOCK EXCHANGE, MONTHLY, OPEN-HIGH-LOW-CLOSE (for each stock listed, for month prior to month of publication). BANK AND QUOTATION RECORD. Published monthly.

STOCK PRICES ON MIDWEST STOCK EXCHANGE, WEEKLY, CLOSE (closing price for week just past and for week before that, for each exclusively listed stock). BARRON'S. Published weekly.

STOCK PRICES ON MIDWEST STOCK EXCHANGE, YEAR TO DATE, HIGH-LOW (current year's price range for each exclusively listed stock). BARRON'S. Published weekly.

STOCK PRICES ON MIDWEST STOCK EXCHANGE, YEAR TO DATE, OPEN-HIGH-LOW (opening price and range for current year for each listed stock). BANK AND QUOTATION RECORD. Published monthly.

STOCK PRICES ON MILAN STOCK EXCHANGE, DAILY, CLOSE (for each of about 16 selected stocks, in Italian lire, for previous trading day). NEW YORK TIMES. Published weekdays.

STOCK PRICES ON MONTREAL STOCK EXCHANGE, DAILY, HIGH-LOW-CLOSE (for stocks traded on previous day). NEW YORK TIMES. Published weekdays. Also published on business days in WALL STREET JOURNAL.

STOCK PRICES ON MONTREAL STOCK EXCHANGE, WEEKLY, CLOSE (closing prices for week just past and week before that). BARRON'S. Published weekly.

STOCK PRICES ON MONTREAL STOCK EXCHANGE, YEAR TO DATE, HIGH-LOW (current year's price ranges). BARRON'S. Published weekly.

STOCK PRICES ON NATIONAL STOCK EXCHANGE, DAILY, HIGH-LOW-CLOSE (for stocks traded on previous day). NEW YORK TIMES. Published weekdays. Also published on business days in WALL STREET JOURNAL.

STOCK PRICES ON NATIONAL STOCK EXCHANGE, WEEKLY, HIGH-LOW-CLOSE (prices for week just past). COMMERCIAL AND FINANCIAL CHRONI-CLE. Monday edition.

STOCK PRICES ON NATIONAL STOCK EXCHANGE, WEEKLY, OPEN-HIGH-LOW-CLOSE (for week just past). BARRON'S. Published weekly.

STOCK PRICES ON NATIONAL STOCK EXCHANGE, YEAR TO DATE, HIGH-LOW (price ranges for current year). BARRON'S. Published weekly.

STOCK PRICES ON NEW YORK STOCK EXCHANGE, DAILY, HIGH-LOW (for each day of week just past, price range is shown for each listed stock). COMMERCIAL AND FINANCIAL CHRONICLE. Monday edition.

STOCK PRICES ON NEW YORK STOCK EXCHANGE, DAILY, OPEN-HIGH-LOW-CLOSE (for previous day, for each stock traded). NEW YORK TIMES. Published weekdays. Also published on business days in WALL STREET JOUR-NAL.

STOCK PRICES ON NEW YORK STOCK EXCHANGE, MONTHLY, HIGH-LOW (for each of twelve months of year just past, price range is given for each list-ed stock). COMMERCIAL AND FINANCIAL CHRONICLE. This data is pub-lished annually in special section of Thursday edition, usually around the end of January or first of February.

STOCK PRICES ON NEW YORK STOCK EXCHANGE, MONTHLY, OPEN-

HIGH-LOW-CLOSE (for month prior to month of publication, for each listed stock). BANK AND QUOTATION RECORD. Published monthly.

STOCK PRICES ON NEW YORK STOCK EXCHANGE, WEEKLY, HIGH-LOW-CLOSE (for week just past, for each listed stock). BARRON'S. Published weekly. Also published weekly in Sunday edition of NEW YORK TIMES.

STOCK PRICES ON NEW YORK STOCK EXCHANGE, YEAR TO DATE, HIGH-LOW (current year's price range for each stock). BARRON'S. Published weekly. Also published daily and on Sunday in NEW YORK TIMES, and daily in WALL STREET JOURNAL.

STOCK PRICES ON NEW YORK STOCK EXCHANGE, YEAR TO DATE, OPEN-HIGH-LOW (current year's opening price and price range for each stock). BANK AND QUOTATION RECORD. Published monthly.

STOCK PRICES ON NEW YORK STOCK EXCHANGE, YEARLY, HIGH-LOW (annual price range for each of past 24 years is shown for each of stocks listed on New York Stock Exchange, including old issues. All stock splits and name changes are indicated). COMMERCIAL AND FINANCIAL CHRONICLE. This data appears in special "Stock and Bond Outlook Supplement" published annually in latter part of year as part of Thursday edition.

STOCK PRICES ON NEW YORK STOCK EXCHANGE, YEARLY, HIGH-LOW (price range for each listed stock for current year and previous year. Exact dates of annual highs and lows given in each case). COMMERCIAL AND FINANCIAL CHRONICLE. Monday edition.

Stock prices on over-the-counter markets.

SEE: Stock prices, over-the-counter. . .

STOCK PRICES ON PACIFIC COAST STOCK EXCHANGE, DAILY, CLOSE (for each stock traded on previous day). NEW YORK TIMES. Published weekdays.

STOCK PRICES ON PACIFIC COAST STOCK EXCHANGE, DAILY, HIGH-LOW-CLOSE (for exclusively listed stocks traded on previous day). WALL STREET JOURNAL. Published business days.

STOCK PRICES ON PACIFIC COAST STOCK EXCHANGE, MONTHLY, OPEN-HIGH-LOW-CLOSE (monthly prices for all stocks traded, for month prior to month of publication). BANK AND QUOTATION RECORD. Published monthly.

STOCK PRICES ON PACIFIC COAST STOCK EXCHANGE, WEEKLY, CLOSE (closing prices for week just past and for week previous to that, for exclusively listed stocks). BARRON'S. Published weekly.

STOCK PRICES ON PACIFIC COAST STOCK EXCHANGE, YEAR TO DATE, OPEN-HIGH-LOW (opening price and price range for current year given for each stock listed). BANK AND QUOTATION RECORD. Published monthly.

STOCK PRICES ON PARIS STOCK EXCHANGE (BOURSE), DAILY, CLOSE (for each of about 18 selected stocks, in French francs, for previous trading day). NEW YORK TIMES. Published weekdays.

STOCK PRICES ON PHILADELPHIA-BALTIMORE-WASHINGTON STOCK EX-CHANGE, DAILY, HIGH-LOW-CLOSE (for each exclusively listed stock traded on previous day). WALL STREET JOURNAL. Published business days.

STOCK PRICES ON PHILADELPHIA-BALTIMORE-WASHINGTON STOCK EX-CHANGE, MONTHLY, OPEN-HIGH-LOW-CLOSE (monthly prices for all stocks traded, for month prior to month of publication). BANK AND QUOTATION RECORD. Published monthly.

STOCK PRICES ON PHILADELPHIA-BALTIMORE-WASHINGTON STOCK EX-CHANGE, WEEKLY, CLOSE (for exclusively listed stocks, shows closing prices for week just past and for week previous to that). BARRON'S. Published weekly.

STOCK PRICES ON PHILADELPHIA-BALTIMORE-WASHINGTON STOCK EX-CHANGE, WEEKLY, HIGH-LOW-CLOSE (for week just past). COMMERCIAL AND FINANCIAL CHRONICLE. Monday edition.

STOCK PRICES ON PHILADELPHIA-BALTIMORE-WASHINGTON STOCK EX-CHANGE, YEAR TO DATE, HIGH-LOW (current year's price range for each exclusively listed stock). BARRON'S. Published weekly.

STOCK PRICES ON PHILADELPHIA-BALTIMORE-WASHINGTON STOCK EX-CHANGE, YEAR TO DATE, OPEN-HIGH-LOW (opening price and price range for current year given for each stock listed). BANK AND QUOTATION REC-ORD. Published monthly.

STOCK PRICES ON PITTSBURGH STOCK EXCHANGE, DAILY, HIGH-LOW-CLOSE (for each exclusively listed stock traded on previous day). WALL STREET JOURNAL. Published business days.

STOCK PRICES ON PITTSBURGH STOCK EXCHANGE, MONTHLY, OPEN-HIGH-LOW-CLOSE (monthly prices for all stocks traded, for month prior to month of publication). BANK AND QUOTATION RECORD. Published monthly.

STOCK PRICES ON PITTSBURGH STOCK EXCHANGE, WEEKLY, CLOSE (clos-ing price for week just past and previous week for each exclusively listed stock). BARRON'S. Published weekly.

STOCK PRICES ON PITTSBURGH STOCK EXCHANGE, YEAR TO DATE, HIGH-LOW (current year's price range for each exclusively listed stock). BARRON'S. Published weekly.

STOCK PRICES ON PITTSBURGH STOCK EXCHANGE, YEAR TO DATE, OPEN-HIGH-LOW (current year's opening price and price range for each listed stock). BANK AND QUOTATION RECORD. Published monthly.

STOCK PRICES ON SALT LAKE CITY STOCK EXCHANGE, DAILY, HIGH-LOW-CLOSE (for each exclusively listed stock traded on previous day). WALL STREET JOURNAL. Published business days.

INVESTMENT INFORMATION

STOCK PRICES ON SYDNEY STOCK EXCHANGE, DAILY, CLOSE (for each of about 18 selected stocks, in Australian dollars and cents, for previous trading day). NEW YORK TIMES. Published weekdays.

STOCK PRICES ON TOKYO STOCK EXCHANGE, DAILY, CLOSE (for each of about 18 selected stocks, in Japanese yen, for previous trading day). NEW YORK TIMES. Published weekdays.

STOCK PRICES ON TORONTO STOCK EXCHANGE, DAILY, HIGH-LOW-CLOSE (for each stock traded on previous day. Three categories: industrials, mines, and oil & gas). NEW YORK TIMES. Published weekdays. Also published on business days in WALL STREET JOURNAL.

STOCK PRICES ON TORONTO STOCK EXCHANGE, WEEKLY, CLOSE (closing price for week just past and week before that, for each exclusively listed stock. Three lists: industrials, banks, and mines-oils). BARRON'S. Published weekly.

STOCK PRICES ON TORONTO STOCK EXCHANGE, WEEKLY, CLOSE (closing prices for week just past for industrials, mines, and oils). COMMERCIAL AND FINANCIAL CHRONICLE. Monday edition.

STOCK PRICES ON TORONTO STOCK EXCHANGE, YEAR TO DATE, HIGH-LOW (current year's price range for each exclusively listed stock. Three lists: industrials, banks, and mines-oils). BARRON'S. Published weekly.

STOCK PRICES ON ZURICH STOCK EXCHANGE, DAILY, CLOSE (for each of about 20 selected stocks, in Swiss francs, for previous trading day). NEW YORK TIMES. Published weekdays.

Stock prices over-the-counter.

SEE: Stock prices, over-the-counter. . .

Stock purchase warrants.

SEE: Warrants. . .

Stock ratings.

SEE: Ratings, stocks. . .

Stock registrars.

SEE: Registrars. . .

Stock sales volume.

SEE: Volume of trading stocks. . .

Stock shares outstanding.

SEE: Shares outstanding. . .

Stock splits.

SEE ALSO: Stock dividends. . . (Current listings of
stock dividends normally include stock splits.)

STOCK SPLITS (month, year, and amount of splits for past 20 years or so are
indicated on price charts for each of over 1,000 actively traded common stocks).
MOODY'S HANDBOOK OF COMMON STOCKS. Published quarterly.

STOCK SPLITS (footnotes indicate amount and year of splits for each of about
4,300 corporations over past five years). STANDARD & POOR'S SECURITY
OWNER'S STOCK GUIDE. Published monthly.

STOCK SPLITS (week, month, year, and amount of splits for past four years or
so are indicated on price charts for each of about 960 listed stocks). TREND-
LINE'S CURRENT MARKET PERSPECTIVES. Published monthly.

STOCK SPLITS (month, year, and amount of splits for past 18 years or so are
indicated on price charts for each of about 1,400 leading common stocks).
VALUE LINE INVESTMENT SURVEY. Part three: published weekly, a few
industries each week.

STOCK SPLITS, AMERICAN STOCK EXCHANGE (stock splits and substantial
stock dividends listed alphabetically by company, for year to date. Amount
and "Date When Admitted to Trading" are given in each case). BANK AND
QUOTATION RECORD. Published monthly.

STOCK SPLITS, CURRENT, PREVIOUSLY ANNOUNCED (all cash and stock
dividends, including splits, previously announced and to be paid in near
future, are listed alphabetically by company. Dates of payment and record are
included). COMMERCIAL AND FINANCIAL CHRONICLE. Monday edition.

STOCK SPLITS, CURRENT, WEEKLY LIST (all cash and stock dividends, including splits, announced during current week, are listed alphabetically by
company. Dates of payment and record are given.) COMMERCIAL AND
FINANCIAL CHRONICLE. Monday edition.

STOCK SPLITS, NEW YORK STOCK EXCHANGE (stock splits and substantial
stock dividends listed alphabetically by company, for year to date. Amount
and "Date When Admitted to Trading" are given in each case). BANK AND
QUOTATION RECORD. Published monthly.

STOCK SPLITS, NEW YORK STOCK EXCHANGE (all stock splits for each
listed company shown for past 24 years). COMMERCIAL AND FINANCIAL
CHRONICLE. This data appears in special annual supplement to Thursday
edition, published in latter part of year.

Stock symbols.
SEE: Ticker symbols. . .

Stock transfer agents
SEE: Transfer agents. . .

STOCK TRANSFER TAXES (currently effective rates, as in New York, Florida,

and South Carolina). STANDARD & POOR'S SECURITY OWNER'S STOCK
GUIDE. Published monthly.

STOCK TRANSFER TAXES, CANADIAN (currently effective rates, as in Ontario
and Quebec). STANDARD & POOR'S SECURITY OWNER'S STOCK GUIDE.
Published monthly.

Stock value of convertible bonds.

>   SEE: Convertible bonds, stock value of bonds. . .

Stock volume.

>   SEE: Volume of trading in stocks. . .

Stock yields.

>   SEE: Dividend yields (percent). . .
>   Also see entries under various stock averages and indexes,
>   such as "Dow-Jones industrial stock average, dividend
>   yield. . ."

Stock yields, high.

>   SEE: High yielding stocks. . .

Stockbrokers.

>   SEE: Brokers. . .
>   Underwriters. . .

Stockholders' equity.

>   SEE: Capitalization stated as dollar amounts. . .
>   Capitalization stated as percentages. . .

STOCKHOLDERS, NUMBER OF (number of current stockholders given for each
of over 1,000 companies with actively traded common stock). MOODY'S
HANDBOOK OF COMMON STOCKS. Published quarterly.

STOCKHOLDERS, NUMBER OF (number of current stockholders given for each
of about 1,400 leading corporations). VALUE LINE INVESTMENT SURVEY.
Part three: published weekly, a few industries each week.

Stockholdings, changes in.

>   SEE: Insider transactions. . .

Stockholdings, institutional.

>   SEE: Institutional holdings. . .

Stores, number of.

>   SEE: Retailers, number of stores. . .

Straight debt value of convertible bonds.

SEE: Convertible bonds, estimated investment worth. . .

Street loans.

SEE: Brokers' loans. . .
Call loan rates. . .

Supermarkets.

SEE: Retailers.

Suspended dealings.

SEE: Dealings suspended. . .

Swings, trading.

SEE: Trading swings. . .

Swiss stocks.

SEE: Foreign stock price indexes. . .
Stock prices on Zurich Stock Exchange. . .

Sydney Stock Exchange prices.

SEE: Foreign stock price indexes. . .
Stock prices on Sydney Stock Exchange. . .

Symbols, ticker.

SEE: Ticker symbols. . .

Tax, income, deferred.

SEE: Deferred income tax. . .

Tax, interest equalization.

SEE: Foreign bonds, foreign basis. . .

Tax equivalent yields.

SEE: Tax-exempt vs. taxable yields. . .

Tax-exempt bonds.

SEE: Municipal bonds. . .
Public authority bonds. . .
Toll revenue bonds. . .

TAX-EXEMPT VS. TAXABLE YIELDS (shows taxable yields required to equal various tax-exempt yields, for various personal and corporate income tax brackets). STANDARD & POOR'S EARNINGS AND RATINGS BOND GUIDE. Published monthly.

Tax-free exchange funds.

SEE: Exchange funds. . .

Tax status, Pennsylvania.

SEE: Pennsylvania tax status. . .

Taxes, bond transfer.

SEE: Bonds, transfer taxes. . .

Taxes, stock transfer.

SEE: Stock transfer taxes. . .

Tentative listings.

SEE: New listings, stocks (pending). . .

TICKER SYMBOLS (for about 2,200 stocks on New York and American Stock Exchanges). MOODY'S HANDBOOK OF COMMON STOCKS. Published quarterly.

TICKER SYMBOLS (for about 700 active stocks on New York and American Stock Exchanges). TRENDLINE DAILY BASIS STOCK CHARTS. Published weekly.

TICKER SYMBOLS (for about 1,000 active stocks on New York and American Stock Exchanges). TRENDLINE'S CURRENT MARKET PERSPECTIVES. Published monthly.

TICKER SYMBOLS (for over 3,000 stocks listed on New York, American, and many other U.S. and Canadian exchanges). STANDARD & POOR'S SECURITY OWNER'S STOCK GUIDE. Published monthly.

TICKER SYMBOLS (for about 1,400 active stocks, mostly New York Stock Exchange). VALUE LINE INVESTMENT SURVEY. Part one, published weekly. Also in part three: published weekly, a few industries each week.

TIME LOAN RATES (PERCENT), DAILY (bid-ask rates on mixed prime collateral loans for 30 days, 60 days, 90 days, four months, five months, and six months. All six rates quoted for each day of month prior to month of publication). BANK AND QUOTATION RECORD. Published monthly.

"Times earned" (times interest charges were earned).

SEE: Earnings to fixed charges ratio. . .

Tokyo Stock Exchange prices.

SEE: Foreign stock price indexes. . .
Stock prices on Tokyo Stock Exchange. . .

Toll revenue bonds.

SEE ALSO: Public authority bonds. . .

INVESTMENT INFORMATION

TOLL REVENUE BONDS, LIST OF (about 85 toll revenue bonds are arranged geographically by state, with quality ratings indicated). STANDARD & POOR'S EARNINGS AND RATINGS BOND GUIDE. Published monthly.

Tops and bottoms (stock price averages).

    SEE: Trading swings. . .

Toronto Stock Exchange.

    SEE: Commission rates, Canadian stock exchanges. . .
           Dividends, amount, indicated annual rate, Tornoto
               Stock Exchange. . .
           Earnings per share, interim, Toronto Stock
               Exchange. . .
           Stock prices on Toronto Stock Exchange. . .
           Volume of trading in stocks, individual stocks on
               Toronto Stock Exchange. . .
           Volume of trading in stocks, total for Toronto
               Stock Exchange. . .

Trading for members' accounts.

    SEE: Member trading. . .

Trading markets.

    SEE: Markets where bonds are traded. . .
           Markets where stocks are traded. . .

TRADING SWINGS, AMERICAN STOCK EXCHANGE PRICE LEVEL INDEX (on daily price chart covering about two years, numerical index figure is indicated at tops and bottoms of rallies and declines). TRENDLINE DAILY BASIS STOCK CHARTS. Published weekly.

TRADING SWINGS, DOW-JONES INDUSTRIAL STOCK AVERAGE (on daily price chart covering about four years, price of Dow-Jones industrial average is shown at tops and bottoms of rallies and declines). TRENDLINE DAILY BASIS STOCK CHARTS. Published weekly.

TRADING SWINGS, DOW-JONES STOCK AVERAGES (amounts, dates, and prices relative to rallies and declines of Dow-Jones industrial, railroad, and utility stock averages. About nine years are covered). This data usually appears in January or February in BARRON'S.

TRADING SWINGS, STANDARD & POOR'S COMPOSITE 500 STOCK INDEX (on daily price chart covering about four years, numerical index figure is shown at tops and bottoms of rallies and declines). TRENDLINE DAILY BASIS STOCK CHARTS. Published weekly.

TRADING SWINGS, STANDARD & POOR'S STOCK INDEXES (amounts, dates, and percentage changes of rallies and declines in Standard & Poor's industrial, railroad, and utility stock price indexes. Period covered is about twelve months).

STANDARD & POOR'S SECURITY OWNER'S STOCK GUIDE. Published monthly. Also published weekly in THE OUTLOOK.

Trading volume.

>   SEE: Volume of trading. . .

Transactions, insider.

>   SEE: Insider transactions. . .

Transactions, investment company.

>   SEE: Investment company transactions. . .

Transfer agents.

>   SEE ALSO: Registrars. . .

TRANSFER AGENTS (name and city of bank serving as transfer agent for each of over 1,000 actively traded common stocks). MOODY'S HANDBOOK OF COMMON STOCKS. Published quarterly.

TRANSFER AGENTS (name and city of bank, where applicable, serving as transfer agent for each of about 26,000 unlisted and listed corporations). NATIONAL MONTHLY STOCK SUMMARY. This data appears in semiannual cumulative volumes, dated April 1 and October 1.

Transfer taxes.

>   SEE: Bonds, transfer taxes. . .
>   Stock transfer taxes. . .

Transportation stock index, New York Stock Exchange.

>   SEE: New York Stock Exchange transportation stock index. . .

Treasury bill averages.

>   SEE: Moody's treasury bill averages. . .
>   Standard & Poor's treasury bill index. . .

TREASURY BILLS, PRICES, DAILY (bid and asked prices in percentage discount form for each of about 40 issues, for previous trading day). NEW YORK TIMES. Published weekdays. Also published on business days in the WALL STREET JOURNAL.

TREASURY BILLS, PRICES, MONTHLY, CLOSE (end-of-month bid and asked prices in dollars and cents for each of about 40 issues. Labeled "United States and Municipal Bonds"). BANK AND QUOTATION RECORD. Published monthly.

TREASURY BILLS, PRICES, WEEKLY, CLOSE (end-of-week bid and asked prices in dollars and cents for each of about 40 issues). COMMERCIAL AND FINANCIAL CHRONICLE. Monday edition.

TREASURY BILLS, YIELDS TO MATURITY, DAILY (percentage yield for each of about 40 issues, for previous trading day). NEW YORK TIMES. Published weekdays.

TREASURY BILLS, YIELDS TO MATURITY, WEEKLY (end-of-week yields shown for each of about 40 issues). COMMERCIAL AND FINANCIAL CHRONICLE. Monday edition.

Treasury bonds.

SEE: Government bonds. . .

TREASURY CERTIFICATES, PRICES, DAILY (bid and asked prices for each of about 50 "Bonds, Notes and Certificates", for previous trading day). NEW YORK TIMES. Published weekdays.

TREASURY CERTIFICATES, YIELDS TO MATURITY, DAILY (percentage yield for each of about 50 "Bonds, Notes and Certificates", for previous trading day). NEW YORK TIMES. Published weekdays.

Treasury notes.

SEE ALSO: Government bonds. . .

TREASURY NOTES, PRICES, DAILY (bid and asked prices for each of about 50 "Bonds, Notes and Certificates", for previous trading day). NEW YORK TIMES. Published weekdays.

TREASURY NOTES, PRICES, DAILY (bid and asked prices for each of about 24 note issues, for previous trading day). WALL STREET JOURNAL. Published business days.

TREASURY NOTES, PRICES, MONTHLY, CLOSE (end-of-month bid and asked prices for each of about 24 U.S. Treasury notes. Labeled "United States and Municipal Bonds"). BANK AND QUOTATION RECORD. Published monthly.

TREASURY NOTES, PRICES, WEEKLY, CLOSE (end-of-week bid and asked prices for each of about 24 U.S. notes). COMMERCIAL AND FINANCIAL CHRONICLE. Monday edition.

TREASURY NOTES, YIELDS TO MATURITY, DAILY (percentage yield for each of about 50 "Bonds, Notes and Certificates", for previous trading day). NEW YORK TIMES. Published weekdays.

TREASURY NOTES, YIELDS TO MATURITY, DAILY (percentage yield for each of about 24 U.S. Treasury notes, for previous trading day). WALL STREET JOURNAL. Published business days.

Trust certificates, railroad equipment.

SEE: Railroad equipment trust certificates. . .

Trusts, investments.

> SEE: Closed-end investment companies. . .
> Investment compnies. . .
> Mutual funds. . .

Turning points of stock prices.

> SEE: Trading swings. . .

Turnpike bonds.

> SEE: Public authority bonds. . .
> Toll revenue bonds. . .

Underwriters.

> SEE ALSO: Brokers. . .
> New issues. . .

UNDERWRITERS OF BOND ISSUES (name of original underwriter--head of syndicate--indicated for each of about 2,600 corporate and 200 foreign bond issues. Original price and year of issue also given). STANDARD & POOR'S EARNINGS AND RATINGS BOND GUIDE. Published monthly.

Underwriters of stock issues.

> SEE: New issues, SEC registrations. . .
> New issues, stocks. . .

Underwriting activity.

> SEE: New issues, number of. . .
> New issues, bonds, total value of. . .
> New issues, stocks, total value of. . .
> New issues, total value of. . .

Unearned premium totals, insurance companies.

> SEE: Insurance companies, unearned premium totals. . .

Uninterrupted dividends, year of beginning.

> SEE: Dividends, uninterrupted, year of beginning. . .

United States Comptroller of the Currency.

> SEE: Comptroller of the Currency. . .

United States government bonds.

> SEE: Government bonds. . .

United States Securities and Exchange Commission.

> SEE: New issues, SEC registrations. . .
> Securities and Exchange Commission. . .

United States securities trading, total market value.

    SEE: Market value total of share sales on all
          registered exchanges. . .

United States Treasury bills.

    SEE: Treasury bills. . .

United States Treasury bonds.

    SEE: Government bonds. . .

United States Treasury certificates.

    SEE: Treasury certificates. . .

United States Treasury notes.

    SEE: Treasury notes. . .

Unlisted bond prices.

    SEE: Bond prices, over-the-counter. . .

Unlisted stock price averages.

    SEE: National Quotation Bureau over-the-counter
          industrial stock average. . .
          National Quotation Bureau over-the-counter insurance
          stock average. . .

Unlisted stock prices.

    SEE: Stock prices, over-the-counter. . .

UPSIDE-DOWNSIDE VOLUME, AMERICAN STOCK EXCHANGE, DAILY ("up"
volume of trading--rising prices--and "down" volume--falling prices--for each
day of week just past. Labeled "Stock Exchange Volume Trends"). BARRON'S.
Published weekly.

UPSIDE-DOWNSIDE VOLUME, NEW YORK STOCK EXCHANGE, DAILY ("up"
volume of trading--rising prices--and "down" volume--falling prices--for each
day of week just past. Labeled "Stock Exchange Volume Trends"). BARRON'S.
Published weekly.

UPSIDE-DOWNSIDE VOLUME, NEW YORK STOCK EXCHANGE, MOVING
AVERAGE, CHART (ten day moving average charted daily for about six months).
TRENDLINE DAILY BASIS STOCK CHARTS. Published weekly.

Utilities, bonds (unlisted).

    SEE: Utility bonds (unlisted). . .

UTILITIES, BOOK VALUE PER SHARE, YEARLY (for each of past eleven years,
for each of large gas, electric, telephone, and water utilities with actively

traded common stock). MOODY'S HANDBOOK OF COMMON STOCKS. Published quarterly.

UTILITIES, BOOK VALUE PER SHARE, YEARLY (for each of past 18 or so years, for each of about 100 leading gas, electric, and water utility companies). VALUE LINE INVESTMENT SURVEY. Part three: published weekly, a few industries each week.

UTILITIES, COMMON STOCK EQUITY (PERCENTAGE), YEARLY (for each of past eleven years, for each of large gas, electric, telephone, and water utilities with actively traded common stock). MOODY'S HANDBOOK OF COMMON STOCKS. Published quarterly.

UTILITIES, COMMON STOCK EQUITY (PERCENTAGE), YEARLY (for each of past 18 or so years, for each of about 100 leading gas, electric, and water utility companies. Labeled "Common Equity Ratio"). VALUE LINE INVESTMENT SURVEY. Part three: published weekly, a few industries each week.

UTILITIES, DEBT RATIO (PERCENTAGE), YEARLY (for each of past 18 or so years, for each of about 100 gas, electric, and water utility companies. Debt ratio represents long term debt as a percentage of total capitalization). VALUE LINE INVESTMENT SURVEY. Part three: published weekly, a few industries each week.

UTILITIES, GROSS FOR COMMON (PERCENTAGE), YEARLY (for each of past eleven years, for each of large gas, electric, telephone, and water utility companies with actively traded common stock. "Gross for common" refers to percentage of gross operating revenues "available for common equity"). MOODY'S HANDBOOK OF COMMON STOCKS. Published quarterly.

UTILITIES, OPERATING INCOME AS PERCENTAGE OF NET PLANT, YEARLY (for each of past eleven years, for each of large gas, electric, telephone, and water utility companies with actively traded common stock. "Net plant" refers to book value "without allowance for working capital and other elements"). MOODY'S HANDBOOK OF COMMON STOCKS. Published quarterly.

UTILITIES, OPERATING INCOME AS PERCENTAGE OF NET PLANT, YEARLY (for each of past 18 or so years, for each of about 100 large gas, electric, and water utility companies. Labeled "Return on Net Plant"). VALUE LINE INVESTMENT SURVEY. Part three: published weekly, a few industries each week.

UTILITIES, OPERATING RATIO (PERCENTAGE), YEARLY (for each of past four years, for each of about 35 major gas, electric, and telephone utility companies. Represents operating expenses expressed as a percentage of gross revenues). TRENDLINE'S CURRENT MARKET PERSPECTIVES. Published monthly.

UTILITIES, OPERATING RATIO (PERCENTAGE), YEARLY (for each of past 18 or so years, for each of about 100 large gas, electric, and water utility companies. Represents operating expenses as a percentage of gross revenues). VALUE LINE INVESTMENT SURVEY. Part three: published weekly, a few industries each week.

Utilities, preferred stock ratings.

> SEE: Ratings, stocks, Standard & Poor's, utilities. . .

UTILITIES, PREFERRED STOCK RATIO (PERCENTAGE), YEARLY (for each of past 18 or so years, for each of about 100 large gas, electric, and water utility companies. Represents preferred stock as percentage of total capitalization). VALUE LINE INVESTMENT SURVEY. Part three: published weekly, a few industries each week.

Utilities, return on net plant.

> SEE: Utilities, operating income as percentage of net
> plant. . .

Utility bond averages.

> SEE: Dow-Jones utility bond average. . .
> Moody's utility bond average. . .
> New York Times utility bond average. . .
> Standard & Poor's utility bond indexes. . .

UTILITY BONDS (UNLISTED), PRICES, MONTHLY, CLOSE (bid prices are given for end of month prior to month of publication, for each of about 1,300 over-the-counter public utility bonds). BANK AND QUOTATION RECORD. Published monthly.

Utility stock averages.

> SEE: Dow-Jones utility stock average. . .
> Moody's preferred stock averages. . .
> Moody's utility stock average. . .
> New York Stock Exchange utility stock index. . .
> Standard & Poor's utility stock index. . .
> Value Line utility stock index. . .

UTILITY STOCKS (UNLISTED), PRICES, MONTHLY, CLOSE (bid and asked prices are given for end of month prior to month of publication, for each of about 450 over-the-counter utility stocks). BANK AND QUOTATION RECORD. Published monthly.

VALUE LINE COMPOSITE STOCK INDEX, DIVIDEND YIELD (PERCENT), CURRENT (estimated yield average for coming year, for a composite of about 1,400 leading common stocks). VALUE LINE INVESTMENT SURVEY. Part one, published weekly.

VALUE LINE COMPOSITE STOCK INDEX, PRICE, DAILY, CLOSE (closing price for each of ten recent days. Labeled "Value Line Averages"). VALUE LINE INVESTMENT SURVEY. Part two. This data appears approximately every other week.

Value Line group indexes.

SEE: Value Line industry group stock indexes . . .

VALUE LINE INDUSTRIAL STOCK INDEX, PRICE, DAILY, CHART (line chart of daily price index for about three years). VALUE LINE INVESTMENT SURVEY. Part two. This data appears approximately every other week.

VALUE LINE INDUSTRIAL STOCK INDEX, PRICE, DAILY, CLOSE (closing price for each of ten recent days. Labeled "Value Line Averages"). VALUE LINE INVESTMENT SURVEY. Part two. This data appears approximately every other week.

VALUE LINE INDUSTRIAL STOCK INDEX, PRICE, WEEKLY, CHART (line chart of weekly price index for about seven years. Labeled "Weekly Value Line Industrial Averages"). VALUE LINE INVESTMENT SURVEY. Part three: published weekly, a few industries each week.

VALUE LINE INDUSTRY GROUP STOCK INDEXES, PRICES, MONTHLY, CHARTS (small line charts of monthly stock prices for about 100 industry groups are shown in "Relative Strength" form over a period of about three years. Each chart shows the ratio of a particular industry to the Value Line composite stock index of 1,400 leading common stocks). VALUE LINE INVESTMENT SURVEY. Part three: published weekly, a few industries each week.

VALUE LINE RAILROAD STOCK INDEX, PRICE, DAILY, CHART (line chart of daily price index for about three years). VALUE LINE INVESTMENT SURVEY. Part two. This data appears approximately every other week.

VALUE LINE RAILROAD STOCK INDEX, PRICE, DAILY, CLOSE (closing price for each of ten recent days. Labeled "Value Line Averages"). VALUE LINE INVESTMENT SURVEY. Part two. This data appears approximately every other week.

VALUE LINE RAILROAD STOCK INDEX, PRICE, DAILY, CLOSE (closing price of weekly price index for about seven years). VALUE LINE INVESTMENT SURVEY. Part three: published weekly, a few industries each week.

VALUE LINE RAILROAD STOCK INDEX, PRICE, WEEKLY, CHART (line chart daily price index for about three years). VALUE LINE INVESTMENT SURVEY. Part two. This data appears approximately every other week.

VALUE LINE UTILITY STOCK INDEX, PRICE, DAILY, CLOSE (closing price for each of past ten days. Labeled "Value Line Averages"). VALUE LINE INVESTMENT SURVEY. Part two. This data appears approximately every other week.

VALUE LINE UTILITY STOCK INDEX, PRICE, WEEKLY, CHART (line chart of weekly price index for about seven years). VALUE LINE INVESTMENT SURVEY. Part three: published weekly, a few industries each week.

Value of all shares listed on New York Stock Exchange.

SEE: Market value total of all shares listed on New York Stock Exchange. . .

Value of total share volume on New York Stock Exchange.

SEE: Market value total of share sales on New York Stock Exchange. . .

Value of trading on all registered exchanges.

SEE: Market value total of share sales on all registered exchanges. . .

Variety stroes.

SEE: Retailers. . .

Volume, advance-decline.

SEE: Advances and declines, volume. . .

Volume, high.

SEE: High volume stocks. . .

Volume, upside-downside.

SEE: Upside-downside volume. . .

Volume of floor trading.

SEE: Floor traders' volume. . .

Volume of member trading.

SEE: Member trading. . .

Volume of odd-lot transactions.

SEE: Odd-lot short sales. . .
Odd-lot volume of trading. . .

Volume of sales.

SEE: Volume of trading. . .

Volume of short sales.

SEE: Short sales. . .

Volume of specialist trading.

SEE: Specialists' trading. . .

Volume of trading in bonds, individual bonds.

SEE ALSO: Volume of trading in bonds, total. . .

VOLUME OF TRADING IN BONDS, INDIVIDUAL BONDS ON AMERICAN STOCK EXCHANGE, DAILY (par value sales for each issue traded on previous day). NEW YORK TIMES. Published weekdays. Also published on business days in the WALL STREET JOURNAL.

VOLUME OF TRADING IN BONDS, INDIVIDUAL BONDS ON AMERICAN STOCK EXCHANGE, MONTHLY (par value amount of sales--$1000 bonds-- for each bond issue listed, for month prior to month of publication). BANK AND QUOTATION RECORD. Published monthly.

VOLUME OF TRADING IN BONDS, INDIVIDUAL BONDS ON AMERICAN STOCK EXCHANGE, WEEKLY (number of $1000 bonds sold, for each issue traded during week just past). BARRON'S. Published weekly. Also published weekly in Monday edition of COMMERCIAL AND FINANCIAL CHRONICLE and Sunday edition of the NEW YORK TIMES.

VOLUME OF TRADING IN BONDS, INDIVIDUAL BONDS ON AMERICAN STOCK EXCHANGE, YEAR TO DATE (current year's sales for each bond listed). BANK AND QUOTATION RECORD. Published monthly.

VOLUME OF TRADING IN BONDS, INDIVIDUAL BONDS ON NEW YORK STOCK EXCHANGE, DAILY (par value dollar sales--$1000 bonds--for each bond traded, for previous day). NEW YORK TIMES. Published weekdays. Also published on business days in the WALL STREET JOURNAL.

VOLUME OF TRADING IN BONDS, INDIVIDUAL BONDS ON NEW YORK STOCK EXCHANGE, MONTHLY (par value dollar sales--$1000 bonds--for each bond issue listed, for month prior to month of publication). BANK AND QUOTATION RECORD. Published monthly.

VOLUME OF TRADING IN BONDS, INDIVIDUAL BONDS ON NEW YORK STOCK EXCHANGE, WEEKLY (number of $1000 bonds sold, for each issue traded during week just past). BARRON'S. Published weekly. Also published weekly in Monday edition of COMMERCIAL AND FINANCIAL CHRONICLE and in Sunday edition of NEW YORK TIMES.

VOLUME OF TRADING IN BONDS, TOTAL FOR AMERICAN STOCK EX-CHANGE, DAILY (total par value bond sales for each day of week just past, for each of the following groups: domestic bonds, foreign government bonds, foreign corporate bonds, and total bonds). COMMERCIAL AND FINANCIAL CHRONICLE. Monday edition.

VOLUME OF TRADING IN BONDS, TOTAL FOR AMERICAN STOCK EX-CHANGE, DAILY (total par value bond sales for previous trading day). WALL STREET JOURNAL. Published business days.

VOLUME OF TRADING IN BONDS, TOTAL FOR AMERICAN STOCK EX-CHANGE, MONTHLY-YEARLY (for month prior to month of publication, and for same month for each of three previous years, shows total par value dollar amount of bonds traded. In addition to grand total, totals are shown for "Domestic," "Foreign Govt.," and "Foreign Corporate"). BANK AND QUO-

TATION RECORD. Published monthly.

VOLUME OF TRADING IN BONDS, TOTAL FOR AMERICAN STOCK EX-
CHANGE, WEEKLY-YEARLY (total par value bond sales for week just past,
and for same week a year ago, for each of the following classes: domestic,
foreign government, foreign corporate, and total bonds). COMMERCIAL AND
FINANCIAL CHRONICLE. Monday edition.

VOLUME OF TRADING IN BONDS, TOTAL FOR AMERICAN STOCK EX-
CHANGE, WEEKLY-YEARLY (total par value sales for week just past and same
week one year ago). NEW YORK TIMES. Sunday edition.

VOLUME OF TRADING IN BONDS, TOTAL FOR AMERICAN STOCK EX-
CHANGE, YEAR TO DATE-YEARLY (for current year up to and including month
prior to month of publication, and for same period for each of three previous
years, shows total par value dollar amounts of bonds traded. In addition to
grand total, totals are shown for "Domestic," "Foreign Govt.," and "Foreign
Corporate"). BANK AND QUOTATION RECORD. Published monthly.

VOLUME OF TRADING IN BONDS, TOTAL FOR AMERICAN STOCK EX-
CHANGE, YEAR TO DATE-YEARLY (total par value bond sales for year to date,
and for same period a year ago, for the following: domestic bonds, foreign
government bonds, foreign corporate bonds, and total bonds). COMMERCIAL
AND FINANCIAL CHRONICLE. Monday edition.

VOLUME OF TRADING IN BONDS, TOTAL FOR AMERICAN STOCK EX-
CHANGE, YEAR TO DATE-YEARLY (total par value sales for current year to
date, and for same period one year ago). NEW YORK TIMES. Sunday edition.

VOLUME OF TRADING IN BONDS, TOTAL FOR AMERICAN STOCK EX-
CHANGE, YEAR TO DATE-YEARLY (total par value sales for current year to
date, and for same period for each of two previous years). WALL STREET
JOURNAL. Published business days.

VOLUME OF TRADING IN BONDS, TOTAL FOR NEW YORK STOCK EX-
CHANGE, DAILY (par value sales total for each day of week just past.
Labeled "Sales, ths $"). BARRON'S. Published weekly.

VOLUME OF TRADING IN BONDS, TOTAL FOR NEW YORK STOCK EX-
CHANGE, DAILY (for each day of week just past, shows par value totals for
"Railroad and Miscel. Bonds," "Foreign Bonds," "Int'l Bank Bonds," "U.S.
Govt. Bonds," and "Total Bond Sales"). COMMERCIAL AND FINANCIAL
CHRONICLE. Monday edition.

VOLUME OF TRADING IN BONDS, TOTAL FOR NEW YORK STOCK EX-
CHANGE, DAILY (total par value volume for all issues combined, for each
of two previous trading days. Separate totals also shown for domestic bonds
and foreign bonds). NEW YORK TIMES. Published weekdays.

VOLUME OF TRADING IN BONDS, TOTAL FOR NEW YORK STOCK EX-
CHANGE, DAILY (total par value volume for all issues combined, for previous

trading day. Separate totals also given for "Corporation Bonds" and "Foreign Bonds"). WALL STREET JOURNAL. Published business days.

VOLUME OF TRADING IN BONDS, TOTAL FOR NEW YORK STOCK EX-CHANGE, DAILY-YEARLY (total par value sales for each day of week just past, and for each day of corresponding week one year ago). NEW YORK TIMES. Sunday edition.

VOLUME OF TRADING IN BONDS, TOTAL FOR NEW YORK STOCK EX-CHANGE, MONTHLY-YEARLY (for month prior to month of publication, and for same month for each of three previous years, shows total par value dollar amount of bonds traded. In addition to grand totals, totals are shown for "Railroad and Mins.," "International Bank," "Foreign Govt.," and "United States Govt."). BANK AND QUOTATION RECORD. Published monthly.

VOLUME OF TRADING IN BONDS, TOTAL FOR NEW YORK STOCK EX-CHANGE, MONTHLY-YEARLY (total par value volume for latest month, previous month, and same month one year ago). BARRON'S. Published weekly.

VOLUME OF TRADING IN BONDS, TOTAL FOR NEW YORK STOCK EX-CHANGE, WEEKLY-YEARLY (total par value volume for latest week, previous week, and some week one year ago). BARRON'S. Published weekly.

VOLUME OF TRADING IN BONDS, TOTAL FOR NEW YORK STOCK EX-CHANGE, WEEKLY-YEARLY (total par value sales for week just past and for same week a year ago, for each of the following classes" U.S. government bonds, International Bank bonds, foreign bonds, railroad & industrial bonds, and grand total). COMMERCIAL AND FINANCIAL CHRONICLE. Monday edition.

VOLUME OF TRADING IN BONDS, TOTAL FOR NEW YORK STOCK EX-CHANGE, WEEKLY-YEARLY (total par value sales for week just past and for same week one year ago). NEW YORK TIMES. Sunday edition.

VOLUME OF TRADING IN BONDS, TOTAL FOR NEW YORK STOCK EX-CHANGE, YEAR TO DATE-YEARLY (for current year up to and including month prior to month of publication, and for same period for each of three previous years, shows total par value dollar amounts of bonds traded. In addition to grand totals, totals are shown for "Railroad and Misc.," "International Bank," "Foreign Govt.," and "United States Govt."). BANK AND QUO-TATION RECORD. Published monthly.

VOLUME OF TRADING IN BONDS, TOTAL FOR NEW YORK STOCK EX-CHANGE, YEAR TO DATE-YEARLY (total par value bond sales for year to date and for same period one year ago, for each of the following classes: U.S. government bonds, International Bank bonds, foreign bonds, railroad and industrial bonds, and grand total). COMMERCIAL AND FINANCIAL CHRON-ICLE. Monday edition.

VOLUME OF TRADING IN BONDS, TOTAL FOR NEW YORK STOCK EX-CHANGE, YEAR TO DATE-YEARLY (total par value sales for current year to date, and for same period last year. Separate totals also shown for domestic bonds and foreign bonds). NEW YORK TIMES. Published weekdays.

VOLUME OF TRADING IN BONDS, TOTAL FOR NEW YORK STOCK EX-CHANGE, YEAR TO DATE-YEARLY (total par value sales for current year to date, and for same period last year). NEW YORK TIMES. Sunday edition.

VOLUME OF TRADING IN BONDS, TOTAL FOR NEW YORK STOCK EX-CHANGE, YEAR TO DATE-YEARLY (total par value sales "since January 1" for current year, and for each of two previous years). WALL STREET JOUR-NAL. Published business days.

Volume of trading in stocks, advances and declines.

    SEE: Advances and declines, volume. . .
           Upside-downside volume. . .

Volume of trading in stocks, Dow-Jones averages.

    SEE: Dow-Jones composite stock average, volume of
           trading. . .
           Dow-Jones industrial stock average, volume of
           trading. . .
           Dow-Jones railroad stock average, volume of
           trading. . .
           Dow-Jones utility stock average, volume of
           trading. . .

Volume of trading in stocks, individual stocks.

    SEE ALSO: Volume of trading in stocks, total. . .

VOLUME OF TRADING IN STOCKS, INDIVIDUAL STOCKS, DAILY, CHARTS (daily volume is charted for about nine months, for each of about 700 active, listed stocks). TRENDLINE DAILY BASIS STOCK CHARTS. Published weekly.

VOLUME OF TRADING IN STOCKS, INDIVIDUAL STOCKS, MONTHLY (for each of about 3,000 listed issues, shows number of shares in hundreds traded during month prior to month of publication). STANDARD & POOR'S SECU-RITY OWNER'S STOCK GUIDE. Published monthly.

VOLUME OF TRADING IN STOCKS, INDIVIDUAL STOCKS, MONTHLY, PER-CENTAGE BASIS, CHARTS (over a period of about ten years, chart shows "per-centage of outstanding shares traded monthly," for each of about 1,400 lead-ing common stocks). VALUE LINE INVESTMENT SURVEY. Part three: pub-lished weekly, a few industries each week.

VOLUME OF TRADING IN STOCKS, INDIVIDUAL STOCKS, WEEKLY, CHARTS (weekly volume is charted for about four years, for each of about 960 listed stocks). TRENDLINE'S CURRENT MARKET PERSPECTIVES. Published monthly.

VOLUME OF TRADING IN STOCKS, INDIVIDUAL STOCKS ON AMERICAN

STOCK EXCHANGE, DAILY (for each issue traded on previous day). NEW YORK TIMES. Published weekdays. Also published on business days in the WALL STREET JOURNAL.

VOLUME OF TRADING IN STOCKS, INDIVIDUAL STOCKS ON AMERICAN STOCK EXCHANGE, MONTHLY (for month prior to month of publication). BANK AND QUOTATION RECORD. Published monthly.

VOLUME OF TRADING IN STOCKS, INDIVIDUAL STOCKS ON AMERICAN STOCK EXCHANGE, WEEKLY (total weekly sales for each listed stock). BARRON'S. Published weekly. Also published in Monday edition of COM-MERCIAL AND FINANCIAL CHRONICLE, and in Sunday edition of NEW YORK TIMES.

VOLUME OF TRADING IN STOCKS, INDIVIDUAL STOCKS ON AMERICAN STOCK EXCHANGE, YEAR TO DATE (up to and including month prior to month of publication). BANK AND QUOTATION RECORD. Published monthly.

VOLUME OF TRADING IN STOCKS, INDIVIDUAL STOCKS ON BOSTON STOCK EXCHANGE, DAILY (for each exclusively listed stock traded on previous day). WALL STREET JOURNAL. Published weekdays.

VOLUME OF TRADING IN STOCKS, INDIVIDUAL STOCKS ON BOSTON STOCK EXCHANGE, MONTHLY (for month prior to month of publication). BANK AND QUOTATION RECORD. Published monthly.

VOLUME OF TRADING IN STOCKS, INDIVIDUAL STOCKS ON BOSTON STOCK EXCHANGE, YEAR TO DATE (up to and including month prior to month of publication). BANK AND QUOTATION RECORD. Published monthly.

VOLUME OF TRADING IN STOCKS, INDIVIDUAL STOCKS ON CINCINNATI STOCK EXCHANGE, DAILY (for each exclusively listed stock traded on previous day). WALL STREET JOURNAL. Published weekdays.

VOLUME OF TRADING IN STOCKS, INDIVIDUAL STOCKS ON CINCINNATI STOCK EXCHANGE, WEEKLY (for week just past). COMMERCIAL AND FI-NANCIAL CHRONICLE. Monday edition.

VOLUME OF TRADING IN STOCKS, INDIVIDUAL STOCKS ON DETROIT STOCK EXCHANGE, DAILY (for each exclusively listed stock traded on previous day). WALL STREET JOURNAL. Published business days.

VOLUME OF TRADING IN STOCKS, INDIVIDUAL STOCKS ON DETROIT STOCK EXCHANGE, MONTHLY (for month prior to month of publication). BANK AND QUOTATION RECORD. Published monthly.

VOLUME OF TRADING IN STOCKS, INDIVIDUAL STOCKS ON DETROIT STOCK EXCHANGE, YEAR TO DATE (up to and including month prior to month of publication). BANK AND QUOTATION RECORD. Published monthly.

VOLUME OF TRADING IN STOCKS, INDIVIDUAL STOCKS ON HONOLULU

STOCK EXCHANGE, DAILY (for each stock traded two days ago). WALL STREET JOURNAL. Published business days.

VOLUME OF TRADING IN STOCKS, INDIVIDUAL STOCKS ON MIDWEST STOCK EXCHANGE, DAILY (for each stock traded on previous day). NEW YORK TIMES. Published weekdays. Also published on business days in the WALL STREET JOURNAL.

VOLUME OF TRADING IN STOCKS, INDIVIDUAL STOCKS ON MIDWEST STOCK EXCHANGE, MONTHLY (for month prior to month of publication). BANK AND QUOTATION RECORD. Published monthly.

VOLUME OF TRADING IN STOCKS, INDIVIDUAL STOCKS ON MIDWEST STOCK EXCHANGE, YEAR TO DATE (up to and including month prior to month of publication). BANK AND QUOTATION RECORD. Published monthly.

VOLUME OF TRADING IN STOCKS, INDIVIDUAL STOCKS ON MONTREAL STOCK EXCHANGE, DAILY (for each stock traded on previous day). NEW YORK TIMES. Published weekdays. Also published on business days in the WALL STREET JOURNAL.

VOLUME OF TRADING IN STOCKS, INDIVIDUAL STOCKS ON NATIONAL STOCK EXCHANGE, DAILY (for each stock traded on previous day). NEW YORK TIMES. Published weekdays. Also published on business days in the WALL STREET JOURNAL.

VOLUME OF TRADING IN STOCKS, INDIVIDUAL STOCKS ON NATIONAL STOCK EXCHANGE, WEEKLY (for week just past). BARRON'S. Published weekly. Also published in Monday edition of COMMERCIAL AND FINAN-CIAL CHRONICLE.

VOLUME OF TRADING IN STOCKS, INDIVIDUAL STOCKS ON NEW YORK STOCK EXCHANGE, DAILY (for each issue traded on previous day). NEW YORK TIMES. Published weekdays. Also published on business days in the WALL STREET JOURNAL.

VOLUME OF TRADING IN STOCKS, INDIVIDUAL STOCKS ON NEW YORK STOCK EXCHANGE, MONTHLY (for month prior to month of publication). BANK AND QUOTATION RECORD. Published monthly.

VOLUME OF TRADING IN STOCKS, INDIVIDUAL STOCKS ON NEW YORK STOCK EXCHANGE, WEEKLY (total weekly sales for each listed stock). BAR-RON'S. Published weekly. Also published in Monday edition of COMMERCIAL AND FINANCIAL CHRONICLE, and in Sunday edition of NEW YORK TIMES.

VOLUME OF TRADING IN STOCKS, INDIVIDUAL STOCKS ON NEW YORK STOCK EXCHANGE, YEAR TO DATE (up to and including month prior to month of publication). BANK AND QUOTATION RECORD. Published monthly.

VOLUME OF TRADING IN STOCKS, INDIVIDUAL STOCKS ON PACIFIC COAST STOCK EXCHANGE, DAILY (for each stock traded on previous day). NEW YORK TIMES. Published weekdays. Also published on business days in the WALL STREET JOURNAL.

VOLUME OF TRADING IN STOCKS, INDIVIDUAL STOCKS ON PACIFIC COAST STOCK EXCHANGE, MONTHLY (for month prior to month of publication). BANK AND QUOTATION RECORD. Published monthly.

VOLUME OF TRADING IN STOCKS, INDIVIDUAL STOCKS ON PACIFIC COAST STOCK EXCHANGE, YEAR TO DATE (up to and including month prior to month of publication). BANK AND QUOTATION RECORD. Published monthly.

VOLUME OF TRADING IN STOCKS, INDIVIDUAL STOCKS ON PHILADELPHIA-BALTIMORE-WASHINGTON STOCK EXCHANGE, DAILY (for each exclusively listed stock traded on previous day). WALL STREET JOURNAL. Published business days.

VOLUME OF TRADING IN STOCKS, INDIVIDUAL STOCKS ON PHILADELPHIA-BALTIMORE-WASHINGTON STOCK EXCHANGE, MONTHLY (for month prior to month of publication). BANK AND QUOTATION RECORD. Published monthly.

VOLUME OF TRADING IN STOCKS, INDIVIDUAL STOCKS ON PHILADELPHIA-BALTIMORE-WASHINGTON STOCK EXCHANGE, WEEKLY (for week just past). COMMERCIAL AND FINANCIAL CHRONICLE. Monday edition.

VOLUME OF TRADING IN STOCKS, INDIVIDUAL STOCKS ON PHILADELPHIA-BALTIMORE-WASHINGTON STOCK EXCHANGE, YEAR TO DATE (up to and including month prior to month of publication). BANK AND QUOTATION RECORD. Published monthly.

VOLUME OF TRADING IN STOCKS, INDIVIDUAL STOCKS ON PITTSBURGH STOCK EXCHANGE, DAILY (for each exclusively listed stock traded on previous day). WALL STREET JOURNAL. Published business days.

VOLUME OF TRADING IN STOCKS, INDIVIDUAL STOCKS ON PITTSBURGH STOCK EXCHANGE, MONTHLY (for month prior to month of publication). BANK AND QUOTATION RECORD. Published monthly.

VOLUME OF TRADING IN STOCKS, INDIVIDUAL STOCKS ON PITTSBURGH STOCK EXCHANGE, YEAR TO DATE (up to and including month prior to month of publication). BANK AND QUOTATION RECORD. Published monthly.

VOLUME OF TRADING IN STOCKS, INDIVIDUAL STOCKS ON SALT LAKE CITY STOCK EXCHANGE, DAILY (for each exclusively listed stock traded on previous day). WALL STREET JOURNAL. Published business days.

VOLUME OF TRADING IN STOCKS, INDIVIDUAL STOCKS ON TORONTO STOCK EXCHANGE, DAILY (for each stock traded on previous day. Three lists: industrials, mines, and oils-gas). NEW YORK TIMES. Published weekdays. Also published on business days in the WALL STREET JOURNAL.

Volume of trading in stocks, low-priced stocks.

SEE: Barron's low-priced stock index, volume of
      trading. . .

Volume of trading in stocks, odd-lot.

SEE: Odd-lot short sales. . .
     Odd-lot volume of trading. . .

Volume of trading in stocks, percentage basis, individual stocks.

SEE: Volume of trading in stocks, individual stocks,
     monthly, percentage basis. . .

Volume of trading in stocks, short sales.

SEE: Short sales. . .

Volume of trading in stocks, total.

SEE ALSO: Volume of trading in stocks, individual
          stocks. . .

VOLUME OF TRADING IN STOCKS, TOTAL FOR AMERICAN STOCK EX-
CHANGE, DAILY (for each day of week just past). BARRON'S. Published
weekly. Also published in Monday edition of COMMERCIAL AND FINANCIAL
CHRONICLE.

VOLUME OF TRADING IN STOCKS, TOTAL FOR AMERICAN STOCK EX-
CHANGE, DAILY (for previous trading day). WALL STREET JOURNAL. Published business days.

VOLUME OF TRADING IN STOCKS, TOTAL FOR AMERICAN STOCK EX-
CHANGE, DAILY, CHART (total volume in shares in charted on daily basis for
about two years). TRENDLINE DAILY BASIS STOCK CHARTS. Published weekly.

VOLUME OF TRADING IN STOCKS, TOTAL FOR AMERICAN STOCK EX-
CHANGE, DAILY-YEARLY (for previous trading day, day before that, and
same day one year ago). NEW YORK TIMES. Published weekdays.

VOLUME OF TRADING IN STOCKS, TOTAL FOR AMERICAN STOCK EX-
CHANGE, MONTHLY, CHART (monthly totals for the Exchange are charted
for about five years). MOODY'S HANDBOOK OF COMMON STOCKS.
Published quarterly.

VOLUME OF TRADING IN STOCKS, TOTAL FOR AMERICAN STOCK EX-
CHANGE, MONTHLY-YEARLY (for month prior to month of publication, and
for same month for each of three previous years). BANK AND QUOTATION
RECORD. Published monthly.

VOLUME OF TRADING IN STOCKS, TOTAL FOR AMERICAN STOCK EX-
CHANGE, WEEKLY, CHART (weekly totals for the Exchange are charted for
about four years). TRENDLINE'S CURRENT MARKET PERSPECTIVES. Pub-

lished monthly.

VOLUME OF TRADING IN STOCKS, TOTAL FOR AMERICAN STOCK EX-
CHANGE, WEEKLY-YEARLY (for week just past, previous week, and same
period one year ago). BARRON'S. Published weekly.

VOLUME OF TRADING IN STOCKS, TOTAL FOR AMERICAN STOCK EX-
CHANGE, WEEKLY-YEARLY (for week just past, and for same week a year
ago). COMMERCIAL AND FINANCIAL CHRONICLE. Monday edition. Also
published in Sunday edition of NEW YORK TIMES.

VOLUME OF TRADING IN STOCKS, TOTAL FOR AMERICAN STOCK EX-
CHANGE, YEAR TO DATE-YEARLY (for current year up to and including
month prior to month of publication, and for same period for each of three
previous years). BANK AND QUOTATION RECORD. Published monthly.

VOLUME OF TRADING IN STOCKS, TOTAL FOR AMERICAN STOCK EX-
CHANGE, YEAR TO DATE-YEARLY (for current year to date, and for same
period one year ago). COMMERCIAL AND FINANCIAL CHRONICLE. Monday edition. Also published daily in NEW YORK TIMES, and in Sunday edition of NEW YORK TIMES.

VOLUME OF TRADING IN STOCKS, TOTAL FOR AMERICAN STOCK EX-
CHANGE, YEAR TO DATE-YEARLY (volume "since January 1" for current
year, and for each of two previous years). WALL STREET JOURNAL. Published business days.

VOLUME OF TRADING IN STOCKS, TOTAL FOR BOSTON STOCK EX-
CHANGE, DAILY (for previous trading day). WALL STREET JOURNAL. Published business days.

VOLUME OF TRADING IN STOCKS, TOTAL FOR BOSTON STOCK EXCHANGE,
MONTHLY-YEARLY (for month prior to month of publication, and for same month
for previous year). BANK AND QUOTATION RECORD. Published monthly.

VOLUME OF TRADING IN STOCKS, TOTAL FOR BOSTON STOCK EXCHANGE,
YEAR TO DATE-YEARLY (for current year up to and including month prior to
month of publication, and for same period one year earlier). BANK AND QUO-
TATION RECORD. Published monthly.

VOLUME OF TRADING IN STOCKS, TOTAL FOR CINCINNATI STOCK EX-
CHANGE, DAILY (for previous trading day). WALL STREET JOURNAL. Published business days.

VOLUME OF TRADING IN STOCKS, TOTAL FOR DETROIT STOCK EXCHANGE,
DAILY (for previous trading day). WALL STREET JOURNAL. Published business
days.

VOLUME OF TRADING IN STOCKS, TOTAL FOR DETROIT STOCK EX-
CHANGE, MONTHLY-YEARLY (for month prior to month of publication, and for
same month one year ago). BANK AND QUOTATION RECORD. Published
monthly.

INVESTMENT INFORMATION

VOLUME OF TRADING IN STOCKS, TOTAL FOR DETROIT STOCK EXCHANGE, YEAR TO DATE-YEARLY (for current year up to and including month prior to month of publication, and for same period one year earlier). BANK AND QUOTATION RECORD. Published monthly.

VOLUME OF TRADING IN STOCKS, TOTAL FOR HONOLULU STOCK EXCHANGE, DAILY (for day before yesterday). WALL STREET JOURNAL. Published business days.

VOLUME OF TRADING IN STOCKS, TOTAL FOR MIDWEST STOCK EXCHANGE, DAILY (for previous trading day). NEW YORK TIMES. Published weekdays. Also published on business days in the WALL STREET JOURNAL.

VOLUME OF TRADING IN STOCKS, TOTAL FOR MIDWEST STOCK EXCHANGE, MONTHLY-YEARLY (for month prior to month of publication, and for same month for previous year). BANK AND QUOTATION RECORD. Published monthly.

VOLUME OF TRADING IN STOCKS, TOTAL FOR MIDWEST STOCK EXCHANGE, YEAR TO DATE-YEARLY (for current year up to and including month prior to month of publication, and for same period one year earlier). BANK AND QUOTATION RECORD. Published monthly.

VOLUME OF TRADING IN STOCKS, TOTAL FOR MONTREAL STOCK EXCHANGE, DAILY (for previous trading day, in two categories: industrials and mines-oils). NEW YORK TIMES. Published weekdays. Also published business days in the WALL STREET JOURNAL.

VOLUME OF TRADING IN STOCKS, TOTAL FOR NATIONAL STOCK EXCHANGE, DAILY (for previous trading day). NEW YORK TIMES. Published weekdays. Also published business days in the WALL STREET JOURNAL.

VOLUME OF TRADING IN STOCKS, TOTAL FOR NEW YORK STOCK EXCHANGE, DAILY ("Big Board Volume" is given for each day of month prior to month of publication). BANK AND QUOTATION RECORD. Published monthly.

VOLUME OF TRADING IN STOCKS, TOTAL FOR NEW YORK STOCK EXCHANGE, DAILY (for each day of week just past). BARRON'S. Published weekly. Also published in Monday edition of COMMERCIAL AND FINANCIAL CHRONICLE.

VOLUME OF TRADING IN STOCKS, TOTAL FOR NEW YORK STOCK EXCHANGE, DAILY (for each of last three trading days). WALL STREET JOURNAL. Published business days.

VOLUME OF TRADING IN STOCKS, TOTAL FOR NEW YORK STOCK EXCHANGE, DAILY CHART (daily total volume charted for about three months. Labeled "Daily Sales in Millions"). NEW YORK TIMES. Published weekdays.

VOLUME OF TRADING IN STOCKS, TOTAL FOR NEW YORK STOCK EXCHANGE, DAILY, CHART (daily total volume charted for about one year). THE OUTLOOK. Published weekly.

VOLUME OF TRADING IN STOCKS, TOTAL FOR NEW YORK STOCK EX-
CHANGE, DAILY, CHART (daily total volume charted for about four years).
TRENDLINE DAILY BASIS STOCK CHARTS. Published weekly.

VOLUME OF TRADING IN STOCKS, TOTAL FOR NEW YORK STOCK EX-
CHANGE, DAILY, CHART (daily total volume charted for about four months.
Labeled "Daily Volume"). WALL STREET JOURNAL. Published business days.

VOLUME OF TRADING IN STOCKS, TOTAL FOR NEW YORK STOCK EX-
CHANGE, DAILY-YEARLY (for previous trading day, day before that, and same
day one year ago). NEW YORK TIMES. Published weekdays.

VOLUME OF TRADING IN STOCKS, TOTAL FOR NEW YORK STOCK EX-
CHANGE, DAILY-YEARLY (for each day of week just past, and for each day
of corresponding week a year ago and two years ago). NEW YORK TIMES.
Sunday edition.

Volume of trading in stocks, total for New York Stock Exchange, dollar value.

> SEE: Market value total of share sales on New York
> Stock Exchanges. . .

VOLUME OF TRADING IN STOCKS, TOTAL FOR NEW YORK STOCK EX-
CHANGE, HOURLY (for each hour of each trading day of week just past).
BARRON'S. Published weekly.

VOLUME OF TRADING IN STOCKS, TOTAL FOR NEW YORK STOCK EX-
CHANGE, HOURLY (for each hour of each of last three trading days). WALL
STREET JOURNAL. Published business days.

VOLUME OF TRADING IN STOCKS, TOTAL FOR NEW YORK STOCK EX-
CHANGE, MONTHLY (DAILY AVERAGE), CHART (average daily volume is
charted for each month over a period of about ten years). MOODY'S HAND-
BOOK OF COMMON STOCKS. Published quarterly.

VOLUME OF TRADING IN STOCKS, TOTAL FOR NEW YORK STOCK EX-
CHANGE, MONTHLY-YEARLY (for month prior to month of publication, and
for same month for each of three previous years). BANK AND QUOTATION
RECORD. Published monthly.

VOLUME OF TRADING IN STOCKS, TOTAL FOR NEW YORK STOCK EX-
CHANGE, MONTHLY-YEARLY (for latest month, preceding month, and same
month one year ago). BARRON'S. Published weekly.

VOLUME OF TRADING IN STOCKS, TOTAL FOR NEW YORK STOCK EX-
CHANGE, WEEKLY, CHART (weekly sales in millions of shares charted for
about two years). NEW YORK TIMES. Sunday edition.

VOLUME OF TRADING IN STOCKS, TOTAL FOR NEW YORK STOCK EX-
CHANGE, WEEKLY, CHART (weekly volume charted over a period of about
five years). TRENDLINE'S CURRENT MARKET PERSPECTIVES. Published
monthly.

INVESTMENT INFORMATION

VOLUME OF TRADING IN STOCKS, TOTAL FOR NEW YORK STOCK EX-CHANGE, WEEKLY-MONTHLY-YEARLY (for latest week, previous week, month ago, and same week one year ago). COMMERCIAL AND FINANCIAL CHRONI-CLE. Thursday edition.

VOLUME OF TRADING IN STOCKS, TOTAL FOR NEW YORK STOCK EX-CHANGE, WEEKLY-YEARLY (for week just past, previous week, and same week one year ago). BARRON'S. Published weekly.

VOLUME OF TRADING IN STOCKS, TOTAL FOR NEW YORK STOCK EX-CHANGE, WEEKLY-YEARLY (for week just past, and for same week one year ago). COMMERCIAL AND FINANCIAL CHRONICLE. Monday edition.

VOLUME OF TRADING IN STOCKS, TOTAL FOR NEW YORK STOCK EX-CHANGE, WEEKLY-YEARLY (number of shares traded during week just past, and during corresponding week for each of two previous years). NEW YORK TIMES. Sunday edition.

VOLUME OF TRADING IN STOCKS, TOTAL FOR NEW YORK STOCK EX-CHANGE, WEEKLY-YEARLY (for week just past, previous week, and same week one year ago. Labeled "Last Week's Markets"). WALL STREET JOURNAL. This data appears in Monday edition.

VOLUME OF TRADING IN STOCKS, TOTAL FOR NEW YORK STOCK EX-CHANGE, YEAR TO DATE-YEARLY (for current year up to and including month prior to month of publication, and for same period for each of three previous years). BANK AND QUOTATION RECORD. Published monthly.

VOLUME OF TRADING IN STOCKS, TOTAL FOR NEW YORK STOCK EX-CHANGE, YEAR TO DATE-YEARLY (for current year so far, and for same period one year ago). COMMERCIAL AND FINANCIAL CHRONICLE. Monday edition. Also published weekdays in NEW YORK TIMES.

VOLUME OF TRADING IN STOCKS, TOTAL FOR NEW YORK STOCK EX-CHANGE, YEAR TO DATE-YEARLY (for current year so far, and for same period for each of two previous years). NEW YORK TIMES. Sunday edition. Also published on business days in the WALL STREET JOURNAL.

VOLUME OF TRADING IN STOCKS, TOTAL FOR PACIFIC COAST STOCK EXCHANGE, DAILY (for previous trading day). NEW YORK TIMES. Published weekdays. Also published on business days in the WALL STREET JOURNAL.

VOLUME OF TRADING IN STOCKS, TOTAL FOR PACIFIC COAST STOCK EX-CHANGE, MONTHLY-YEARLY (for month prior to month of publication, and for same month for previous year). BANK AND QUOTATION RECORD. Published monthly.

VOLUME OF TRADING IN STOCKS, TOTAL FOR PACIFIC COAST STOCK EXCHANGE, YEAR TO DATE-YEARLY (for current year up to and including month prior to month of publication, and for same period one year earlier). BANK AND QUOTATION RECORD. Published monthly.

VOLUME OF TRADING IN STOCKS, TOTAL FOR PHILADELPHIA-BALTIMORE-WASHINGTON STOCK EXCHANGE, DAILY (for previous trading day). WALL STREET JOURNAL. Published business days.

VOLUME OF TRADING IN STOCKS, TOTAL FOR PHILADELPHIA-BALTIMORE-WASHINGTON STOCK EXCHANGE, MONTHLY-YEARLY (for month prior to month of publication, and for same month for previous year). BANK AND QUOTATION RECORD. Published monthly.

VOLUME OF TRADING IN STOCKS, TOTAL FOR PHILADELPHIA-BALTIMORE-WASHINGTON STOCK EXCHANGE, YEAR TO DATE-YEARLY (for current year up to and including month prior to month of publication, and for same period one year ago). BANK AND QUOTATION RECORD. Published monthly.

VOLUME OF TRADING IN STOCKS, TOTAL FOR PITTSBURGH STOCK EXCHANGE, DAILY (for previous trading day). WALL STREET JOURNAL. Published business days.

VOLUME OF TRADING IN STOCKS, TOTAL FOR PITTSBURGH STOCK EXCHANGE, MONTHLY-YEARLY (for month prior to month of publication, and for same month for previous year). BANK AND QUOTATION RECORD. Published monthly.

VOLUME OF TRADING IN STOCKS, TOTAL FOR PITTSBURGH STOCK EXCHANGE, YEAR TO DATE-YEARLY (for current year up to and including month prior to month of publication, and for same period one year earlier). BANK AND QUOTATION RECORD. Published monthly.

VOLUME OF TRADING IN STOCKS, TOTAL FOR SALT LAKE CITY STOCK EXCHANGE, DAILY (for previous trading day). WALL STREET JOURNAL. Published business days.

VOLUME OF TRADING IN STOCKS, TOTAL FOR TORONTO STOCK EXCHANGE, DAILY (for previous trading day). NEW YORK TIMES. Published weekdays. Also published on business days in the WALL STREET JOURNAL.

Volume trends.

    SEE: Advances and declines, volume. . .
          Upside-downside volume. . .

WARRANTS (basic terms, expiration dates, and monthly prices of many stock purchase warrants--interfiled alphabetically). NATIONAL MONTHLY STOCK SUMMARY. Published monthly.

WARRANTS (basic terms, expiration dates, and monthly prices of many stock purchase warrants--interfiled alphabetically). STANDARD & POOR'S SECURITY OWNER'S STOCK GUIDE. Published monthly.

Where traded.

    SEE: Markets where bonds are traded. . .
          Markets where stocks are traded. . .

WORKING CAPITAL, YEARLY (shown for each of past eleven years for each of over 1,000 companies having actively traded common stock, and for most recent year only for over 1,200 companies with less actively traded stock). MOODY'S HANDBOOK OF COMMON STOCKS. Published quarterly.

WORKING CAPITAL, YEARLY (for each of past 18 or so years, for each of about 1,300 leading industrial and transportation companies). VALUE LINE INVESTMENT SURVEY. Part three: published weekly, a few industries each week.

World Bank bonds.

>SEE: International Bank for Reconstruction and Development bonds. . .

Year, fiscal.

>SEE: Fiscal year. . .

Year in which uninterrupted dividends began.

>SEE: Dividends, uninterrupted, year of beginning. . .

Year of incorporation.

>SEE: Founding dates. . .

Year of issue for bonds.

>SEE: Bonds, year of issue. . .
>Foreign bonds, year of issue. . .

Year of maturity for bonds.

>SEE: Bonds, due dates. . .
>Convertible bonds, due dates. . .
>Foreign bonds, due dates. . .
>Government bonds, due dates. . .

Yearly dividends.

>SEE: Dividends, amount, yearly. . .

Yearly earnings per share.

>SEE: Earnings per share, yearly. . .

Yield averages (dividends).

>(See cross references under "Dividend yield averages.")

YIELD SPREAD (PERCENT), BONDS AND STOCKS, WEEKLY-YEARLY (yield spread between Barron's high-grade bond index and Dow-Jones industrial stock average, for end of latest week, previous week, and same week one year ago). BARRON'S. Published weekly.

YIELD SPREAD (RATIO), BONDS AND STOCKS, WEEKLY-YEARLY (yield spread ratio between Barron's high-grade bond index and Barron's 50-stock average, for end of latest week, previous week, and same week one year ago. Labeled "Bond-Stock Ratio," and compiled by using stock earnings yield rather than dividend yield). BARRON'S. Published weekly.

Yields, bond averages.

> See entries under various bond averages--Barron's, Dow-Jones, Moody's and Standard & Poor's.

Yields, bonds.

> SEE: Bond yields. . .
> Convertible bonds, yields. . .
> Foreign bonds, yields. . .
> Government bonds, yields. . .

Yields, dividends (percent).

> SEE: Dividend yields (percent). . .

Yields, high (stocks).

> SEE: High yielding stocks. . .

Yields, stock averages.

> (See cross references under "Dividend yield averages.")

Yields, tax exempt vs. taxable.

> SEE: Tax exempt vs. taxable yields. . .

Zurich Stock Exchange prices.

> SEE: Foreign stock price indexes. . .
> Stock prices on Zurich Stock Exchange. . .